OXFORD
UNIVERSITY PRESS

INSIGHT

Intermediate Workbook

Second Edition

Lucy Holmes • Paul Hancock

OXFORD
UNIVERSITY PRESS

Great Clarendon Street, Oxford, OX2 6DP, United Kingdom

Oxford University Press is a department of the University of Oxford. It furthers the University's objective of excellence in research, scholarship, and education by publishing worldwide. Oxford is a registered trade mark of Oxford University Press in the UK and in certain other countries

First published in 2022
2026 2025 2024 2023 2022
10 9 8 7 6 5 4 3 2

ISBN: 978 0 19 426260 6

Printed and bound in Portugal by Gráfica Maiadouro

This book is printed on paper from certified and well-managed sources

ACKNOWLEDGEMENTS

Cover images by: Shutterstock/James Aloysius Mahan V/Stockfotografie/VicW.

The publisher would like to thank the following for their permission to reproduce photographs: Alamy pp.39 (Graham Prentice), 48 (blickwinkel), 49 (Doug Diamond), 76 (*The Angel of the North*/Gavin Hellier), 109 (Adam Burton), 113 (*Sense and Sensibility* 1995/AF archive); Bridgeman Images p.6 (skull/Illustration for The Picture Magazine, 1894/Look and Learn, clown/Illustration from The Boy's Own Annual (The Boy's Own Paper Office, London, 1913)/Look and Learn, Cat's Head c.1810 (colour woodblock print) by Japanese School, (19th century)/Galerie Janette Ostier/Archives Charmet); Getty Images pp.4 (boy/Sven Hagolani, girl/The Photo Commune), 6 (bird prints/Diep Vi Hoa), 8 (David M. Benett), 9 (Andreja Pejic/Daniele Venturelli, 1960s models/ Mondadori Portfolio, 1990s catwalk/Victor VIRGILE), 17 (C/Ashit Desai), 29 (evgenyatamanenko), 30 (laptop/CHUYN), 31 (WPA Pool), 41 (Bastøy Prison library/Marco Di Lauro), 46 (B/123ducu), 55 (DOUGLAS MAGNO), 56-57 (golubovy), 62 (Christophel Fine Art), 73 (Matt Winkelmeyer), 76 (Antony Gormley/Zoe Norfolk), 77 (skater/Stanislav Krasilnikov), 78 (Chuck Close *Mosaics* at MAR Art Museum of Ravenna. 2019/Roberto Serra/Iguana Press), 79 (Peter Macdiarmid), 80 (China News Service), 107 (F. J. Mortimer/ Stringer/Hulton Archive), 115 (Catherine Ledner), 116 (C/LightFieldStudios, 3/digitalskillet), 177 (food bank/SDI Productions, repair/Jose Luis Pelaez Inc, clean up/SDI Productions, protest/China News Service), 121 (Huntstock), 123 (hip hop/gradyreese), 126 (Giuseppe Lombardo/EyeEm); The Guardian p.53; Oxford University Press pp.17 (D/Shutterstock/Sean Pavone), 21 (Shutterstock/ Monkey Business Images), 22 (athlete/Shutterstock/LifetimeStock, girl with phone/Getty/svetikd), 24 (head/Shutterstock/agsandrew, x-ray/Shutterstock/ wonderisland, heart rate/Shutterstock/Jeff Metzger, syringe/Getty/C Squared Studios), 26 (Shutterstock/Gena Melendrez), 30 (students/Shutterstock/ michaeljung), 34 (Shutterstock/PR Image Factory), 38 (woman/Shutterstock/ Lewis Tse Pui Lung), 54 (man/Shutterstock/fizkes), 74 (Shutterstock/Stuart Jenner), 82 (Shutterstock/Mega Pixel), 104, 105 (Getty/James Brey), 106, 108, 110, 112, 119 (laptop/Shutterstock/Teo); Shutterstock pp.5 (kitten/ Olhastock, owl/FotoRequest), 6 (horse prints/Steven Collins, bear prints/ Dan Kosmayer), 7 (A/Chiyacat, B/Nadi, C/Borislav Bajkic, D/Michael Kraus), 9 (inclusive models/UfaBizPhoto), 10 (Rawpixel.com), 13 (Chantal de Bruijne), 15 (Nyokki), 16 (Mindscape studio), 17 (B/Boris Stroujko), 20 (Boontoom Sae-Kor), 28 (Zebra-Studio), 32 (Anton Gvozdikov), 33 (Getty/tobkatrina), 38 (girls/Blanscape), 40 (eyal granith), 41 (cell/Ann Kosolapova), 46 (A/Marques, rucksack/Pixel-Shot, holdall/Morok), 52 (LookerStudio), 54 (trainers/jjaf), 57 (researcher/fizkes), 64 (Salty View), 65 (RossHelen), 70 (A/Irina Neftenova, B/Golubovy, C/leungchopan), 81 (mural/nuu_jeed), 116 (A/LStockStudio, B/ Robert Kneschke, 1/Laurin Rinder, 2/Prostock-studio, 4/AJP, 5/Prostock-studio), 119 (books/Lub4yk, paint/Sergey Robins, sports/kot, desk), 123 (ballet/Evgeny Atamanenko, Latin/Billion Photos, folk/Stanislaw Tokarski), 125 (Matej Kastelic), 127 (Viktoriia Hnatiuk), 128 (ASDF_MEDIA); Shutterstock Editorial p.47 (Charles Sykes/AP), 77 (*The Lord of the Rings* 2001/Pierre Vinet/New Line/ Saul Zaentz/Wing Nut/Kobal), 111 (*The Secret Garden* 1993/Am Zoetrope/Warner Bros/Kobal).

Illustrations by: John Haslam pp.54 (train board, envelope), 62.

The authors and publisher are grateful to those who have given permission to reproduce the following extracts and adaptations of copyright material: p.53 Adapted from 'I felt my twin sister's labour pains' by Sally Keeble, 21 March 2009, *The Guardian*, Copyright Guardian News & Media Ltd 2021, reprinted by permission; p.105 From Oxford Bookworms Library Level 4: *Treasure Island* by Robert Louis Stevenson, retold by John Escott, © Oxford University Press 2008, reprinted by permission; p.107 From Oxford Bookworms Library Level 4: *Silas Marner* by George Elliot, retold by Clare West, © Oxford University Press 2008, reprinted by permission; p.109 From Oxford Dominoes Level 3: *The Moonstone* by Wilkie Collins, retold by Merinda Wilson, © Oxford University Press 2010, reprinted by permission; p.111 From Oxford Bookworms Library Level 3: *The Secret Garden* by Frances Hodgson Burnett, retold by Clare West, © Oxford University Press 2008, reprinted by permission; p.113 From Oxford Bookworms Library Level 5: *Sense and Sensibility* by Jane Austen, retold by Clare West, © Oxford University Press 2008, reprinted by permission.

Although every effort has been made to trace and contact copyright holders before publication, this has not been possible in some cases. We apologise for any apparent infringement of copyright and, if notified, the publisher will be pleased to rectify any errors or omissions at the earliest possible opportunity.

Contents

1 First impressions

Vocabulary

V Insight Describing appearance

1 Choose the correct words.

1 This painting is quite **attractive** / **plain**! I thought it would be more colourful.
2 Some people think tattoos are attractive, but I think they're really **stunning** / **ugly**!
3 My sister is looking **plain** / **slim** and healthy these days! She's been training for a marathon.
4 Everyone looked round when Jafari came in wearing that suit. He was so **plain** / **handsome**!
5 Expensive clothes are not necessary if you want to look **elegant** / **ugly** and stylish.
6 Boxers can't be **beautiful** / **overweight** before a fight.

V Insight Compound adjectives: appearance

2 Complete the compound adjectives, each with a different ending. Then use them to complete the sentences.

- blue-__________ ■ broad-__________
- fair-__________ ■ pale-__________
- short-__________ ■ sun-__________

1 Most of my family are __________, apart from my dad, who has dark hair.
2 Charles spent most of his summer holiday lying on the beach – look how __________ he is!
3 Most professional swimmers are very __________!
4 If both parents are __________, there is a 60% chance that their children will also need glasses.
5 Because I am __________, I either have to wear sun cream or get sunburnt!
6 Ursula hasn't got brown eyes and black hair – she's __________ with grey hair.

Vocabulary extra Describing hair

3 Complete the text with the words below.

■ bob ■ bun ■ curly hair ■ plaits ■ ponytail ■ shaved head ■ spiky

4 Choose the correct answers.

1 Many swimmers are __________-shouldered.
 a ugly **b** broad **c** big
2 My brother has __________ skin and dark eyes like me.
 a elegant **b** fair **c** straight
3 It's good that models can be all shapes and sizes. They all used to be __________.
 a plain **b** handsome **c** slim
4 For centuries, a sun-__________ face indicated that someone worked all day in the fields.
 a skinned **b** sighted **c** tanned
5 These days, clear skin and __________ eyes are important signs of a healthy body.
 a bright **b** fair **c** broad
6 Everyone has completely different ideas about what they find __________ in people.
 a slim **b** pale **c** attractive
7 You have to run around so much in your new job, you don't need to worry about getting __________.
 a overweight **b** pale **c** sun-tanned
8 I'm fairly __________-skinned, unlike my twin.
 a short **b** pale **c** medium

5 TASK Use the adjectives for appearance and hairstyles to describe how the boy and girl look different to each other.

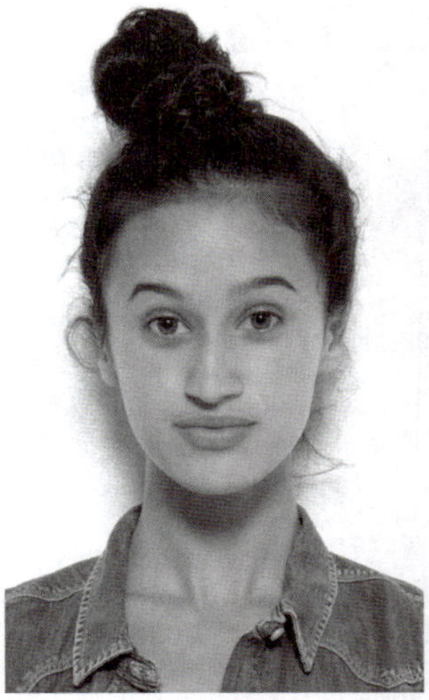

As far as hairstyles go, I think my twin brother has tried them all. When he was a small boy, he had lovely [1]__________. I was always jealous of him because mine was straight! Then, when he started school, he decided to grow it. Soon he had a [2]__________, like me. People said we looked very similar with our hair pulled back and tied up but I didn't want this when I was seven, so I would make mine into [3]__________! It took longer in the mornings, but Mum helped me. And when I took them out, my hair was really wavy.

When we started secondary school, we couldn't look more different. He used gel to make his hair go up. He put so much in, it wouldn't move and his [4]__________ hairstyle would last all day! I had a [5]__________, you know, all the same length, or a [6]__________ on the top of my head when it grew, especially when I couldn't be bothered to brush it. I thought it made me look more grown up.

Now he's older, he isn't able to be so flexible with his hair, and now has a [7]__________. I think it's the easiest hairstyle he's ever had and it suits him.

Grammar

Present simple and present continuous

1 Which tense will come next in these sentences? Write PS (present simple) or PC (present continuous).

1 These days, people in the UK … ______
2 You can use the kitchen now – no one … ______
3 A butterfly always … ______
4 These days I have so much work that … ______
5 At the moment, the world's population … ______
6 Young people nowadays … ______
7 The majority of old people usually … ______
8 In your country this week, … ______

2 Match sentence endings a–h to 1–8 in exercise 1.

a … is growing by 80 million a year.
b … are often more comfortable with technology than their parents.
c … is using it right now.
d … sleep less than they did when they were younger.
e … are most school children on holiday?
f … I'm finding it hard to meet my deadlines.
g … uses its feet to taste things.
h … spend around £1,000 on learning to drive.

3 Complete the phone dialogue between a vet and a pet owner. Use the present simple or present continuous form of the verbs in brackets.

A Hello, Amy. How's the new kitten? Is he better? [1] ______ (walk) OK now?
B Yes, I [2] ______ (watch) him now in the garden. I think he [3] ______ (be) all right. He [4] ______ (play) with my son!
A Oh good. And what about the other cats? [5] ______ (make) friends with him?
B Well, they [6] ______ (try) to, but he [7] ______ (hide) from them a lot. He [8] ______ (not know) them and is a bit scared. It will take time.

4 Complete the sentences. Use the present simple or present continuous form of the verbs in brackets. Use your own ideas to complete the statements.

1 We always ______ (learn) a lot in our ______ classes.
2 How ______ (you / travel) to school this week?
3 I usually ______ (believe) what my ______ tells me.
4 I often ______ (watch) ______ on TV.
5 Right now, I ______ (do) my homework in the ______.
6 I regularly ______ (save up) money for ______.
7 I ______ (eat) a lot of ______ these days.

5 Complete the text. Use the present simple or continuous form of the verbs below

be ▪ brush ▪ close ▪ consider ▪ have ▪ leave ▪ love ▪ open ▪ search ▪ seem ▪ take ▪ think ▪ try ▪ want ▪ work

Home | About | Destinations | Gallery | **Blog**

My name's Carlos and I volunteer at a pet rescue centre in my town. I usually [1] ______ all day on Saturdays. The centre [2] ______ from 9 until 5 every day but today we [3] ______ early because it's Christmas Eve. It's ten o'clock now and I [4] ______ the horses. This one's called Willow. We [5] ______ six horses at the moment so it usually [6] ______ about three hours. I [7] ______ looking after the horses because they always see me coming and welcome me. Did you know that they [8] ______ able to see really well and have almost 360-degree vision? All the other horses [9] ______ to get my attention now. They [10] ______ to go into the field, but they'll have to wait.

After this, I'm going to see the Barred Owl. I've never seen one up close. We think it escaped from being eaten by another owl. I never knew that owls hunt owls! It [11] ______ wrong, but here in the US, the Great Horned Owl hunts the smaller Barred Owl!

As well as the usual cats and dogs, we also have rats. Some people [12] ______ they're awful, but they actually make really good pets. They're very intelligent and can be trained to do things like dogs!

If you [13] ______ taking an animal home, there are a number of checks. You can't just take them. The main thing is that we have to be sure you'll look after them. There's a special application form. If you [14] ______ for a pet and find one, we want to know you're right for the animal, too. And after you [15] ______ with them, you'll receive support from the centre and have a home visit over the following months.

6 TASK Write sentences about your life using the verbs below. Use the present simple and the present continuous.

feel ▪ have ▪ live ▪ think ▪ work / study

Listening, vocabulary and speaking

V Insight Words often confused: personality adjectives

1 Read the sentences. Tick (✓) the sentences that are correct. Replace three incorrect adjectives.

1 Stop telling me how to live my life! You're very **arrogant** if you think you have all the answers! ☐
2 Jacob could do a lot better at school if he worked harder – he's very **easy-going**. ☐
3 I like the way your mum knows when to give advice and when to say nothing – she's very **sensitive**. ☐
4 I don't think Sofia is afraid of giving interviews, she's just very **stubborn** about her success. ☐
5 It's good to have strong opinions, but if you never change your mind, that's just being **determined**. ☐

2 Complete the sentences with the words below.

assertive ▪ determined ▪ easy-going ▪ emotional ▪ shy

1 My mum is ____________ and doesn't like to be the centre of attention.
2 He cries a lot. He's very ____________.
3 Sheila will say no when someone asks her to do things she doesn't want to do. She's ____________.
4 A ____________ person, like Ali, will never stop trying, even when something seems impossible.
5 My cousin is very ____________ and isn't difficult to please.

Speaking

Speculating

3 🔊1.01 Listen to the dialogue and look at the pictures. Are the sentences true (T) or false (F)? Correct the false ones.

1 Dan is avoiding work he should be doing.
2 Dan has known about the Italian artist for a while.
3 Lily doesn't see the second clown to begin with.
4 Lily is less interested in the images than Dan.

4 🔊1.01 Listen again and complete the phrases.

1 It ____________ two children and a puppy.
2 It ____________ it, doesn't it?
3 He ____________ a great imagination ...
4 The girls ____________ they're the eyes now ...
5 It doesn't ____________ that strange ...
6 It ____________ a picture of any sad clown.
7 Oh, it ____________ one clown because ...
8 It ____________ the clown is unhappy this way, and ...
9 I thought it ____________ a picture ...
10 But there ____________ more cats in the image.

5 Choose the words to complete the dialogue.

Mark Hey look, I've found this old photo of our great-grandparents and their family!
Vicky Wow, that [1]**can't** / **look** / **must** be about 50 years old!
Mark Look, that's our great-grandfather, Edward. He [2]**looks like** / **looks** / **could** really nice and friendly.
Vicky But who's that woman? It [3]**can't** / **might** / **may** be our great-grandmother; she [4]**might** / **looks like** / **looks** too young.
Mark No, that [5]**might** / **looks as if** / **can** be her. I think she was very young when she got married.
Vicky And do you think that [6]**seems** / **looks** / **could** be our grandfather?
Mark Yes, I've seen photos of him as a child, and that [7]**must** / **looks like** / **might** him.
Vicky They [8]**look as if** / **might** / **seem** they're on holiday in France. What are they eating?
Mark It [9]**can** / **looks as if** / **could** be some kind of cake.

6 TASK Look at the prints below and guess the animal that made them using the language of speculating. Think about:

- what the animal looks like.
- what size it is.
- where it lives.
- what it eats.

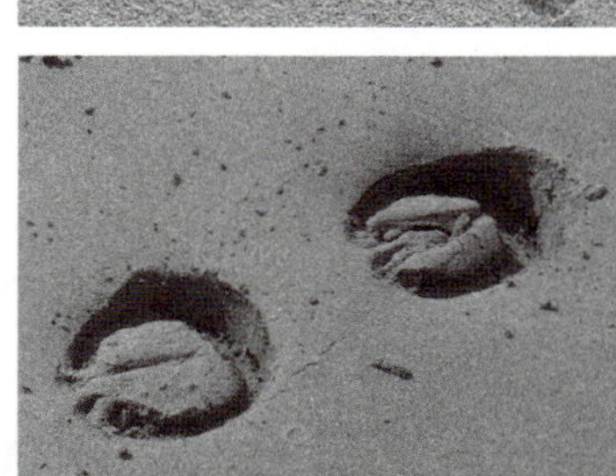
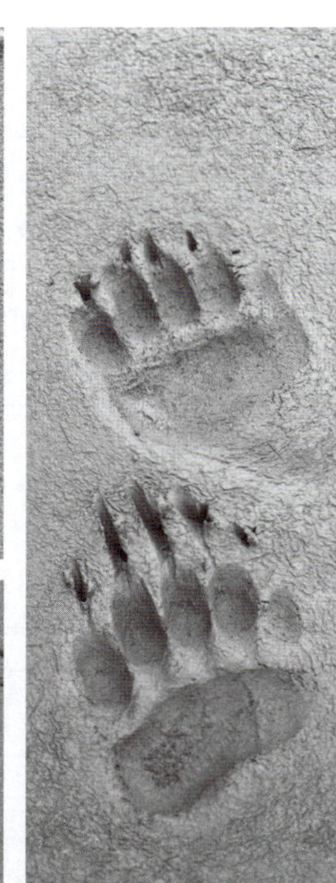

Vocabulary and grammar

V Insight Clothes and fashion

1 Complete the sentences with adjectives to describe fashion.

1 I sometimes buy expensive d__________ clothes, but I will always wait for the sales.
2 New technology could bring some very i__________ ideas for future fashion, including clothes that change colour!
3 I like it when people manage to look very s__________ even when they buy things from charity shops.
4 This dress looks new, but I bought it from a s__________ shop in Camden Market.
5 I love v__________ clothes, especially 70s dresses. The quality was so much better then than nowadays.
6 Punk was such an o__________ fashion movement. I think a lot of fashion since then has just copied it.

Vocabulary extra Clothes

2 Match items of clothing a–f to descriptions 1–6 of why people might wear them.

1 This will keep you warm, but is easy to take off, with buttons down the front.
2 This jacket can be really light and easy to wear, but it's incredibly warm.
3 You can wear these in the gym or around the house when you're relaxing.
4 Perfect for a camping or walking holiday, and all those pockets are useful, too.
5 On a cold day, this will even keep your ears warm!
6 They can be worn on the beach.

a cargo pants / trousers
b fleece
c cardigan
d Bermudas
e joggers
f hoody

3 Label the photos with the correct item of clothing.

A

____

B

____

C

____

D

____

Verb patterns

4 Choose the correct verbs to complete the sentences. Remember to use the correct verb patterns.

ban ▪ dress ▪ pay ▪ see ▪ steal ▪ wear (×2)

1 I can't imagine __________ a suit to work every day. I live in casual clothes.
2 In cold weather, I need __________ my hoody more, now that I've got a shaved head!
3 A 16-year-old girl admitted __________ some trainers from a London store.
4 You can avoid __________ the highest prices for stuff if you shop in markets.
5 In the past, Harrods, an upmarket department store, decided __________ people wearing jeans. It isn't like that anymore.
6 We expected __________ men wearing kilts in Scotland, but there weren't that many.
7 I love __________ in really bright colours. My students always comment on it!

5 Match 1–8 to a–h.

1 I stopped drinking coffee.
2 I forgot to meet Sumire.
3 I tried running twice a week, but I didn't enjoy it.
4 I regret telling you that the party was cancelled – it was a stupid lie.
5 I stopped to drink a coffee.
6 I tried to run fast but I didn't have enough energy.
7 I regret to tell you that the party has been cancelled.
8 I won't forget meeting Sumire!

a I stopped working and had a break.
b I met Sumire and it was an amazing experience.
c I wasn't able to run fast.
d I'm sorry about something I told you in the past.
e I didn't meet Sumire.
f I ran a few times, but it wasn't fun.
g I don't drink coffee any more.
h I'm sorry about something I'm telling you now.

6 TASK Use the correct form of a verb to complete the comments from an online survey so they are true for you.

1 I don't need __________ when ...
2 I prefer __________ at weekends.
3 I don't like __________ because ...
4 I wish I could __________ but ...
5 I've tried __________ and people said I looked good!
6 I often avoid __________ because ...

Reading

1 Look at the title of the reading. What do you think the article is about?

a Learning to make the most of your appearance.
b How models have become more like you and me.
c Accepting that the fashion world is unrealistic.

2 Study the highlighted words in the article. Then match them to definitions 1–9.

1 look like RESEMBLE
2 small brown spots, often on people with pale skin FRECKLES
3 feeling embarrassed or guilty ASHAMED
4 being young YOUTH
5 size and shape of a human body PHYSIQUE
6 has two sides that are the same in shape or size SIMMETRICAL
7 put importance on something EMPHASIS
8 act in a way because of how someone treated you REACT
9 looking at something quickly, without reading FLICKING TROUGH

3 Choose the correct answers.

1 In paragraph one, what is true about the writer?
  a She often had problems sleeping.
  b She wasn't keen on her appearance.
  c She didn't think it was possible to be a model.
  d She didn't understand the fashion choices in magazines.
2 What is the overall message in paragraph two?
  a The change experienced in the nineties was limited.
  b The nineties signalled big changes in the fashion industry.
  c Many normal people began to relate to images they saw.
  d Difference was celebrated in the supermodels of the time.
3 How has social media had a negative impact?
  a Young people have started to change their appearance.
  b The pressure to look good has become even greater.
  c Many people don't recognize when filters are used.
  d We're less likely to talk to each other face to face.
4 What is true about boys and girls?
  a Almost 50% of boys decided to change their diets.
  b Their reaction differs in relation to negative comments.
  c Girls didn't often discuss their appearance as teenagers.
  d Boys don't tend to care as much about how they look.
5 What statement is true in paragraph five?
  a Change is happening throughout the fashion industry.
  b The industry is easier for original female fashion models.
  c The rate of change has been quicker with female models.
  d The male fashion industry doesn't seem to want to change.
6 In the last paragraph, how does the writer feel about the future?
  a realistic
  b pessimistic
  c extremely positive
  d somewhat optimistic

Finally, a reflection of reality

1 I remember growing up in the eighties and flicking through magazines and wondering why the people who were chosen to wear certain clothes on fashion shoots looked nothing like me. I had red hair, glasses and freckles. It didn't make me have sleepless nights or worry too much. Instead, I thought that I'd never be able to do that kind of job. 'You've got to see it to be it', as they say.

2 Then the nineties came along and gave birth to the supermodels. Sure, there was Kate Moss, who at a comparatively tiny 1.7 m was different, but only in the sense of her height. Then there was Naomi Campbell, who had dark skin, but again everything else was not unusual. This sent the message that you had to be slim and your skin had to be flawless. A symmetrical face was preferred and beauty was all about youth. The images of both women and men in magazines mostly reflected a very small percentage of people we see in our everyday lives.

3 Since social media has become popular, there has been even more emphasis on what people consider to be perfection regarding looks. On top of this is the ability to add filters. They change a person's face so much that I'm not sure I'd recognize some people in real life! It's no surprise that this has all had a negative effect on young people. A YouGov survey of 1,118 teenagers in Britain found that 37% felt ashamed or upset by their appearance.

4 And it isn't just girls. Credos, an advertising industry think tank, surveyed over 1,000

eight- to eighteen-year-old boys. Over half of them said that they'd think about changing what they ate in order to look better. While girls may cry or talk about it if someone said something about their appearance, boys react differently. They may pretend it didn't hurt them and are less likely to talk to anyone.

5 Having said this, slowly but surely things are moving in the right direction. Thanks to models like Winnie Harlow, who has vitiligo*, Andreja Pejić, who became the first transgender model in Vogue in 2015, and Jacky O'Shaughnessy, who is over 60, we are starting to see a shift. They have all fought against the fashion world's idea of beauty and made a successful career from what they look like. Male modelling seems to have been slower to move from tradition: a slim, muscular physique. However, Nemar Parchment, who became the first plus size male model signed by IMG in 2018, is leading the way.

6 As much as we'd all like to see changes happen overnight, this isn't realistic. If you look at images of the eighties and compare them to today, however, there is visible change. Social media appears to have advantages and disadvantages. On the one hand, there is pressure to resemble the narrow ideas of beauty that we see. On the other hand, the nature of social media means that you can reach a wide audience. Seeing a variety of body types will help to give people the confidence to believe in themselves no matter what they look like.

Glossary

* Vitiligo is a condition where white patches appear on the skin

4 Write the noun forms of the adjectives. Check your answers in the article.

1 beautiful BEAUTY
2 perfect PERFECTION
3 able ABILITY
4 traditional TRADITION
5 confident CONFIDENCE

5 Complete the sentences with the correct form of the words in exercise 4.

1 Leonardo da Vinci studied anatomy. That's why he drew the human body to PERFECTION.
2 CONFIDENCE is something particularly popular in Hollywood. Older actresses in particular complain about this.
3 Jake's ABLE to look good in anything is annoying!
4 It isn't always the most ~~BEAUTIFUL~~ CONFIDENT people who succeed. It often those who have the ABILITY to make the most of their skills.
5 It's TRADIONAL for Japanese women to wear a kimono when they become 20 years of age.

6 TASK Look at the images taken from different magazines. Use *look*, *looks like*, *appear*, *seem*, *look as if* and some of the adjectives and nouns you have just learned to guess when the photos were taken. Do they show traditional beauty or a wider, more modern idea of beauty?

Writing An informal email

1 **Read the email and correct the mistakes. Write your corrections in the correct category. There are two items in each category.**

To: Oscar **Subject:** Photo from Bruno!

Hi Oscar!

I took this photo of my family yesterday, so I send it to you now. Say me if you like it. I'm very sun-taned! Thats my grandparents' house, and you can see that it's big old and very beautyful. My brother and I go often there. I really like their garden, and we're often playing volleyball in it. My brother plays really good. You are studying hard right now? I want to write to you more often. Please reply soon.

Love, Bruno

Punctuation: ______, ______
Spelling: ______, ______
Grammar: ______, ______
Word order: ______, ______
Vocabulary: ______, ______

2 **Read the advert on a school sports website. Then read Marsha's email and label the photograph.**

Sports teams looking for partners!

If you want to contact sports teams in other countries, send us some information and an email address. Or just write to one of the people already in our sports team partnership project.

3 **Complete Marsha's email.**

Subject: Sports team partnership

Hi Nadine,

My name's Marsha and I'm 17. I [1] ______ to you as part of the sports team partnership project. I play rugby for my school team. There are 20 people in our rugby club, and we try to practise at least twice a week after school. Twice a month, on Saturday, 15 of us [2] ______ in the first team.

I [3] ______ you a photo of a few of us after training. I'm in the middle of the photo, the one with dark skin and my hair up in a bun on top of my head. I'm quite tall – I [4] ______ and holding the rugby ball! My best friend, Debbie, is the one with [5] ______ hair on the right – yes, she's tall as well and a great defender. She's very funny and easy-going. My other good friends are Amber – she's the one at the back on the left – and Zahra. Zahra's the one with dark hair next to me. She looks younger and smaller than the rest of us, but she's actually really strong. Write and tell me something about you and your team and send me a photo. I hope to [6] ______ from you soon.

Bye for now, Marsha

A ______
B ______
C ______
D ______

Writing guide

TASK **Write an informal email in reply to the online forum post.**

> Do you and your friends want to get in touch with other fans of your favourite bands? Post a photo of you and your friends below!

PLAN 1 **Think about the following:**

- bands which you and your friends like
- your favourite songs
- concerts you've been to
- how the bands influence the clothes and the hairstyles of you and your friends

PLAN 2 **Decide which ideas you are going to use and make notes for each paragraph.**

Paragraph 1: Introduction. Write about which band you and your friends are fans of, and why you like them.
Paragraph 2: Describe a photo of you and your friends and say where you are in the photo. Describe clothes and hairstyles and their connection with different bands.
Paragraph 3: Ask for more photos and information.
Paragraph 4: Ask for another email and sign off.

WRITE **Write your email.**

REVIEW **Check the following points.**

- Have you used the correct email format and register?
- Have you included all the information asked for in the task?
- Have you checked grammar, vocabulary, punctuation and spelling?

U1 Assess your progress

Give yourself a mark 1–3 for each Learning Objective from the lesson.
1 I found this difficult. **2** This was OK. **3** I can do this well.

Lesson	Learning Objective	Mark
Lesson 1A	I can scan a text for specific information.	2
	I can use context to understand new words.	1
	I can use adjectives to describe appearance.	2
	How can I improve?	
Lesson 1B	I can recognize numbers and measurements.	2
	I can use the present simple to talk about routines, facts and general truths.	3
	I can use the present continuous to talk about current activities and planned future events.	3
	How can I improve?	
Lesson 1C	I can understand the main points in a radio interview.	
	I can use personality adjectives.	
	I can use key language to speculate.	
	How can I improve?	
Lesson 1D	I can understand cohesion in a text.	
	I can use clothes and fashion words to describe clothing and style.	
	I can recognize and use different verb patterns.	
	How can I improve?	
Lesson 1E	I can consider audience, genre and purpose to plan and write an email.	
	I can use appropriate language and register in an informal email.	
	I can use phrases to describe position in a photo.	
	How can I improve?	

Action plan

Make a plan for what you can do next to improve. Discuss your ideas with your classmates / teacher.

2 On the move

Vocabulary

Insight Compound nouns: travel

1 Complete the compound nouns with the words below.

destination ▪ guide ▪ package ▪ park ▪ resort ▪ transport ▪ trap

1 We went to a beach __________ in Portugal but, to be honest, it was a bit of a disappointment.
2 Casablanca, in Morocco, has trams as part of the city's public __________ system.
3 It's a good idea to visit some of the other art galleries in Italy, as Rome is a bit of a tourist __________.
4 __________ holidays are less popular now that people can book flights and accommodation online.
5 The whole of Yellowstone National __________ in the US is actually a giant supervolcano.
6 A tour __________'s salary often isn't very high, but they often get tips at the end of a trip.
7 France is the world's number one travel __________.

Insight Travel

2 Match verbs 1–7 to nouns a–g.

1 take part in	a the sun
2 escape	b the sights
3 take	c the beaten track
4 soak up	d people
5 get off	e time out
6 see	f the crowds
7 get to know	g guided tours

3 Complete the adverts with the phrases in exercise 2.

1 **No travel companions? No problem! __________ while you see the famous European cities with Adventures Abroad.**

2 __________ in the popular places! Our expert guides know places the tourists don't!

3 We've all had a cold, dark winter. It's time to __________ on a holiday to the Greek islands.

4 Do you need to __________ and just relax? Book one of our spa days today and you get a 25% discount.

5 *__________ of London in our open-top double-decker bus!*

6 __________ one of our __________ and there's no need for a guidebook. Our guides will be happy to answer all your questions.

7 Hire one of our jeeps, and __________. Discover the beautiful coves that make Minorca such a special place.

Vocabulary extra Types of holiday

4 Match types of holiday 1–6 to descriptions a–f.

1 a working holiday
2 a house swap
3 a backpacking holiday
4 a city break
5 a honeymoon
6 an adventure holiday

a When you see the most famous sights of a place in a couple of days.
b When you do jobs, often to help local people.
c When a couple goes on holiday after their wedding.
d When people live in each other's homes.
e When you explore new places and do unusual and exciting things, such as a safari.
f When you travel to many places, carrying all your things on your back.

5 Complete the email with the words below.

adventure holiday ▪ beach resort ▪ coach tour ▪ get off the beaten track ▪ got to know ▪ national park ▪ package holiday ▪ self-catering ▪ soak up the sun ▪ take some time out ▪ tour guide

Hi Priti

Thanks for your email. Yes, we're finally back from South Africa.

As you know, we started off on safari at the Kruger [1]__________ near Johannesburg. We had a great [2]__________ called Arno. He had amazing knowledge about all the wild animals and we were lucky enough to see some lions. We [3]__________ him quite well and invited him to our house in Ireland next year.

Then we were going to take a [4]__________ all the way down to Cape Town, but we decided to hire a car instead. It took several days as we stopped off along the way. We went horse-riding and had a beach day where we could [5]__________ on our way there.

We were in [6]__________ accommodation for the whole holiday, but we mainly just ate out as we didn't feel like cooking.

When we got to Cape Town, we had a couple of days at a [7]__________. It was the perfect end to a fabulous holiday: the spa meant we had a bit of luxury, and we had the sea a short walk away, too. It was great to [8]__________ and relax after our busy year at work.

Thanks for suggesting an [9]__________. I'd never have done it without your encouragement. It's much better to [10]__________. You can't do this on a [11]__________ with 150 other tourists!

See you soon.

Sophie

6 TASK Think about the best holiday or the worst holiday you have ever had. What kind of holiday was it and what did you do? What made it so good or so bad?

Grammar

Narrative tenses

1 Match the sentence halves. Then write them as one sentence using one past continuous phrase, one past simple phrase and *when*.

1 the sun / not shine
2 you / leave / your bag on the coach
3 the coach / reverse / into the entrance
4 we / have / dinner in the hotel restaurant
5 you / stay / in Dubai
6 the sun / set / over the mountains

a the fire alarm / go off.
b it / hit / a car in the hotel car park.
c we / arrive / at the ski resort.
d you / go / hot air balloon?
e I / wake up.
f you / travel / to the airport?

1 *The sun wasn't shining when I woke up.*
2 ______
3 ______
4 ______
5 ______
6 ______

2 Choose the option that has a similar meaning to the first sentence.

1 We'd crossed the river when we saw the crocodiles.
  a We crossed the river and then we saw the crocodiles.
  b We saw the crocodiles when we were crossing the river.
  c We saw the crocodiles before we crossed the river.
2 Will was eating when I got to the restaurant.
  a Will started eating when I got to the restaurant.
  b I got to the restaurant and then Will started eating.
  c Will had started eating when I got to the restaurant.
3 I'd learned a lot of Cantonese when I left Hong Kong.
  a I learned Cantonese when I was in Hong Kong.
  b I learned a lot of Cantonese after I left Hong Kong.
  c When I left Hong Kong I was learning Cantonese.
4 I heard a loud noise when the plane was taking off.
  a I heard a noise before the plane took off.
  b The plane started taking off and I heard a noise.
  c After the plane had taken off, I heard a noise.
5 We visited the art gallery and had tea in a hotel.
  a We had tea and then went to the art gallery.
  b We went to the art gallery and then to a hotel.
  c We were visiting the art gallery when we had tea.
6 We were walking to the station because our taxi hadn't come when we saw Vicki crossing the road.
  a We walked to the station, then the taxi didn't come, then we saw Vicki.
  b The taxi didn't come, then we arrived at the station, then we saw Vicki.
  c The taxi didn't come, then we saw Vicki, then we got to the station.

3 Complete the sentences. Use the correct past perfect or past simple form of the verbs in brackets.

1 When the snow ______ (stop), we ______ (go) out to build a snowman.
2 When the train came, I ______ (realize) I ______ (lose) my ticket.
3 Unfortunately, the film ______ (start) by the time we ______ (arrive).
4 When we ______ (pack) our bags, we ______ (call) a taxi to take us to the airport.
5 Everyone ______ (finish) eating the meal before we ______ (get) to the café.
6 I ______ (not be able to) go to Hiro's party because I ______ (promise) to go to Elena's!

4 Complete the text using the correct form of the verbs in brackets.

A few years ago, I [1] ______ (travel) to the airport. I [2] ______ (be) so excited! I [3] ______ (spend) most of the previous year saving up the money to visit my friend in Greece. Before I [4] ______ (leave) home, I [5] ______ (check) that I had my money and my passport. I [6] ______ (not want) anything to stop me going. I [7] ______ (relax) on the airport bus when I [8] ______ (realize) that I [9] ______ (forget) the gift for my friend. After a few minutes I [10] ______ (decide) that it wasn't the end of the world and I would buy something at the airport.

When the bus [11] ______ (arrive), I went straight to check-in. Lucky me. There [12] ______ (not be) a queue. I handed over my passport. The man looked at it. Why [13] ______ he ______ (shake) his head? My heart sank when he [14] ______ (tell) me that my passport was out of date.

I can laugh now as I got an emergency passport a couple of days later, but it really wasn't funny at the time!

5 TASK You are a travel writer. You have just returned from a trip. Using one of the examples below, write about what you did on the trip for a travel magazine.

- a trek in the Himalayas in Nepal
- looking after elephants in Thailand
- a diving course in the Caribbean

Listening, vocabulary and speaking

V Insight Types of journey

1 Choose the correct words.

1 I'd love to do **a voyage** / **an expedition** across the Pacific Ocean on a big ship.
2 My language school had an **expedition** / **excursion** every weekend to other places in Canada.
3 Antarctica **expeditions** / **excursions** have become popular – does it ever get crowded?
4 My sister bought this lovely sari for me on her business **voyage** / **trip** to India.
5 The longest non-stop **flight** / **tour** is from New York to Singapore – nearly 19 hours!
6 You need to be very fit if you want to do that **excursion** / **trek** through the Alps.
7 It's worth taking a guided **trek** / **tour** along the Great Wall of China. Our guide told us it's believed to be over 21,000 kilometres long!

2 Complete the sentences with words from exercise 1.

1 In 2018, Jade Hameister, from Melbourne, became the youngest person to complete an unsupported and unassisted ____________ to the South Pole from the coast on skis.
2 I saw my favourite pop group when they did a ____________ of the UK last year.
3 When I was 18, I did a three-month ____________ across the Atlantic from the Caribbean.
4 Would you like to go on an ____________ to Brighton at the weekend?
5 We went on a seven-day ____________ in Nepal from Pokhara to Annapurna base camp, which sits at an altitude of 4,130 metres.
6 The shortest commercial ____________ takes just 90 seconds to go between two Scottish islands, Westray and Papa Westray.

Persuading and negotiating

3 🔊2.01 Study the lines from a dialogue. Then answer the questions. Listen and check.

Katie Dad was asking me where we'd like to go away this year …
Katie That climbing wall is nearby, and you loved when we got a boat on the lake.
Joe Well, maybe if you're small kids, but not for us. I feel like we've outgrown it a bit.

1 What's the relationship between Joe and Katie?
____
2 How old do you think they are?
____
3 What are they discussing?
____

4 🔊2.01 Listen again. Write J (Joe) or K (Katie) next to the phrases that they use in the dialogue. Which phrase do they not use?

1 ________ That sounds brilliant! But I'm not so sure about that youth hostel.
2 ________ OK, you've convinced me. I'll agree if you promise that we can spend a weekend there another time.
3 ________ Let's say we want to go there. Come on, you won't be sorry.
4 ________ OK, let's go for it! It will be a laugh like it was before.
5 ________ It's always great to get in a tent, make fires and cook for ourselves. What do you think?
6 ________ And anyway, you've got nothing to lose – we can go to the campsite for a weekend at some point.
7 ________ I'd like to try something different. Why don't we have a bit more luxury?

5 🔊2.02 Listen and complete the dialogue with parts of the phrases in exercise 4.

A I think [1]____________ try that new Japanese restaurant in town. They have really low tables and you sit on the floor!
B [2]____________ interesting, but I don't like Japanese food. Why [3]____________ for an Indian?
A [4]____________ sure about Indian food since I had that curry that was way too hot.
B Well, try something different, then. You won't [5]____________, I promise.
A Mmmm. I'm not convinced.
B Look, if you come to the Indian restaurant, I'll pay, so you've got [6]____________.
A OK, you've [7]____________. And I'll pay for ice creams in Gelato Mio's afterwards.
B OK, let's [8]____________ it!

6 TASK You and a friend have decided to go on an adventure holiday, but you want to go on different ones. Write a dialogue in which you persuade each other, negotiate and reach an agreement.

ICELAND – *the land of fire and ice*

If you're looking for everything nature has to offer, Iceland is for you. This seven-day trip will let you explore the waterfalls, glaciers and the famous geothermal pools of the Blue Lagoon. You may even be lucky enough to see the Northern Lights on our evening excursion. If you love the great outdoors, this is the trip for you. You won't be disappointed.

SWIMMING AND TREKKING IN Croatia

Enjoy swimming in the clear waters of the Adriatic Sea, to and from the beautiful islands of Kornati National Park. Get off the beaten track and back to nature across land and sea. Meet new friends while you explore these mostly uninhabited islands. It will be an unforgettable experience, and you'll get fit at the same time!

Vocabulary and grammar

V Insight Verbs + prepositions: travel

1 Complete the sentences with the correct form of the verbs below.

connect with ▪ cut through ▪ drive along ▪ lead to ▪ travel down ▪ wind around

1 If you ________ Route 66 from Chicago to Los Angeles, you'll travel over 3,600 kilometres through some spectacular scenery.
2 When you ________ the Wainui River in New Zealand, you'll experience some of the most challenging white water in the world.
3 One of the oldest roads in the world, The King's Highway, ________ the north of Jordan ________ the south and passes through the historic city of Petra.
4 The Atlantic Road in Norway ________ eight kilometres of beautiful Norwegian coastline and is an example of impressive engineering.
5 The Guoliang Tunnel Road in China ________ the Taihang Mountains and was created by local villagers.
6 Twelve roads ________ the Arc de Triomphe in Paris and form the shape of a star from above.

Vocabulary extra Travel and transport

2 Choose the correct words.

1 The San Francisco Bay cruise leaves from **platform** / **pier** 39 on Fisherman's Wharf.
2 Flight BA 161 is now boarding at **stand** / **gate** 12.
3 Excuse me, is there a **cabin** / **buffet car** on this train?
4 The Cambridge coach goes from **platform** / **stand** 11. It's a bit late today.
5 Would you like a window or **deck** / **aisle** seat?
6 Please put all hand luggage in the **carriages** / **overhead lockers** and prepare for take-off.
7 A 21-year-old man was arrested after driving in the wrong direction on the **runway** / **motorway**.
8 The ship will stop at Cape Town, so that passengers can go **ashore** / **land** there.
9 I don't think I would enjoy a six-week **flight** / **cruise** – I don't like the sea that much.
10 The boat will **set sail** / **take off** at 6.00 p.m., so please make sure you're back in time.

used to and *would*

3 Complete the sentences with the correct form of the verbs in brackets and *used to* or *would*.

1 People ________ (often drive) without seat belts before it became illegal.
2 People ________ (run) long distances to deliver messages – that's how the marathon began.
3 Before the Panama Canal was built, ships ________ (sail) all the way around South America.
4 Until cheap flights appeared in the 1960s, most people ________ (not travel) by plane.
5 Britain ________ (have) 32,000 kilometres of railway tracks. It now has 16,000.
6 People ________ (have) much worse diets in the past, which is why they were smaller.

4 Complete the text with the correct form of the verbs below and *used to* or *would*.

be ▪ go ▪ have ▪ meet ▪ not live ▪ stay ▪ take ▪ travel

We are all aware of how technology has changed over the last 100 years. No one [1]________ a phone or computer, but what about everything else?

For a start, people [2]________ as long as they do now. In 1920 in the USA, the average life expectancy was your mid-50s and now it's almost 80.

And life [3]________ very different for women. It wasn't until 1918 that women were allowed to vote in the UK. Can you imagine that? It was also when the car industry was born. Before that, people [4]________ long distances by train and short distances on foot. Companies like Ford in the United States were now using factories to build cars. This made the process cheaper.

Holidays were different as well. Although there was commercial air travel in the 1920s, it [5]________ only the richest members of society to destinations abroad. Most people [6]________ local and travel to tourist places nearby.

And now we all have many forms of entertainment. Back then, the family [7]________ in the living room to listen to the radio. It seems strange, doesn't it? Without a TV, cinema was also popular. Many people [8]________ every week.

5 TASK Write sentences about when you were at primary school using *would* and *used to*. Think about:

- food and drink.
- lessons.
- friends.
- sport.
- weekends.

Reading

1 Look at the four holidays below and decide which you would most like to go on. Then read the magazine article. Have you changed your mind?

1 an excursion to a winter park in Norway
2 a cycle ride from Rotterdam to Vienna
3 a trip to the temple of Angkor Wat in Cambodia
4 a trek through the Grand Canyon

2 In which description do people:

1 say that things seem to be from a children's story? A, B
2 talk about very big buildings? ______, ______
3 travel by river? ______, ______
4 say they got a good night's rest? ______, ______
5 travel by animal? ______, ______
6 travel by bicycle? ______, ______
7 see the sun go up or down? ______, ______
8 look at the night sky? ______, ______
9 talk about the cost of the holiday? ______, ______

3 Read the article again. Answer the questions.

1 When does the Winter Park open?
______
2 Why is it easier to cycle along the side of rivers?
______
3 Why doesn't the Riverside Ride have much environmental impact?
______
4 How was Angkor Wat built as quickly as it was?
______
5 Why is it a good idea to get to Angkor Wat early?
______
6 What do people on the Grand Canyon holiday do in the evenings?
______

4 Study the highlighted words in the article. Then match them to definitions 1–7.

1 flat boats that go along rivers, especially where the water moves very fast ______
2 a person owned by another person and made to work for them ______
3 shining brightly and then less brightly, like stars ______
4 how fast you do something ______
5 quite cold ______
6 the parts of a tree that are in the ground ______
7 very sentimental and romantic ______

5 TASK Write a paragraph saying which of the holidays would suit ONE of the below.

- An older couple
- A family
- A group of friends

Unforgettable getaway

We asked you to send us your stories about holiday trips that were truly unforgettable. Here are some of our favourites.

(A)

Hunderfossen Winter Park – Norway

We went here on our half-term holiday, and it was by far the best thing I've ever done! We had to wait until after sunset for the park to open, and as we were getting near, we could see the lights of the log cabins twinkling in the white snow, with the stars twinkling in the black sky above them. You travel around by horse-drawn sleigh, past the huge Fairytale Castle and I did feel like I was in a fairy tale! If this all sounds a bit soppy, then how about some ice-climbing, ice-bowling, snow-rafting or driving around on snowmobiles (they have special ones that kids can drive)? We spent a night in the ice hotel, and although it's pretty chilly (about -5°C), they have really warm sleeping bags, and I had one of the best nights of sleep ever. It was a fantastic experience!

Paula, 15

(B)

Riverside Ride, Rotterdam to Vienna

I did this ride with student friends from university. It sounds like a cycling marathon for sporty types, but that wasn't us! We'd discovered a really important secret … the roads that follow rivers are usually pretty flat and easy to cycle on! We followed the Rhine and Danube most of the way (with just one short boat ride!), and there are cycle tracks and quiet country roads that wind along the riverside and keep you off the beaten track. We stayed in B&Bs and it wasn't very expensive. The views were amazing, especially the fairy-tale castles overlooking the river. There were plenty of sights to see, but it was mostly about taking time out and going at a nice, slow pace through a landscape full of history and natural beauty. It's also a good way to get to know people, as we chatted most of the time we were cycling. Finally, you won't find a holiday with less environmental impact!

Dan, 23

(C)

Angkor Wat – Cambodia

I spent my gap year backpacking around Asia. I loved Cambodia, and the most unforgettable experience was Angkor Wat, which is an amazing ruined temple. Some people call it the eighth wonder of the world, and it's on the Cambodian national flag! It's unbelievably enormous – more than one square kilometre in size. It took around 30 years to build, but a modern engineer said it would take about 300 years to build today, probably because you couldn't use thousands of unpaid slave workers! I'd recommend getting there early to escape the crowds. I cycled there and arrived just as the sun was rising – it was awesome! I love the fact that nature is taking back parts of the temple, with huge tree roots growing up through them.

Jenny, 19

(D)

Grand Canyon – USA

If you don't think the Grand Canyon is the most unforgettable thing you've ever seen, then you haven't been there! I'd never thought of it as a family holiday, but it certainly is. We did a trek-and-bike camping holiday, with a guide who set up camp every night, cooked and organized games. We camped right on the edge of the Grand Canyon. The next day the adults headed down the 14-kilometre trail into the canyon on foot, and our 14-year-old son decided to go by mule! We slept well that night, after we'd spent a couple of hours lying on our backs looking up at the stars! We also went through the Bryce Canyon National Park, which has incredible rock formations, and then went down the canyon on rafts along the Colorado River! It wasn't cheap, but it's a memory we'll have for life.

Ricardo, 42

Writing A story

1 Read the first two paragraphs of Kerry's story. Number the order in which the following things are mentioned. There are two things that you do not need.

_____ **a** a description of the weather
_____ **b** the time of day
_____ **c** the time of year
_____ **d** the location
_____ **e** a description of the other people around
_____ **f** how the person was feeling
_____ **g** a quote

It was around four o'clock in the afternoon. It was still hot, but it was beginning to get a bit cooler. I was hungry and tired from sightseeing, so I bought something to eat and sat down. I was travelling around South Africa for a month and I had just finished looking around Cape Point. This is where the Atlantic Ocean meets the Pacific.

There were a lot of tourists, all looking as hot and as hungry as me. But I managed to find somewhere quiet to sit on some rocks and admire the view. A couple were there too, doing the same as me. I hadn't eaten all day, so I opened my sandwiches and some water and ate quickly.

2 Look at the first two paragraphs again. Find examples of the following tenses.

1 past continuous to give background to the story
_____

2 past perfect to say what happened before the story began
_____

3 past simple to begin the story
_____

3 Read the third paragraph of the story. Why did Kerry think the couple might be crazy?

1 _____ I saw the couple pointing at me. They were looking at me very strangely. To my surprise, they started shouting angrily at me in a foreign language. They seemed a bit crazy, to be honest. 2 _____ I tried smiling nervously at them. I hadn't done anything wrong and didn't want to shout back. 3 _____ they stopped, but I decided it would be better to go and eat somewhere else. I quietly walked away and, although it was crowded, I 4 _____ found another spot. It wasn't as nice, but at least no one was trying to have an argument with me!

4 Read the last paragraph of the story. Why had the couple shouted at Kerry angrily? Why did Kerry feel embarrassed?

I heard some footsteps coming up behind me. 5 _____ I realized the couple had followed me. And this time someone else was with them. I tried to leave, but 6 _____ the other person started speaking in English. He told me that the couple wanted to explain their behaviour but needed a translator. A monkey had been behind me trying to take my food, and they were shouting at it, not me. I was embarrassed, but happy that I hadn't done anything wrong!

5 Complete the paragraphs in exercises 3 and 4 with the words below.

a few seconds later ■ after a while ■ at first ■ eventually ■ just then ■ that's when

6 Match the verbs to the adverbs. Check your answers in the story paragraphs.

1 eat	**a** nervously
2 look	**b** quietly
3 smile	**c** strangely
4 shout	**d** quickly
5 walk away	**e** angrily

Writing guide

TASK **Write your own embarrassing story which happened to you when travelling.**

PLAN 1 **Think about the following:**
- who you were with and the reason for travelling
- how the situation began
- the embarrassing thing that happened
- how you felt and what you did afterwards

PLAN 2 **Make notes for each paragraph.**
Paragraph 1: Try to write an interesting opening sentence that makes the reader want to know more. Include background details in this paragraph, using the past continuous and past perfect.
Paragraph 2: Describe the events which led up to the embarrassing event.
Paragraph 3: Finish the story of the event.
Paragraph 4: Say what you did afterwards and how you felt.

WRITE **Write your story.**

REVIEW **Check the following points.**
- Have you used a variety of narrative tenses?
- Have you used enough adjectives and adverbs to bring the story to life?
- Have you checked grammar, vocabulary, spelling and punctuation?

U2 Assess your progress

Give yourself a mark 1–3 for each Learning Objective from the lesson.
1 I found this difficult. **2** This was OK. **3** I can do this well.

Lesson 2A

	Mark
I can recognize attitude and point of view in a text.	
I can scan a text for specific information.	
I can use compound nouns and phrases to talk about travel.	
How can I improve?	

Lesson 2B

	Mark
I can use the past simple to describe completed actions or states in the past, and past habits.	
I can use narrative tenses to describe the past.	
How can I improve?	

Lesson 2C

	Mark
I can use different strategies to identify purpose in a listening text.	
I can use verbs and prepositions to talk about travel.	
I can use phrases to persuade, negotiate and agree in a discussion.	
How can I improve?	

Lesson 2D

	Mark
I can find and understand relevant information in a text.	
I can use verbs + prepositions to talk about travel.	
I can use *used to* and *would* to talk about the past.	
How can I improve?	

Lesson 2E

	Mark
I can write an effective opening sentence to a story.	
I can order events in a story.	
How can I improve?	

Action plan

Make a plan for what you can do next to improve. Discuss your ideas with your classmates / teacher.

3 Health matters

Vocabulary

Insight Idioms: happiness and sadness

1 Match the words and phrases to make idioms.

1 ☹ down in the
2 ☺ feeling
3 ☹ be on cloud
4 ☹ down in
5 ☺ on top of

a the world
b mouth
c the dumps
d blue
e nine

Insight Noun suffixes: *-ness*, *-ity*

2 Write the noun or adjective form of the words below. Then use one of the forms to complete sentences a–h.

1 ___________ / generosity
2 lazy / ___________
3 able / ___________
4 tired / ___________
5 ___________ / necessity
6 ___________ / kindness
7 ___________ / prosperity
8 happy / ___________

a Money doesn't make you ___________, but it can certainly help.
b Bob Kerrey said 'Unexpected ___________ is the most powerful, least costly, and most underrated agent of human change.'
c My father is so ___________, both with his time and money.
d We were all so ___________ after travelling from the UK to New Zealand.
e My boss has no time for ___________; she demands hard work and leads by example.
f It's ___________ for people to remove their shoes when entering a house in Japan.
g The majority of people from the island of Mauritius in the Indian Ocean have the ___________ to speak both French and English fluently.
h In China, red is the colour of ___________, and traditionally children receive money in red packets every Chinese New Year.

Vocabulary extra Feelings

3 Match feelings 1–6 with situations a–f to complete the sentences.

1 I was disgusted by
2 I was furious when
3 I was petrified when I
4 I was astonished when someone told me
5 I was pleased when I opened the envelope and
6 I was very upset that you

a my new laptop broke within a month.
b saw the invitation to the wedding.
c that Anya was Serbian – her English is perfect!
d had to give a lecture in front of 200 students.
e went to the cinema with Jacob instead of me.
f how dirty the room was at the hotel.

4 Complete the report with the words below.

ability ▪ appalled ▪ astonished ▪ cross ▪ devastated ▪ happiness ▪ kind ▪ necessity

Time to put your phone down?

Do you get [1] ___________ when people use their smartphones when they're talking to you? Do you worry that the art of conversation has gone?

I'm constantly [2] ___________ by this kind of behaviour, especially when I have to repeat myself! When did the phone become a [3] ___________ you have to check every five minutes? Although, I have to tell myself this as well!

My daughter is probably like a lot of other teenagers when she says that she has the [4] ___________ to talk and look at her phone at the same time. She says she can live without it, but she'd be [5] ___________ if I took it away.

I was [6] ___________, then, that last week she suggested a 'digital detox' holiday. It's for some mother and daughter time, apparently, which is a [7] ___________ thing to do.

So, we're going to a hotel without any internet access for a couple of nights. I'm hoping it brings us both [8] ___________ and relaxation, but I'm also slightly afraid that my daughter will cope with no technology better than I will!

5 TASK Complete the comments from an online feedback form for things for young people to do in your local area. Use your own ideas.

Post a comment

I'm appalled that ___________.
The ability to ___________
is very important in life.
I get furious when ___________.
I'm astonished that ___________.
I'm really excited about ___________.

Grammar

Past simple and present perfect

1 Complete the world records using the past simple or present perfect form of the verbs below.

become ▪ never beat ▪ play ▪ run ▪ teach ▪ win

1 In 2018, Kyle Jackson (UK) ________ the youngest professional *Fortnite* gamer at the age of 13.
2 Brazil ________ in every FIFA World Cup since the tournament began.
3 NBA star Kevin Durant (USA) ________ 3,459 Indian children basketball, which became a new world record in 2017 for the largest basketball lesson. It took place in various venues all over India.
4 On 2 December 2017, Sophie Goodwin (UK) ________ her 100th marathon, which made her, at the age of 21, the youngest person in the world to do this.
5 Nearly two thirds of all international rugby teams ________ New Zealand.
6 No one ________ more Paralympic gold medals than Trischa Zorn (USA), who has 41 for swimming.

2 Complete the sentences. Use the present perfect form of the verbs in brackets and choose the correct words.

1 Ms Davies ________ (be) our science teacher **for** / **since** seven months.
2 I ________ **already** / **yet** ________ (read) *Romeo and Juliet.*
3 I ________ (not tell) my parents about the party **already** / **yet**.
4 ________ (you / work) very hard **this week** / **last week**?
5 Sofia ________ **yet** / **just** ________ (leave) the house – she'll be back in about ten minutes.
6 I ________ (watch) every Portsmouth match **for** / **since** 2008.
7 We've **ever** / **never** ________ (travel) in Africa, but we'd love to.

3 Tick (✓) the sentences that are correct. Rewrite the five sentences that are incorrect.

1 We've lived in Bolivia for two years before my dad got a job here. ☐
2 Did you watch that series yet? ☐
3 My twin sister and I have never worn the same clothes. ☐
4 Did you ever see a live rugby match? ☐
5 I haven't bought any clothes at the weekend. I couldn't find anything I liked. ☐
6 'How long have you had your laptop?' 'Since I was at university.' ☐
7 Did you ever go to Vancouver? It's my favourite city. ☐
8 Lily's been to dance lessons every day this week. ☐

4 Complete the text about Spinning™. Use the present perfect or past simple form of the verbs in brackets.

Get fit by cycling nowhere!

1 ________ (try) Spinning yet? 2 ________ (ever / hear) of it? It's a form of bike-aerobics which South African Johnny Goldberg 3 ________ (create) in the USA in the late 1980s. Since then it 4 ________ (become) popular in many countries.

In 1989, fitness instructor Goldberg 5 ________ (want) to prepare himself better for cycling events. For this reason, he 6 ________ (invent) a bike you could train on like a real bike, but which 7 ________ (not travel) anywhere.

He 8 ________ (take) his idea to a class and it was an instant success, and he soon 9 ________ (expand) his idea. In 1991, he 10 ________ (open) a studio in Hollywood which is when it really took off.

Spinning 11 ________ (develop) a lot since then, and many gyms now have a special room with Spinning bikes for lessons. Technology 12 ________ (play) a big part as well. People who come to classes can now go up- and downhill, and instructors can set different challenges to suit different levels of fitness.

And if you are far away from a gym, no problem. You might want to invest in an at-home Spinning bike. Peloton has not only produced a bike, but they also have workout videos that you can live-stream. There are even a number of accessories to choose from: weights, heart rate monitors and resistance bars!

So, if you 13 ________ (never experience) this type of class, go along to your local gym and sign up today. But be prepared for a hard workout! Don't say I 14 ________ (not warn) you!

5 TASK Write a short blog post about an activity you have tried recently to get fit. Why do you prefer it to things you have tried in the past and why would you recommend it to others? Remember to use the past simple and present perfect correctly.

Listening, vocabulary and speaking

V Insight Values

1 **Complete the text with the words below.**

commitment ■ discipline ■ self-esteem ■ self-reliance ■ single-mindedness ■ sportsmanship ■ stamina ■ team spirit

If you want to be a professional athlete, it isn't easy. The following values are just as important as the talent itself:

- [1]__________ Are you prepared to give most of your free time to training and turn down social events?
- [2]__________ You'll need follow a strict diet and make sure you get enough sleep.
- [3]__________ You need to focus on your sports goal – there isn't room for anything else!
- [4]__________ Your manager and trainer will support you, but sometimes it will be down to you alone.
- [5]__________ Can you push yourself to the limit and keep going? Because that is what it takes.
- [6]__________ Will you put your team before your own needs? Sometimes the group is more important than the individual.
- [7]__________ Fair play and respect for your opponents is something that shouldn't be ignored.

If you think this sounds like you, you just might have what it takes to become a successful athlete. In return, you'll get a boost to your [8]__________, as well as success in your field.

Giving and reacting to news

2 **Match lines giving news 1–6 to lines reacting to it a–f.**

1 I lost my phone in the park and found it two days later!
2 I'm not happy about having to give a presentation in class this afternoon.
3 I've had my hair cut and I hate it!
4 I've run 100 metres in 11.3 seconds!
5 My mum's taking me out for a meal as a reward for working so hard.
6 Our teacher said we all had to stay behind because a couple of students didn't do the homework.

a Oh well, it's not the end of the world.
b You deserve it!
c Well done!
d That's so unfair! Just those two should be punished!
e Cheer up! It'll all go really well, I'm sure!
f You're kidding! That's so lucky!

3 **3.01 You are going to listen to Fiona telling Callum that she has been accepted into Oxford University. Tick (✓) the expressions you think you will hear. Then listen and check.**

1 You'll never guess what! ☐
2 Cheer up! ☐
3 You deserve it! ☐
4 That's so unfair! ☐
5 That's fantastic news! ☐
6 Try and look on the bright side. ☐
7 Well done! ☐
8 Poor you! ☐
9 Congratulations! ☐
10 It's not the end of the world. ☐
11 I'm really pleased for you! ☐
12 How exciting! ☐

4 **3.01 Listen to the dialogue again. Are the sentences true (T) or false (F)? Correct the false ones.**

1 Callum already knew that Fiona was trying to get into Oxford University.
2 Fiona had to have an interview before she was accepted.
3 Callum spends a lot of time in the library like Fiona.
4 Callum and Fiona are related to each other.

5 **3.02 Put the words in the correct order to make sentences from a dialogue between Ben and his friend Joe. Then listen and check.**

1 some / got / I've / news / afraid / I'm / bad / .
____
2 happened / ! / no / what's / oh / ?
____
3 to / sorry / really / that / hear / I'm / !
____
4 be / must / you / terrible / feeling / .
____
5 on / well, / the / look / try / side / oh / bright / to / .
____

6 **TASK** **Read the text to Emma from her sister. Write the dialogue when Emma tells her friend, Kester, the news.**

Hi Emma! Can't come to concert! Had an accident. My arm broken, bike not good either! But good news – got onto my university course! Speak soon. Sophie xx

V Insight Adverbs

1 Choose the correct adverbs.

1. **Extremely** / **Clearly**, the computers which we bought very **cheaply** / **surprisingly** were of an inferior quality and have proven to be **incredibly** / **similarly** slow.
2. **Surprisingly** / **Extremely**, for such a powerful car, it goes from zero to 100 km/h relatively **worryingly** / **slowly**. The seats are good quality and **rapidly** / **extremely** comfortable, especially for long journeys.
3. The Prime Minister needs to respond **rapidly** / **comfortably** to prevent pollution levels from becoming **similarly** / **worryingly** high.

2 Match sentences 1–3 in exercise 1 to places a–c you would read them.

a a newspaper report ________

b an email from an IT teacher ________

c a magazine review ________

3 Choose the correct answers.

1. Clearly, the fact that the company uses teenagers to test their games shows that
   - **a** they aren't sure who will be their biggest customers.
   - **b** they think that young people will be their biggest customers.
2. Surprisingly, the study showed that people who studied the longest
   - **a** didn't achieve the best results.
   - **b** had the best grades overall.
3. Cyclists are always in greater danger than car drivers on the roads. Similarly, motorcyclists are
   - **a** more likely to be killed in accidents than car drivers.
   - **b** less likely to be killed in accidents than car drivers.
4. Worryingly, many young people say that they
   - **a** expect to find work when they leave school.
   - **b** don't expect to find work when they leave school.

Present perfect continuous

4 Complete the sentences using the present perfect continuous form of the verbs below.

build ▪ buy ▪ fix ▪ lie ▪ play ▪ talk ▪ wash ▪ work

1. My eyes are tired because I ________________ on a computer all weekend.
2. We don't have any money left because we ________________ lots of presents.
3. Rob is wet because he ________________ the car.
4. Sulaiman is really exhausted because he ________________ football all afternoon.
5. Mike's hands are really cold because he ________________ a snowman.
6. Cecile and Mo are sunburned because they ________________ on the beach all day.
7. Leyla's hands are dirty because she ________________ her bike.
8. I ________________ to Simran and I can't wait to tell you his news!

Present perfect simple and present perfect continuous

5 Complete the newspaper article with the correct form of the verbs in brackets. Use the present perfect simple or present perfect continuous.

Watch your portions!

Over the last 20 years, I [1] ________________ (always take) the time to exercise. I [2] ________________ (run) several marathons and half-marathons. My weight [3] ________________ (not change) much for the majority of this time. And for someone who is almost 50, I feel as fit as I was in my 20s. As a result, I'm lucky that I [4] ________________ (never watch) what I eat. I love my food and couldn't go on a diet if I tried.

But recently, I [5] ________________ (think) more and more about how much I eat. I might be able to run long distances, but am I eating more than I need? In the last 30 years, there [6] ________________ (be) a gradual increase in portion size, from takeaways to chocolate bars to meals in restaurants. This is perhaps why, up till now, a large percentage of us [7] ________________ (eat) more than is needed to maintain a healthy weight.

Everyone knows how popular certain diets [8] ________________ (become) recently. They're certainly big business. But if we simply look at the size of the portion we are being given, this would be enough for most people to be a healthy weight. And it's a pretty cheap option!

How much I eat [9] ________________ (not be) something that I [10] ________________ (ever consider) much before now. I'm not saying I'm going to go on a diet. I've already mentioned this would be impossible for me. But it may just be time that I looked at portion sizes at least.

6 TASK Write about some of the activities below in relation to your life. Say how long you have been doing them (present perfect continuous + *for* or *since*), and talk about some of your results or achievements (present perfect simple).

- live / your house
- study / English
- play / instrument
- have / your phone
- know / your friend
- do / your hobby

Reading

1 Read the article and choose the most suitable title.

a Is individualized healthcare the future?
b Computers can't make us better
c Medical treatment – past and present

2 Read the article again. Then read the first sentence from paragraphs 1–5. Match them to the paragraph summaries a–f. There is one summary that you do not need.

1 In recent times, the way we use technology in our everyday lives has become more individualized.
2 Some people would say that this change has already begun, with wearable technology that allows us to track our health and daily habits.
3 Despite this, we still don't have the kind of technology that can create detailed treatment plans for each individual.
4 This is where artificial intelligence (AI) can help.
5 Looking ahead, there is a real sense of optimism in the field of medicine.

a Individualized healthcare technology is not yet a reality.
b How modern technology adapts to our personal preferences.
c Taking responsibility for the way we live.
d A smart solution to the problem.
e Using technology to watch our health.
f Looking forward to better things.

3 Match headings A–E to paragraphs 1–5.

A Monitoring our lifestyles
B A bright future is possible
C Technology that knows what we like
D The challenges of personalized treatment
E An answer to the need for speed

4 Are the sentences true (T) or false (F) or not given (NG)? Correct the false ones.

1 Music streaming services have a loyalty point system for their members.
2 Wearable technology can save money spent on healthcare.
3 The reduction in sick days has been because of people monitoring the number of hours they work.
4 Data processing is important for developing personalized healthcare.
5 AI can analyse medical data more quickly.
6 Minor illnesses or injuries can lead to more urgent conditions.
7 The writer believes that everybody would be happy to hand over personal information.

1 ______________

In recent times, the way we use technology in our everyday lives has become more individualized. We now expect a unique experience to suit our own personal tastes. Take music, for example. The days of millions of people listening to the same few radio stations are long gone, replaced with music streaming services like Spotify, Apple Music and others. These services use algorithms to make suggestions based on our individual preferences, and even create specific playlists for each user. Experts believe that there will soon be a similar individualized approach in the field of healthcare.

2 ______________

Some people say that this change has already begun, with wearable technology that allows us to track our health and daily habits. We can now get a visible record of our daily step count, heart rate and the number of hours we slept the previous night. It is estimated that around 20% of healthcare costs are the result of a lack of exercise and sleep, or overconsumption of alcohol and nicotine, and people who monitor their lifestyle are often rewarded with real savings. One study even showed that people who tracked their health with wearable technology saved 18% in healthcare costs and reduced their annual number of sick days by 44%.

3 ______________

Despite this, we still don't have the kind of technology that can create detailed treatment plans for each individual. Part of the problem is the need to collect and analyse vast amounts of data about each individual patient. Given how

unique and complicated the human body is, this means that extremely advanced technology is necessary. However, the desire to develop such technology is certainly there.

4 ______________

This is where artificial intelligence (AI) can help. AI is able to analyse new data as it is added to a database, which allows research to be much faster and more efficient. It would also be able to offer each patient tailor-made treatments based on their personal data – even calculating the exact combinations and amounts of different medicines that will be most effective for each person. While this may not be necessary for minor symptoms like headaches and stomach aches, it could be used to treat more serious illnesses. AI could also be used to identify patterns between illnesses and lifestyle factors like sleep, exercise and nutrition. The earlier these patterns are found, the more effectively the illnesses can be treated or prevented.

5 ______________

Looking ahead, there is a real sense of optimism in the field of medicine. Researchers continue to gain greater insight into the possibilities of individualized medical treatment, and AI is leading the way. We're not there yet, though, and there is still much work to be done. There are also concerns about privacy, and it is difficult to predict whether the general public will be in favour of personalized healthcare. Indeed, the healthcare industry may still need to convince people that the benefits of individualized treatments are worth the cost of sharing such personal data.

5 Match the highlighted words in the article to definitions 1–8.

1 a strong wish to do something ______________
2 to be given something because you have done something good or worked hard ______________
3 to make someone believe that something is true ______________
4 able to be seen ______________
5 a deeper understanding of a situation ______________
6 made for a particular person or purpose ______________
7 sets of rules that are given to a computer to solve a problem ______________
8 extremely large ______________

6 Complete the sentences with words in exercise 5.

1 Search engines have ______________ that can rank websites according to key words used.
2 Recently I've had a ______________ to escape this country and see the world.
3 The book offers a valuable ______________ into the family relationships of elephants.
4 Uranus is the furthest planet ______________ to the naked eye.
5 We didn't expect to be ______________ with a bonus at work, so it was a lovely surprise.
6 The lawyer was able to ______________ the jury that the man was innocent.
7 The Amazon rainforest is so ______________ that it covers 40% of the South American continent.
8 We create ______________ holidays for our clients to some of the most beautiful places in the world.

7 TASK Write a list of some of the most important medical developments in history. How do you think the technology described in the article compares to the ideas in your list?

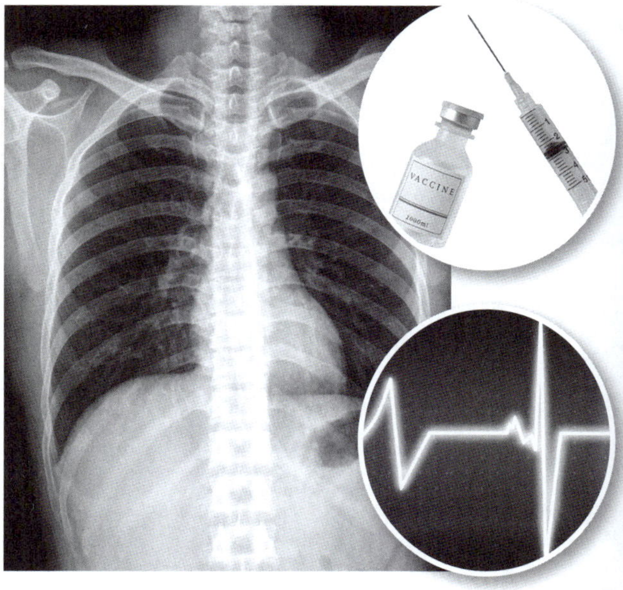

Writing An email to share news

1 Match 1–8 to a–h to make sentences.

1 You need to speak more clearly
2 Maybe you should be an author
3 Fruit is good for you
4 You need to have some hard times in life
5 People eat fast food
6 We should all work
7 Dad's been to the supermarket
8 Since you've all had dinner,

a because it contains vitamins, minerals and fibre.
b so that we don't have to shop while he's away.
c because it's quick and easy to get.
d I'll just make something for myself.
e so that everyone can understand what you're saying.
f in order to get money for nice experiences.
g since you seem to enjoy writing stories.
h in order to recognize and appreciate the good times.

2 Read Claudia's email to her friend Dirk. How will Claudia change her eating and drinking patterns before the open-water swim? Choose the correct answer.

a She will reduce the amount of water she drinks.
b She will eat much more than she usually does.
c She will change her diet completely.

Hi Dirk,

Sorry I haven't been in touch recently. I've been really busy.

I've decided to do a big open-water swim! As you know, I've been on swimming teams for many years. I thought I'd try sea and lake swimming [a]____________ my new friend, Becky, does it. I first swam in open water a couple of months ago. [1]**Luckily / Unfortunately**, I found out that I love it. There's a kind of freedom you don't get in the pool. I did my first competitive swim with her on Sunday, which was exhausting but fun. Most of the other swimmers had been doing it for years, but [2]**surprisingly / to be honest**, I won it! I couldn't believe it!

Anyway, I've been entered for this big race in the summer. I've got to do some hard training now and I have to go on a diet [b]____________ get stronger. [3]**Obviously / Certainly**, it's a bit different from what I usually eat. A few days before the event, I need to increase my carbohydrates, protein and fat. Carbohydrates are especially necessary for endurance. And I have to drink a lot of water [c]____________ I don't get dehydrated. People often forget that swimmers sweat!

[4]**Unfortunately / Luckily**, like most people, I don't drink enough water so I've got a special app on my phone to remind me when and how much I should be drinking.

I will even need to eat during the swim, [d]____________ I need the equivalent of 150–400 calories of carbohydrates every hour after the first one. And it'll probably take me around three hours.

[5]**To be honest / Sadly** I'm enjoying the challenge but it takes up a lot of my time. I'm already dreaming of a sofa day!

Anyway, how are you?

Write soon and let me know your news.

Claudia

3 Read the text again and choose the correct adverbs.

4 Write the ways of expressing reason and purpose in gaps a–d.

because ■ in order to ■ since ■ so that

Writing guide

■ **TASK You have recently started a new activity. Write an email to a friend or relative telling them your news.**

■ **PLAN 1 Think about the following.**
- Decide what the new activity is.
- Think about why you've started doing it, what changes it has made to your lifestyle, and why those changes are necessary.

■ **PLAN 2 Make notes for each paragraph.**

Paragraph 1: Start the email and ask how the person has been.
Paragraph 2: Tell them about your new activity and the reasons for doing it.
Paragraph 3: Describe the changes it has made to your lifestyle, and why.
Paragraph 4: Ask the person for information about their life and ask for a reply.

■ **WRITE Write your email.**

■ **REVIEW Check the following points.**
- Is the style and tone of the email informal?
- Have you begun and ended the letter appropriately?
- Have you used the correct expressions to show the reason and purpose of the changes in your life?
- Have you used some adverbs which show your attitude to the things you describe?
- Have you checked grammar, vocabulary, spelling and punctuation?

U3 Assess your progress

Give yourself a mark 1–3 for each Learning Objective from the lesson.
1 I found this difficult. **2** This was OK. **3** I can do this well.

Lesson	Learning Objective	Mark
Lesson 3A	I can identify the main ideas in a paragraph.	
	I can use idioms to talk about happiness and sadness.	
	I can use noun suffixes.	
	How can I improve?	
Lesson 3B	I can use the past simple and present perfect to talk about experiences.	
	I can use the past simple and present perfect with different adverbs and time words.	
	How can I improve?	
Lesson 3C	I can understand the main points in a radio interview.	
	I can use words relating to values.	
	I can give and react to news.	
	How can I improve?	
Lesson 3D	I can scan a text for specific information.	
	I can use adverbs of manner and degree, and sentence adverbs.	
	I can use the present perfect simple and the present perfect continuous.	
	How can I improve?	
Lesson 3E	I can write an informal email.	
	I can use adverbs and prepositional phrases to show my attitude.	
	I can use words and phrases to express reason and purpose.	
	How can I improve?	

Action plan

Make a plan for what you can do next to improve. Discuss your ideas with your classmates / teacher.

4 Stand up, speak out

Vocabulary

V Insight The environment

1 Choose the correct words.

1 Since 1970, 60% of the world's birds, mammals, fish and reptiles have **relocated** / **died out** because of humans.
2 Why is it that, so often, the public has to pay to clean the land **contaminated** / **evacuated** by private companies?
3 In 2020 some communities in Kenya and Uganda were lucky to **survive** / **die out** after severe flooding.
4 In dry conditions, forest fires can **contaminate** / **spread** faster than 14 miles per hour.
5 We need to **preserve** / **survive** what's left of our natural environment before it disappears.
6 In 1939, 1.5 million children in Britain were **evacuated** / **washed away** from cities to rural locations over a period of three days because of World War II.
7 Part of California's Highway 1, known for its spectacular coastal views, **relocated** / **washed away** in January 2021.
8 The 600 inhabitants of Shishmaref in Alaska will have to **spread** / **relocate** due to rising sea levels caused by climate change.

V Insight Prefixes: *semi-*, *under-*, *over-*, *re-*, *co-*, *inter-*

2 Complete the words with the correct prefixes below.

co ▪ inter ▪ over (×2) ▪ re ▪ semi

1 As well as learning about other subjects, school teaches pupils social skills, like how to ______act with other children.
2 I'm going to start cycling to work. The trains are so ______crowded.
3 I have no idea why Alan won't ______operate with us and work as a team.
4 We lived in a ______-detached house on a housing estate when I was a child.
5 I thought I'd lost my wallet, and then it suddenly ______appeared on my dining table!
6 This spaghetti is soft – you've ______cooked it!

3 Complete the sentences with the words in brackets and the correct prefix.

1 The last part of your report needs to be ______ (written) because it doesn't make much sense.
2 The problem many employers have is that they want ______ (educated) people straight out of university who have work experience.
3 I think that director's films are ______ (rated). I'm not sure why they're so popular.
4 I love the ______ (action) between the two main characters in this programme.
5 I think delivery drivers are ______ (paid) – they deserve more money given the amount of parcels they have to deliver every day.

Vocabulary extra Global issues

4 Match global issues 1–8 to nouns a–h.

1 deforestation	a money
2 disease	b cities
3 drought	c jobs
4 famine	d rivers
5 floods	e trees
6 poverty	f virus
7 unemployment	g food
8 urbanization	h rain

5 Complete the text with the words below.

climate change ▪ disease ▪ drought ▪ famine ▪ flooding ▪ global issues ▪ interacting ▪ overcrowded ▪ overspending ▪ relocate ▪ rethink ▪ spread ▪ survive ▪ urbanization

There are many [1] ______ which we face in the world today.

Firstly, [2] ______ – that is an increase in the Earth's temperature – causes [3] ______ and without water, crops will fail. And when this happens people won't have enough to eat, causing [4] ______.

The opposite problem is rising water levels causing [5] ______. People will no longer be able to live in some coastal towns and cities and will be forced to [6] ______ inland or to higher ground.

On top of this is the threat of [7] ______ from new viruses. As we saw in 2020's global pandemic, because of international travel and [8] ______, Covid-19 could [9] ______ quickly and easily. People [10] ______ made the situation worse and so limiting this was the only way to [11] ______ and stop the spread.

Then there's population growth. Many cities are already [12] ______ and need to provide vital services for their population. Government [13] ______ is rarely on education and healthcare, and this only leads to more problems.

It is clear we need to [14] ______ the way we do things. But with challenge and difficulty comes creativity. And this creativity will result in change for the better.

6 TASK Make a list of global issues in countries around the world. Which ones are you most worried about and why? What can be done to solve them?

Grammar

Expressing the future

1 Complete the sentences with the correct future forms below.

'll see ▪ 'm going to see

1 a I hope I 'll see Sami at the demonstration on Saturday.
b I 'm going to see the new Avengers film tomorrow.

comes ▪ is coming

2 a Alicia is coming for dinner at 7.30.
b The train comes at 10.05.

'm travelling ▪ 'm going to travel

3 a I 'm travelling around Canada in my gap year before university.
b I 'm going to travel to Edinburgh by train for New Year – I've just got the tickets.

will win ▪ are going to win

4 a Manchester United are going to win. They're 2–0 up and there's only extra time to play.
b I think Manchester United will win tomorrow's match.

'm helping ▪ might help

5 a I can't play tennis today – I 'm helping my mum prepare for the party.
b I might sleep you do the shopping. It depends if I finish my work.

2 Complete Chris's post on social media using the correct future form of the verbs in brackets.

Hi everyone!

As you know, some of us [1] will get (get) together at the weekend to talk about the clean-up club we [2] are going to start (start). The intention [3] is going to be (be) to pick up rubbish in areas where people meet and drop litter, like the parks and sports fields. Don't worry; if you aren't sure [4] ________ (be) available every weekend, it isn't a problem. Hopefully we [5] ________ (have) some kind of timetable and you can just join where you have some spare time to volunteer. We [6] ________ (meet) in Westgate Café at 2 p.m. on Saturday to discuss ideas. The weather forecast isn't good. It [7] might rain (rain). I hope I'll [8] be able to (be able to) use my mum's car, so if you're coming from Monkton, I might be able to give you a lift. Just let me know.

See you all then,

Chris

3 Match the answers in exercise 2 to the ways of expressing the future below.

a uncertain prediction 4, 7
b hope 8
c intention 2, 5
d arrangement 1, 6
e prediction based on evidence 3

4 Complete the dialogue with the correct future form of the verbs below.

be ▪ can come ▪ explain ▪ join ▪ might make ▪ plan ▪ take ▪ understand

A [1] ARE you JOIN the food bank protest we've organized for Saturday? We're meeting outside the city hall at 9 a.m.

B I might come. I'm not sure if I [2] will be free. What exactly are you going to do there?

A We [3] 're going to take a big list of all the residents in the local area who have to use food banks. We have a big poster with loads of names on it.

B And what are you hoping that people [4] will understand by that?

A Well, we [5] are going to explain that these people have jobs and still don't have enough food for their families. It isn't just the unemployed. We need to have a living wage. Who knows? It [6] might make a difference. We're [7] planning to take our idea to other towns if we're successful.

B That's cool! I hope I [8] can come.

5 TASK Write a list of your plans and predictions for the next 5, 10 and 20 years. Use different future forms depending on how sure you are that these things will happen.

Listening, vocabulary and speaking

V Insight Verbs + prepositions

1 Match 1–8 to a–h to make sentences.

1 We need to focus
2 We're going to protest
3 I belong
4 We decided to set
5 My teacher insisted
6 Most people believe
7 Many students rely
8 Many politicians don't seem to care

a to a group that demonstrates against climate change.
b on their parents to help with university fees.
c about anyone but themselves.
d on the school campaign to clean up the local area.
e in the right to have free speech. It's so important.
f on us having a knowledge of world issues.
g up a meeting with the mayor.
h against the number of cars allowed into the city centre.

2 Complete the sentences with the correct prepositions and your own ideas.

1 I don't believe ______.
2 I belong ______.
3 I really care ______.
4 I often insist ______.
5 I can always rely ______.

Asking for and expressing opinions

3 Choose the best definition of digital piracy.

a stealing files from another person's computer and sharing them
b illegally copying and selling music, film and software files
c illegally playing music and films in public places for profit

4 🔊4.01 Listen to the dialogue between Jerry and Diane. Who is against digital piracy?

5 Are these lines from the dialogue opinion (O), fact (F), or speculation (S)?

a Maybe they just don't want to know. ______
b Well, it could be a problem when people stop making so many films. ______
c I read that the countries with the most illegal downloads now have the fewest new artists. ______
d I think it's fantastic. ______
e There are lots of people working in those industries who don't get paid much. ______
f I really don't think it's a problem. ______

6 Put phrases 1–10 into the correct category a–c.

1 I'm not so sure about that!
2 If you ask me, it's wrong.
3 What do you reckon?
4 It isn't a problem for stream-ripping software, in my opinion.
5 OK, OK! I take your point.
6 What was your view on downloading that film last week, then?
7 Well, as far as I'm concerned, it doesn't do any harm.
8 I see what you're saying, but I really don't think it's a problem.
9 Well, to tell you the truth, that was probably a wrong thing to do, too.
10 I agree with you about that.

a Asking for opinions ______ , ______
b Expressing opinions ______ , ______ , ______ , ______
c Reacting to opinions and suggestions ______ , ______ , ______ , ______

7 Put the dialogue in the correct order 1–6.

______ a I'm not so sure about that. You can cycle really carefully and still get hit by a car that hasn't seen you.
______ b To tell you the truth, I don't think it really matters what you wear. If you ask me, I think we need more cycle lanes.
______ c I agree with you about that. But until they build more, I'm happy to carry on cycling anyway.
______ d In my opinion, cycling is too dangerous in this town.
______ e I take your point, drivers aren't good at noticing cyclists. But in my opinion, you're fine if you wear a high-visibility jacket.
______ f Really? As far as I'm concerned, it's perfectly safe as long as you pay enough attention.

8 TASK Look at the words and phrases below. Put + after the points which are *for* wearing a school uniform and – after the points which are *against*. Then use the points to write a dialogue between two people asking for and expressing opinions about wearing a school uniform.

- individual ☐
- equality of students ☐
- expensive ☐
- more choice ☐
- feeling of belonging to a place ☐
- doesn't mean better grades ☐
- some students can't afford designer clothes ☐

Vocabulary and grammar

V Insight Collocations: charities

1 Which of the nouns in each group below cannot be used with the verbs?

1 address
  a an issue **b** a campaign **c** a problem
2 transform
  a a situation **b** someone's life **c** a donation
3 donate
  a a charity **b** money **c** unwanted clothes
4 take part in
  a a problem **b** a marathon **c** an event
5 volunteer
  a time **b** money **c** unwanted clothes
6 support
  a a situation **b** a campaign **c** a charity
7 raise
  a awareness **b** a campaign **c** money
8 aid
  a developing countries
  b poor people
  c help

Vocabulary extra Charities

2 Write the words in brackets in the correct form to complete the sentences.

1 The Invictus Games, created by Prince Harry in 2014, is a sports competition. The ____________ are sick or injured members of the armed forces. (compete)
2 The ____________, who are all volunteers, hand out hot meals to homeless people in the area. (distribute)
3 Famous people are often asked to ____________ campaigns for charities. (promote)
4 Leonardo DiCaprio's foundation has been a major ____________ to ocean conservation and has given away more than $100 million to over 200 different projects. (donate)
5 The annual Moon Walk takes place in London and Edinburgh and raises money for breast cancer. ____________ can walk a half marathon or full marathon distance. (participate)
6 We're going to ____________ an event where people can bring unwanted toys and games. (organize)
7 Australian Adam Garone is a co-founder of Movember, which ____________ for men's health by encouraging men to grow a moustache every November. (campaign)

Future continuous and future perfect

3 Write sentences using the future continuous or the future perfect.

1 We / not move / to other planets / 100 years from now.
____
2 People / soon / live / closer to wildlife as green spaces become smaller.
____
3 By 2035, more / driverless cars / invent.
____
4 In 2030, almost 9 billion / people / live / on Earth.
____
5 Hopefully by 2030, scientists / find / a vaccine for HIV.
____
6 By 2050, / USA / become / the largest Spanish-speaking country in the world.
____
7 In 2035, it is believed that / sports programmes / use / holograms / when they show sports events.
____

4 Complete the email with the future continuous or future perfect form of the verbs below.

arrive ▪ check ▪ hand out ▪ hear ▪ publicize ▪ shop

Subject: A Congo tax protest!

Hello everyone!

Most of you know the plan. We'll meet outside the main Congo store next Saturday to peacefully protest against the company avoiding their tax payments. A lot of people [1] ____________ on Saturday because it's the start of their annual sales, and we [2] ____________ leaflets and hoping customers shop elsewhere. The local newspaper [3] ____________ the protest and we're still hoping that the local band, Direction, will give us some support – we [4] ____________ from them by Tuesday. We are expecting our main organizer, Laura Mason, to speak at about midday, as we think the local TV reporters [5] ____________ by then. And, as I said before, this is a peaceful protest – we [6] ____________ that no one is doing anything violent.

Thanks and see you then.

James

5 TASK Imagine that you are being interviewed about life in the future. Complete the sentences with your predictions. Use the future continuous or the future perfect.

1 In five years' time, I think education ____________ .
2 I hope that cars ____________ when I'm 40.
3 In a few years' time, cities ____________ .
4 I don't think people ____________ in 2030!
5 Many animals ____________ before 2050.

Reading

1 Look at the title and subtitle. What do you think the blog post is about?

- **a** Developing countries can't reduce global problems without support from other nations.
- **b** Developing countries need to ask themselves where they can help with global problems.
- **c** The solution to global problems may be found in developing countries.

2 Read the blog post. Decide if sentences A–E are opinion (O), fact (F), or speculation (S).

- **A** It's my view that a more accurate name for developing countries would be 'appropriately developed'.
- **B** Compare that to the 8 hectares an American consumes or the 4.7 hectares a European consumes.
- **C** Companies watch consumer trends very closely and if enough people change their habits, they will probably be forced to follow suit.
- **D** Today I'm going to write about an issue which isn't addressed enough.
- **E** It's doubled since then, to more than seven billion.

3 Look at the sentences A–E in exercise 2 again. Then match them to gaps 1–5 in the blog post.

4 Read the blog post again. Choose the correct answers.

1. Some people say that overpopulation isn't a problem because
   - **a** the global population is getting smaller.
   - **b** there is more awareness of the problem now.
   - **c** the population is growing less quickly than in the past.
   - **d** people aren't worried about it.
2. Global population *is* a problem because
   - **a** it's more than seven billion.
   - **b** it's less than double what it was in 1970.
   - **c** the growth rate is getting higher.
   - **d** it's still increasing by a huge amount every year.
3. In paragraphs 5 and 6, the writer highlights the problem of
   - **a** certain countries being more responsible for overconsumption than others.
   - **b** certain countries being unable to catch up with progress of others.
   - **c** people needing more things in their lives in order to be happy.
   - **d** countries around the world having less land to produce food.
4. How does the writer feel our idea of progress should change?
   - **a** We should concentrate on improving the quality of the products made.
   - **b** We should focus on things in our lives which money can't buy.
   - **c** We should make sure we buy things we need in our lives.
   - **d** We should only have things in our lives that are of a good quality.
5. What can we, as individuals, do to help the global problem?
   - **a** learn about the source of the things we consume
   - **b** think about the amount of things we can give to others
   - **c** ask companies to change the way people shop
   - **d** make sure others have enough of what they need

Overpopulation and overconsumption

Are developing countries the answer rather than the question?

1 I've been discussing the issues behind our continuing economic problems and the increase in extreme weather events in some of my recent blogs. Thanks for all your comments.

2 [1] ________ We passed the 7 billion mark for global population not long ago, which raised some awareness of the issue. Some people were saying that we needn't worry because the rate of population growth has actually been going *down* since 1970.

3 That's true, but in 1970, there were 3.5 billion people on the Earth. [2] ________ Even though the percentage growth rate is lower, we're still adding 80 million people to the planet every year. And thanks to such things as better healthcare, diet and technology, people are living longer.

4 In actual fact, the world's problem isn't so much overpopulation, but *overconsumption*, and it's westerners who use most of the planet's resources. Here's an amazing fact: if developing countries reached the same levels of consumption as the West, that would be the same as the global population increasing to **72 billion!**

5 Did you know that at the moment, Earth has enough resources for each individual to consume around 1.8 global hectares each year? This is what a typical person from Ghana consumes. [3] ________ Developed countries are obviously taking the lion's share.

6 Rather than trying to encourage developing countries to catch up, it would therefore make sense for developed countries to *de*-develop. Isn't it time we moved the focus from how advanced developed countries are, to what we can learn from developing countries? They could definitely teach developed countries a thing or two about how to live happy lives with relatively small salaries and low levels of consumption. [4] __________

7 I think the trickier question is how best to do this. Terms like *de-development* and *zero growth* tend to go against what we consider human progress. That's why our vision of what progress is must change. It shouldn't be how much money we can make, how much we can produce or how much we can buy. We should start looking at progress in terms of the quality of non-material things like family and friendships rather than the quantity of stuff we own. Ghandi once said, 'There is enough for everyone's need, but not everyone's greed.'

8 So, what can we do as consumers? We can do a lot I believe, and it starts with education. Teach yourself about what's behind a label. Where has your food or clothing come from? Did you know that the ice cream company Ben & Jerry's™ use fair-trade ingredients or that Fair Indigo is both eco-friendly and organic? You'll soon start to buy from those companies and become an ethical consumer. [5] __________ Never underestimate the power of the individual.

9 You can also learn about living simply. It is possible to take less from the Earth while still having an enjoyable life. We just have to know when we have enough of what we need rather than more than our fair share. People can always have more, but do they really need it? Probably not!

10 One thing's for sure, if we don't become more aware of the problem of overconsumption and take responsibility for our own personal role in this, nature will force us to anyway!

Let me know your thoughts.

5 Find words and phrases in the text which match definitions 1–8.

1 unusually bad storms and floods ____________________ (paragraph 1)
2 became twice as many ____________________ (paragraph 3)
3 using too much of something ____________________ (paragraph 4)
4 things which are there for people to use ____________________ (paragraph 4)
5 the greatest part of something ____________________ (paragraph 5)
6 image or idea ____________________ (paragraph 7)
7 wanting a lot more than you need ____________________ (paragraph 7)
8 an equal amount of something ____________________ (paragraph 9)

6 Complete the sentences with words and phrases in exercise 5.

1 My ____________________ for the future is one where we can live in harmony with nature.
2 I always have to do ____________________ of the housework at home because my sister's lazy.
3 The rate at which this city has grown is incredible – the population in 1990 was 20,000. Now in 2020 it has more than ____________________ to 45,000.
4 Saudi Arabia is a small country, yet it is very rich in natural ____________________.
5 ____________________ are becoming so much more common these days because of climate change.
6 ____________________ is often caused by advertisers making us believe we need certain products.
7 If everyone took their ____________________, we would all have an equal amount.
8 ____________________ causes some people to have great quantities of something and others to have nothing.

7 TASK Write a paragraph about the problem of overconsumption and suggest how it might be solved.

Writing An opinion essay

1 Which of these things can you recycle?

a takeaway food containers
b glass bottles
c plastic bags

2 Read the first paragraph of the essay. Which sentence summarizes the writer's opinion about cheap clothing?

a The writer thinks that fashionable people often consider the damage to the environment.
b The writer thinks that cheap clothing is necessary in the fashion industry.
c The writer thinks you can be fashionable without destroying the environment.

3 Complete the essay with the phrases below.

- I am convinced that
- in my opinion
- it's also important to note that
- my final point is that
- the main argument against
- to my mind

Writing guide

- **TASK** **Write an essay in support of the charity Friends of the Earth which campaigns for the natural world and everyone in it.**
- **PLAN 1** **Think about the following.**
  - global population
  - sustainable living
  - climate change
  - overconsumption
- **PLAN 2** **Decide which ideas you are going to use and match them to these paragraphs. Make notes.**
  Paragraph 1: Write an introduction and state your opinion.
  Paragraphs 2, 3 and 4: Write an argument for your opinion in each paragraph, giving support and examples. Include an opposing viewpoint sometimes.
  Paragraph 5: Conclude by restating your opinion and summarizing the reasons for it.
- **WRITE** **Write your essay.**
- **REVIEW** **Check the following points.**
  - Do your paragraphs contain separate points?
  - Have you used phrases for introducing arguments and giving opinions?
  - Have you checked grammar, vocabulary, spelling and punctuation?

Does being fashionable mean we can't protect the environment?

Some people believe that buying cheap fashionable clothes is a necessary part of their lives. Although this may be important for them, 1 ____________, there are better and more sustainable ways to be fashionable.

2 ____________ buying cheap clothes is that you are supporting bad conditions for those who produce them. Workers often have to work long hours for little pay.

3 ____________, if we all decided to stop buying such clothes, this type of cheap labour would have to end.

Having said this, 4 ____________ it's natural for people to want to look nice and follow fashion to fit in with their peers.

However, 5 ____________, you can achieve the same kind of image by searching online for second-hand clothes or looking for bargains in charity shops. In fact, you can often buy high-quality clothes for a price you might not normally be able to afford.

6 ____________ by reducing the amount of cheap fashionable clothing we buy on a regular basis, we will reduce the damage the clothing industry causes to the environment. Producing clothes not only uses a lot of water but it also creates large landfills when we throw the items away.

U4 Assess your progress

Give yourself a mark 1–3 for each Learning Objective from the lesson.
1 I found this difficult. **2** This was OK. **3** I can do this well.

Lesson 4A

	Mark
I can find and understand relevant information in a text.	
I can use words relating to the environment.	
I can use the prefixes to change the meaning of words.	
How can I improve?	

Lesson 4B

	Mark
I can scan a text for specific information.	
I can use present tenses, *will*, *going to* and *may* / *might* to express the future.	
How can I improve?	

Lesson 4C

	Mark
I can identify facts, opinions and speculation in a radio programme.	
I can use verbs with prepositions.	
I can ask for, express and react to opinions.	
How can I improve?	

Lesson 4D

	Mark
I can understand cohesion in a text.	
I can use collocations relating to charity work.	
I can use the future continuous and the future perfect to talk about the future.	
How can I improve?	

Lesson 4E

	Mark
I can write an opinion essay.	
I can organize an opinion paragraph.	
I can use different phrases for introducing arguments and giving opinions.	
How can I improve?	

Action plan

Make a plan for what you can do next to improve. Discuss your ideas with your classmates / teacher.

5 Do the right thing

Vocabulary

V Insight Influence

1 Complete the sentences with the words below.

bias ■ control ■ impact ■ impression ■ inspiration ■ reputation

1 I think I made a bad first ____________ when I met my new teacher.
2 You need to take ____________ of your own life!
3 He has a bad ____________ because he was in prison for a year.
4 Her speech made a big ____________ on us all.
5 We must consider all candidates without ____________.
6 Her charity work is an ____________ to us all.

2 Match 1–6 to a–f to make sentences.

1 Sam finally took
2 Can you trust someone who has
3 You shouldn't trust first
4 There's a strong
5 Van Gogh's work has had a huge
6 She is a true

a a bad reputation?
b control of the situation.
c bias against some types of music.
d impressions as they're often wrong.
e inspiration to all young people.
f impact on me as an artist.

V Insight Noun prefixes: *mis-* and *dis-*

3 Rewrite the sentences. Use the correct form of the words in brackets and *mis-* or *dis-*.

1 Acting badly in school can sometimes lead to criminality. (behave)
____
2 Knife crime is often the result of gangs having arguments. (agree)
____
3 Young offenders have often had bad luck in their lives. (fortune)
____
4 You mustn't be untruthful in court. (honest)
____
5 Apologize for your rudeness towards your mother! (respect)
____
6 Many prisoners complain about being treated badly by prison officers. (treat)
____

Vocabulary extra Crime and punishment

4 Complete the compound nouns. Then use them to answer questions a–f.

1 community ____________
2 life ____________
3 internet ____________
4 speeding ____________
5 prison ____________
6 armed ____________
7 traffic ____________

a What do you call a period of time in prison? a ____________
b What's one of the greatest dangers of paying for things online? ____________
c What is a possible punishment for murder? a ____________
d What's the main punishment for driving too fast? a ____________
e When people don't go to prison for minor crimes, what might they do instead? ____________
f What do you call breaking the rules while driving? ____________

5 Read the passage about crime. Choose the correct words.

It has been said that all crime is [1]**theft / vandalism** of some sort. Murder is taking someone's life, [2]**violence / fraud** is taking someone's money and so on.

However, there have always been differences regarding how each crime should be punished. Anything with a weapon is considered to be a serious crime. For that reason, [3]**armed robbery / shoplifting** carries a longer [4]**speeding fine / prison sentence** than minor crimes. Most people can understand the reason why these punishments are given.

But what about less serious crimes? This is often where opinions are different. There is [5]**disagreement / disobedience** over how to punish [6]**vandals / misbehaviour**, for example. It is clearly a crime, until we think of graffiti. Some people think this is a form of art that decorates boring buildings or poor areas of a city. In fact, Banksy is famous all over the world for his street art. Others believe the people who did it should have to pay a fine or do [7]**a life sentence / community service**.

In this way, the question of what is and isn't a crime and how it should be punished is difficult for lawmakers to decide.

6 TASK What are the factors that lead people to commit crime? Think about the below.

boredom ■ family ■ friends ■ poverty ■ where you live

Grammar

First conditional

1 Complete the first halves of the sentences 1–6 with the correct form of the verbs in brackets and match them to the second halves a–f.

1 If you ______ (tell) lies about something,
2 I'm sure your teacher ______ (forgive) you
3 If you ______ (not take) your ticket,
4 If you ______ (apologize),
5 It ______ (not make) you happy
6 Your skin ______ (age) quicker

a if you have a lot of money, but it will help!
b you won't be able to enter.
c you'll have to remember them.
d if you don't wear sun cream
e if you explain what happened.
f your mum will be happy.

Second conditional

2 Complete the sentences with the correct form of the verbs below.

be ▪ do ▪ have ▪ know ▪ lie ▪ live ▪ not have to ▪ print ▪ shave ▪ switch ▪ take ▪ work

1 You ______ 31,709 years old if you ______ for a trillion seconds.
2 I'm sure your computer ______ perfectly if you ______ it off and on again.
3 If you ______ everything on the internet, it ______ 57,000 years.
4 You ______ in bed all morning if you ______ go to school.
5 If you ______ that today was the last day of your life, what ______?
6 If you ______ a tiger, it ______ still ______ stripes. They are on its skin, not in its fur.

First and second conditionals

3 Choose the correct words.

1 If I **call** / **called** my parents later, I **'ll** / **'d** ask them if you can come to stay.
2 Rasila and I won't / wouldn't be friends if we **don't have** / **didn't have** so much in common.
3 I'm 18 and can vote in Britain. If I **live** / **lived** in Japan, I **will** / **would** have to be 20.
4 If my brother **doesn't** / **didn't** leave the party soon, he **'ll** / **'d** miss the last bus.
5 If you **can** / **could** be any animal, what **would** / **will** you be?
6 If anyone **wants** / **wanted** me, I **won't** / **wouldn't** be free until the evening.
7 What **would** / **will** you do if you **have** / **had** an unlimited amount of money?
8 If you **don't** / **didn't** tell anyone my secret, I **won't** / **wouldn't** tell yours.

4 Rewrite the sentences.

1 If you don't put the chicken in the oven at the right temperature, it won't cook well.
Unless ______.
2 You must use the correct username to get onto the website.
Unless ______.
3 If you didn't make mistakes in life, you would never learn from them.
Unless ______.
4 You won't know if you can do it unless you try.
If ______.
5 Unless the taxi arrives soon, we'll be late for the wedding.
If ______.
6 I would take the weekend position if they allowed me to finish at 2 p.m.
Unless ______.

5 Complete the question and reply on an internet advice forum with the correct form of the verbs in brackets.

Dear Morag,

I need your help. I told my sister I couldn't go on holiday with her because I didn't have the money. Now she's angry with me because I'm going away with my friend.

The truth is she has young kids and if I [1] ______ (go) away with her, we [2] ______ (spend) the whole time with her two young daughters. Don't get me wrong, I love my nieces, but a whole ten days won't be a holiday at all. I have a very stressful job and have very little time off. If I [3] ______ (tell) her the truth, she [4] ______ (be) very upset.

What [5] ______ (you do) in my situation?

Thanks

Sheila

Hi Sheila,

You could invent another story but if you [6] ______ (do), you [7] ______ (have) to tell another lie. I always believe honesty is the best policy.

If you [8] ______ (explain) that you love spending time with her and the kids but that you really need to relax because of your job, I'm sure [9] ______ (understand). Maybe suggest going away for a weekend? If you did, it [10] ______ (not be) so tiring for you. She would probably love it, too.

Let me know how it goes, and good luck!

Morag

6 TASK You saw a woman stealing some food from a supermarket. When you left the supermarket, you noticed her giving it to her children. They looked hungry and ate it all straight away. What would you do and why?

Listening, vocabulary and speaking

V Insight Three-part phrasal verbs with *to* and *with*

1 Replace the words in bold with the correct form of the phrasal verbs below.

4 come up with 3 fall out with 6 get away with 1 get round to 8 live up to 5 own up to 7 put it down to 2 put up with

1 We finally **found the time to start** watching *This Country*. It's such a funny series. 1
2 I really don't know how she **tolerates** his antisocial behaviour.
3 I've **had an argument with** my parents about what to do at New Year.
4 Nasser **thought of** a brilliant excuse as to why he missed the football match.
5 Lance Armstrong **admitted to** using banned substances in his cycling competitions.
6 I can't believe Joyce vandalized the community centre and **wasn't punished for** it.
7 Dominique is obviously disappointed she didn't get the job, but she'll have to **say it's caused by** a lack of work experience.
8 This new laptop isn't as good as they say! Sadly, it **hasn't matched** my expectations.

Apologizing and accepting apologies

2 🔊5.01 Match sentences 1–6 to the situations a–f. Then listen and check your answers.

d 1 We regret to inform you that the store is now closing. Please take your purchases to the nearest till.
a 2 I'm very sorry I'm late. The bus was full and I had to wait for another one.
b 3 Don't worry about it, Suzy. It won't show on that dark brown carpet. I'll get you another glass.
c 4 We'd like to apologize for the poor audio quality of that last programme.
f 5 That's OK. I haven't got French today, so you can give it back to me tomorrow.
e 6 That's quite all right, Dan. You're pretty quiet normally, so a bit of loud music from your house every now and then isn't a problem.

a Talking to a teacher
b Visiting grandparents
c Watching TV
d Buying things in a department store
e Talking to a neighbour
f Talking to a school friend

3 🔊5.01 Complete the lines from the dialogues. Then listen again and check.

1 A That's your apologiase ______ for being so slow!
B I'm sorry! I didn't expect ______ take so long. I couldn't find the book that Mum wanted.
2 A Let's say no more ______ about it. Just try to be on time tomorrow.
3 B Oh, no! I'm sorry ______, Gran! I've spilled my lemonade on the floor!
4 A It doesn't metter ______. You can watch it again on your computer. It might be better on that.
5 B Oh, I'm really sorry ______, Anne! I've forgotten to bring your French dictionary back!
6 A I'd like to apologiate ______ for all the noise this afternoon, Mr Tate. I had some friends round and one of them kept turning the music up really loud.

4 Rewrite the dialogues. Make the formal ones informal, and the informal ones more formal.

1 A I'm sorry to have to inform you that the performance is going to start later than expected.
I regret to inform you ______
B Don't worry. We can get something to drink.
That's quiate allright ______
2 A Please accept our apologies for taking up so much of your time.
I feel very bad ______
B That's quite all right.
That's ok ______
3 A We do apologize. It wasn't very considerate of us to act in that way.
We are sorry ______
B Let's say no more about it.
Never mind ______
4 A I'm really sorry I got your address wrong.
I apologise for ______
B It isn't a problem.
Let it doesn't metter ______

5 TASK Read Asha's text to Bruno. Write the dialogue when Bruno phones Asha and apologizes.

New text message:

Are you nearly here? We were meant to meet 30 mins ago. Did you forget? I don't have that long – have to get back to work ... Call me.
Asha x

Vocabulary and grammar

V Insight Synonyms: the law

1 Choose the correct answers.

1 This diet is quite ____________. There are lots of things you can't eat.
a voluntary **b** restrictive **c** optional

2 The lawyer said that the person had acted in a(n) ____________ manner.
a limiting **b** illegal **c** obligatory

3 Maths, science, and English are the only ____________ subjects for 14–16-year-olds in England.
a prohibited **b** restrictive **c** compulsory

4 People in Singapore are ____________ from chewing gum.
a prohibited **b** optional **c** limiting

5 Regular exercise isn't ____________ – your body needs it.
a voluntary **b** legal **c** optional

6 Military service is ____________ in the UK from the age of 16, but teenagers who choose to become soldiers must serve until they're 22.
a compulsory **b** voluntary **c** restrictive

2 Match 1–6 to a–f to make phrases.

1 a fair election
2 compulsory
3 optional
4 restrictive
5 prohibited
6 a legal

a right that everyone has
b books that you aren't allowed to read
c gun laws that ban certain weapons
d means that nobody cheated
e education between the ages of 5 and 16
f features that you can pay more for

Vocabulary extra Law and order

3 Complete the text with the prepositions *for*, *from*, *of* or *to*.

In my opinion, prisons aren't the right way to punish criminals. I don't approve [1]____________ locking people in rooms for most of the day. Of course, they should be punished [2]____________ the crime they've committed. The thing is, I just don't think it deters them [3]____________ making the same mistakes again. When people are sentenced [4]____________ a period of time in prison, they aren't taught anything.

That's why when people are released [5]____________ prison, they don't know what to do. They may not have the skills to find a job and may return to crime. Prison also gives them the chance [6]____________ make new criminal contacts. On top of this, you need to take account [7]____________ how being locked up makes people feel. I know I'd be angry and you can't blame them [8]____________ feeling like that.

There must be a better way. As long as they haven't robbed someone [9]____________ their life or committed a violent crime, community work and educational programmes help people to take responsibility [10]____________ their crime and better prepare them [11]____________ the real world.

Modals of obligation, prohibition and permission

4 Complete the sentences using the correct modal verbs.

1 Supermarket shoppers only may park here.
People who aren't using the supermarket ____________ park there.

2 Only audience members over the age of 16 must pay full price.
Children ____________ pay full price.

3 Passengers must not talk to the bus driver when the bus is moving.
You ____________ talk to the bus driver when the bus has stopped.

4 Under-tens have to be accompanied by a parent in the pool.
Over-tens ____________ be accompanied by an adult in the pool.

5 Customers cannot enter without a face mask.
You ____________ only go in there wearing a face mask.

6 You don't have to pay to park here in the evening.
You ____________ pay if you park here in the daytime.

5 TASK Write sentences about rules and customs in your country. Use *have to*, *don't have to*, *can*, *can't*, *must* and *mustn't*.

You can learn to drive when you're 17 in England …
You don't have to carry an ID card …

Reading

1 Read the first paragraph of the text. What do you think *The Future of prisons?* will be about? Then read the article and check your answer.

a the increasing number of people in prison
b finding prisoners work after they leave
c changing the current prison system
d giving prisoners shorter sentences

2 Read the article again. Match sentences A–E to gaps 1–5. What do the underlined words in the sentences refer to?

A They operate in a way that doesn't involve being locked up for most of the day.
B They have moved from more secure prisons for the last few years of their sentences.
C Over 2 million people were behind bars there in 2020.
D This leads to a large percentage of them being locked up again.
E In comparison to traditional prisons, it appears to work.

3 Are the sentences true (T) or false (F)? Correct the false ones.

1 The writer suggests that money is wasted every year on keeping people in prison.
2 Community service involves working in and around the prison.
3 There is tight security on the island where Bastøy Prison is located.
4 The number of people who return to prison after leaving Bastøy is lower than in traditional prisons.
5 The writer suggests that society isn't ready for big changes to the prison system.

4 Look at the highlighted words in the text. What do they refer to?

1 this ____________
2 it (paragraph 2) ____________
3 that ____________
4 Here ____________
5 they ____________
6 it (paragraph 6) ____________

The Future of prisons?

1 If you do something bad, you go to prison. If you burgle a house, commit murder or steal cars, that's where you go. In fact, in the UK, there were a massive 78,000 people in prison in 2019. But this is a relatively small number when compared to the USA. [1]________ Does this mean the system works or does this mean the system is broken?

2 There are many reasons to believe prison isn't the answer and we must find other ways to punish those in society who break the law. In 2020, it was estimated that the average cost of keeping someone in prison was almost £45,000 a year. All this money and yet offenders often feel lost when they are released from prison because they have been ill-prepared for fitting back into society. [2]________ And so the cycle continues. While the public may feel safe that the 'bad guy' is behind bars, it does little to reduce crime.

3 However, there are alternatives. There are open prisons, or category D prisons. [3]________ Quite the opposite. Some even have permission to leave for a limited time in order to work or spend some time at home. For non-violent criminals there's also community service, that is, doing jobs for the council rather than being in prison.

4 So, this all seems to be moving in a more positive direction. But has Bastøy Prison in Norway gone too far? It's situated on an island a few miles from Oslo and is home to 100 prisoners. [4]________ Here, there are no high fences, and prisoners live together in normal houses. There's also a library, a church and a football pitch. They work for a small salary, learn new skills and the prisoners are responsible for buying their own food to prepare their meals. There's even free time where they can swim, ski and fish. Relatives are allowed to visit at certain times and although there are around 70 staff, only a few guards stay overnight. They don't even have guns!

5 The situation at Bastøy leads many people to use words such as 'holiday camp', 'luxury' and 'easy life'. In short, many regard this type of prison as a positive environment instead of a negative one. But here's the thing. [5] ________ The numbers speak for themselves: Two years after their release, only one in five prisoners go on to reoffend. This is much lower than in both the USA and the UK. The reason is not difficult to see: At this place they don't just sit in a cell, but instead they can get used to living as they will on the outside. It's like a halfway house until they become functional members of society when they leave.

6 If we just looked at the statistics, the example set by Bastøy would be enough to change the whole system, as well as saving the taxpayer a lot of money. However, while the public is keen to reduce crime, it seems to want a visible form of punishment more.

5 Match the collocations 1–6 to the definitions a–f. Use the article to help you.

1 a positive environment
2 look at the statistics
3 commit murder
4 break the law
5 go too far
6 have permission

a kill someone
b ignore the rules of a country
c be allowed to do
d behave in a way that annoys people
e a situation that gives people hope
f study the numbers and percentages

6 Complete the sentences with the collocations from exercise 5. You may have to change the form of the verb.

1 Many of the prisoners in this maximum security prison have ________________.
2 Why do you have to ________________? You really upset Mum.
3 If the classroom is ________________, students often perform better.
4 Does that man ________________ to use that computer?
5 By ________________, we can see most people want to change the current system.
6 If you ________________ by parking in the wrong place, you will get a fine.

7 TASK In your opinion, how can we best treat people who commit crimes? Are there any crimes that should not be punished?

Writing A cause–effect essay

1 Complete the sentences with the words below.

▪ because ▪ because of ▪ results in ▪ therefore ▪ this means ▪ why

1 The glass was smashed. ____________ that the thief entered through the window.
2 We had a vote and that's ____________ the law was changed.
3 It was ____________ he campaigned so hard that the group were successful.
4 Lying in court ____________ serious consequences for those involved.
5 It was ____________ her connection to the politician that she was investigated.
6 My daughter is only 15; ____________ she can't drive to school.

2 Read Max's cause–effect essay and answer the questions.

1 When do young people get involved in crime?
2 Where do criminals look for young people?
3 If street crime reduces, what type of crime will be affected?
4 Why can't police be both on the streets and investigating other crimes?
5 In the final paragraph, why does the writer think it's better to have more police on the streets?

The effect of having more police on our streets

By **MAX WEBB**

This essay will consider the effect of having more police on our streets.

The introduction of more police officers on the streets in local communities will improve life in areas with high crime. One ongoing issue with young people is being involved in crime outside of school hours, which results in problems later on in life. Criminals would find it harder to target young people hanging around parks and communal areas because police would be more visible. This will mean that there will be a reduction in the number of children joining gangs. Therefore, the crime rate will go down and the effect of this is that local people will probably feel safer in their everyday lives as well.

If every area had more police on the streets, there would be other problems. Having a police presence in every part of a town or city would make people feel safer and discourage young people from going into crime. However, due to more police officers on the street, there would be fewer officers investigating more serious crimes like murder and armed robbery. Consequently, the police would spend a large amount of their time walking around the streets rather than catching violent criminals. This would therefore have an impact on how many serious crimes are solved quickly and efficiently. There simply aren't the numbers of police officers to do both.

This essay has highlighted the main features of having more police on our streets. Since serious crime can be the result of getting into crime at a young age, I think the effects are definitely more positive than negative.

3 Read phrases 1–7 which appear in the essay. Do the phrases express cause (C) or effect (E)?

1 ... which results in problems ...
2 ... because police would be more visible.
3 This will mean that ...
4 ... and, the effect of this...
5 However, due to more police ...
6 Consequently, the police ...
7 This would therefore have an impact ...

4 Read the letter again. Which paragraph of the essay includes these causes and effects? ____________

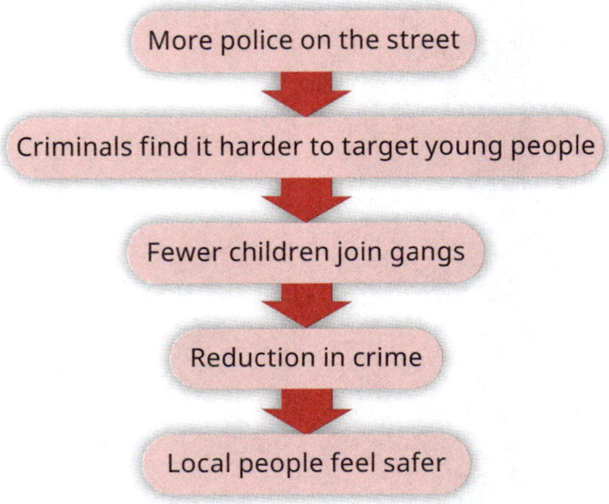

Writing guide

▪ **TASK Write an essay about the cause and effect of having security officers at school or university.**

▪ **PLAN 1 Make notes about the following.**
- what crimes are reported at schools
- why security is needed
- why security isn't needed
- what effect security at a school or university would have on staff and students

▪ **PLAN 2 Decide which ideas you are going to use and match them to these paragraphs.**

Paragraph 1: Introduce the topic briefly and explain the purpose of your essay.
Paragraph 2: Introduce your first point and link the causes and effects.
Paragraph 3: Introduce your second point and link the causes and effects.
Paragraph 4: Summarize, make a suggestion or prediction, or give your opinion.

▪ **WRITE Write your essay. Use the plan to help you.**

▪ **REVIEW Check the following points.**
- Did you use a visual organizer to help you to organize your ideas?
- Did you organize your essay into the correct number of paragraphs?
- Did you use words and expressions for cause and effect?
- Have you checked grammar, vocabulary, spelling and punctuation?

Assess your progress

Give yourself a mark 1–3 for each Learning Objective from the lesson.
1 I found this difficult. **2** This was OK. **3** I can do this well.

Lesson 5A

	Mark
I can use referencing to understand a text.	
I can use words relating to influence.	
I can use the prefixes *mis-* and *dis-* to form nouns with a negative meaning.	
How can I improve?	

Lesson 5B

	Mark
I can use the first conditional to talk about a possible future situation and probable results.	
I can use the second conditional to talk about an unreal, unlikely or imaginary situation and its results.	
How can I improve?	

Lesson 5C

	Mark
I can understand the main points in a radio interview.	
I can use three-part phrasal verbs with *to* and *with*.	
I can apologize and accept apologies.	
How can I improve?	

Lesson 5D

	Mark
I can understand and identify paraphrasing in a text.	
I can use words relating to the law.	
I can use modal verbs to express obligation, prohibition and permission.	
How can I improve?	

Lesson 5E

	Mark
I can write a cause and effect essay.	
I can use a visual organizer to structure my writing.	
I can use words and phrases to express cause and effect.	
How can I improve?	

Action plan

Make a plan for what you can do next to improve. Discuss your ideas with your classmates / teacher.

6 At a price

Vocabulary

Insight Advertising

1 **Match the verbs to the situations.**

display ▪ launch ▪ promote ▪ research ▪ target ▪ trick

1 We're going to have adverts for this new product in popular magazines and newspapers. ______________
2 We're making people think that it's a lot cheaper to buy two, when there's actually very little difference in price. ______________
3 We're finding out exactly what shoppers are looking for when they buy electronic equipment. ______________
4 We're going to start selling the product in the summer. ______________
5 We're aiming the advertising campaign at 12-year-old girls. ______________
6 We're putting the Halloween stuff right next to the entrance of all our department stores. ______________

Insight Collocations: advertising

2 **Complete the sentences with the words below.**

campaign ▪ image ▪ knowledge ▪ magazines ▪ offer ▪ samples

1 I hate being off school, but I do like looking at all the glossy ______________ Mum buys me.
2 If famous labels are underpriced, it can be bad for the brand ______________.
3 I got this for only £1 – it was on special ______________.
4 Oh, look! They're giving out free ______________ at the ice cream counter.
5 Every new iPhone™ product is launched with a huge marketing ______________.
6 I'd advise you to buy this book on how to become a journalist – the author clearly has insider ______________.

Vocabulary extra Types of advertising

3 **Choose the correct answers.**

1 OXFORD UNIVERSITY PRESS

a slogan b logo c jingle

2 'I recommend these trainers. You won't find any more comfortable to run in.' – Cath, City Runners Club

a banner b endorsement c billboard

3 Congratulations! You're one of our lucky winners! Claim your prize by following this link!

a slogan b spam c logo

4 SALE! This weekend only! 50% off all walking boots!

a flyer b endorsement c jingle

5 Something to sell, then come to Aldwell! ♫

a billboard b endorsement c jingle

6 Evan's Electronics CLICK HERE

a banner b stealth marketing c jingle

4 **Complete the text with the words below.**

billboard ▪ brand image ▪ classified ads ▪ displayed ▪ endorsements ▪ flyers ▪ jingles ▪ luxury goods ▪ marketing campaigns ▪ persuade ▪ slogan

Nowadays, we are bombarded with [1] ______________ trying to get us to buy something. Turn on the radio and we hear catchy [2] ______________, walk down the high street of any city and people are trying to give us [3] ______________, or drive down a major road and see a massive [4] ______________ with a memorable [5] ______________.

And the more expensive the product, the bigger the budget. For example, the [6] ______________ market spends an incredible amount to try and get us to buy their products: It is estimated that Gucci spent approximately $567 million on digital marketing and advertising in 2020 alone.

And much of the marketing is now done online via the big social media giants. Companies have seen the benefit of receiving [7] ______________ from famous faces. Kim Kardashian charges around $13,000 to promote a product on Twitter™! It seems celebrities can [8] ______________ the public to buy something relatively easily. Match the [9] ______________ to a lifestyle you want to copy and it's a winning formula for sales.

Even dating, which at one time was limited to [10] ______________ in the pages of a newspaper, is big business these days. Websites for those looking to find love are now [11] ______________ in the same way as other products on the internet. Demanding monthly fees to help you to find a partner makes people believe everything and anything is for sale.

5 **TASK** **Describe an advert you remember from your childhood. Why do you think it was so memorable? Do you think it made people buy the product?**

Grammar

The passive

1 Choose the correct answers.

1 Katherine Johnson __________ by NASA, and she helped to send astronauts to the moon and back in 1968.
   a is employed   b has been employed
   c was employed
2 Lab-grown meat __________ in Singapore.
   a is being serving   b is being served
   c is been served
3 Fair-trade products __________ in over 70 countries around the world.
   a selling   b are sold
   c sold
4 The Oxford MINI™ plant __________ cars since 1913.
   a is being made   b was making
   c has been making
5 Formal sign language __________ by a Spanish monk, Pedro Ponce de León, in the 16th century.
   a was being invented   b was invented
   c is invented
6 The word *champo* __________ in India in the 18th century and is where the word 'shampoo' comes from.
   a was already being used   b used already
   c has already been used

2 Put the words in the correct order to make sentences in a dialogue.

A this / made / the / in / UK / cheese / is / ?
   Excuse me? 1 __________
B was / that / from / cheese / Latvia / imported / .
   No, 2 __________
A stated / why / the packet / isn't / on / that / ?
   3 __________
   Look! 'UK' is written on the label!
B the / made / the / are / rules / Food Standards Agency / by / .
   4 __________
   It's because the packaging was made in the UK.
A being / are / this / tricked / shoppers / by / .
   Well, I think 5 __________

3 Complete the sentences. Use the active or passive form of the verbs below.

already deliver ▪ encourage ▪ provide ▪ sting ▪ stop ▪ use

1 You __________ never __________ by a male bee.
2 More than 16 million animals __________ for transport and communication in the First World War.
3 This is your driver speaking. We __________ in half an hour for a lunch break.
4 The drivers __________ the toys. The problem wasn't noticed before they went out.
5 Australians __________ to eat more kangaroo meat as the animal's population is becoming too big – around 50 million.
6 Calculators __________ for students in the maths test tomorrow.

4 Rewrite the active sentences using the passive. Only use an agent if it is important.

1 Polish farms grow most of Europe's apples nowadays.
   were grown
2 People are not promoting fair trade enough around the world.
   isn't being promoted
3 They've made over 20 James Bond films since 1962.
   have ~~med~~ been made
4 A 19-year-old woman called Mary Shelley wrote *Frankenstein*.
   was called
5 We will only give refunds with a receipt.
   will been given
6 They were still using small children to clean chimneys in the 1860s.
   were been use

5 Complete the text with the correct passive or active form of the verbs in brackets.

CHILD LABOUR

Consumers in the West are keen to buy fair-trade products, and are horrified to hear of child workers 1 beeing used (use) in developing countries. However, let's remember that before 1940, many children aged between five and fourteen 2 worked (work) in Europe and the US. Child labour 3 has been used (use) widely in Britain during the Industrial Revolution, when children as young as four 4 were employed (employ) in factories. Most workers 5 WERE PAIED (pay) according to how much they produced, and a child's working day often 6 LASTED (last) 16 hours.

In 1833, children under the age of nine 7 WEREN'T PERMITED (not permit) to work any longer, and in 1870, the Education Act 8 BROUGHT (bring) huge changes. By the late 19th century, children's lives 9 HAD BEEN TRANSFORM (transform) completely – children were studying instead of working, and 10 WERE SEEN (see) as children instead of 'little adults'.

Today, the highest rates of child labour 11 ARE FOUND (find) in some African nations, with 25% of children aged five to fourteen working. The International Labour Organization stated that the worst forms of child labour 12 WAS DROPED (drop) by nearly 40% from 2000 to 2016, but there was still a long way to go.

6 TASK Imagine you are starting a new ethical business. What will your business be and what steps will you take to make it ethical? Remember to use passive forms.

I've decided to start a new business. All the honey will be made locally and will come from local farmers …

Listening, vocabulary and speaking

V Insight Describing amounts

1 Choose the correct words.

1 There was a **majority** / **significant** number of sales for the new smartphone.
2 A **large proportion** / **tiny minority** of Swiss people speak Romansh – around 60,000 out of a population of more than 8 million.
3 The **tiny** / **vast** majority of TikTok users are under 30.
4 The annual event, Children in Need, had raised a **whopping** / **modest** £1 billion for children's charities between 1980, when it started, and 2018.
5 **An overwhelming** / **A significant** number of students voted for a change to the testing system at the school – around 70%.
6 Her latest concert only sold a **modest** / **massive** number of tickets, proving the singer isn't as popular as she once was.

Expressing contrast

2 6.01 Listen to Helen and Ed talking about the bicycles. Which bike (A or B) would each person choose?

Helen ________ Ed ________

Ⓐ

3 6.01 Listen again. Are the sentences true (T) or false (F)? Correct the false ones.

1 None of Helen's friends are serious cyclists.
2 Helen doesn't think that bike B is good for long distances.
3 Helen could use bike B to go to school.
4 Ed thinks that bike A's design is interesting.
5 Ed likes the colour of bike A.

4 6.01 Complete the sentences with the words and phrases for expressing contrast. Then put the sentences in the correct order 1–6. Listen again and check.

on the other hand ▪ unlike ▪ whereas

____ **a** Bike A looks fairly normal, ________________ the other bike is quite unusual.
____ **b** I could use it for the short journey to school and, ________________ other bikes, I could put it in my locker when I get there!
____ **c** ... it's a racing bike with drop handlebars, and I don't like those. ________________, I think a lot of my friends would like it ...

although ▪ however ▪ in contrast

____ **d** It looks very futuristic. ________________, I'd never choose it because it isn't really a bike, more of a gadget, ...
____ **e** ... it looks a bit like those exercise bikes you see in a gym. ________________, bike A looks a bit boring, ...
____ **f** ________________ I said that the first bike is more normal, it isn't the kind of bike I would choose.

5 TASK It is your friend's birthday and they have asked for a new bag for college. Which would you choose as a gift? Write a short email to another friend and explain your reasons.

Vocabulary and grammar

V Insight Trade

1 Choose the correct words.

1 We need to get more workers if we're going to **manufacture** / **profit** more products next year.
2 The company will still make €11 **industry** / **profit** per item if they sell it for the lower price.
3 I like the **design** / **trend** with the small logo – the big one is too much.
4 We've sold loads of these sunglasses because of the recent **industry** / **trend** for nineties fashion.
5 This isn't a charity – we're a **commercial** / **profit** business and need a price that reflects the quality.
6 It isn't just our company – the whole **industry** / **retailer** is making a lot of money right now.
7 More and more **retailers** / **consumers** are buying on the internet rather than in high street shops.
8 We're looking for a big **industry** / **retailer** that can sell the product all over the country.

Vocabulary extra Consumerism

2 Complete the phrases with the verbs below. Use each verb twice.

give ▪ have ▪ make ▪ put on

1 ________ a promise		5 ________ an influence	
2 ________ a refund		6 ________ the market	
3 ________ display		7 ________ a present	
4 ________ a bad experience		8 ________ a purchase	

3 Match phrases 1–8 in exercise 2 to what the people are saying in a–h.

a 'I'll buy it!' ________
b 'It was terrible!' ________
c 'Place it at the front of the shop window.' ________
d 'Would you like your money back?' ________
e 'We're going to launch it next week.' ________
f 'I won't forget to buy it for you.' ________
g 'Happy Birthday! This is for you!' ________
h 'We're going to change the way people think.' ________

4 Complete the text with the correct form of the words and phrases below.

commercial ▪ design ▪ do some research ▪ have a bad experience ▪ have an influence ▪ launch ▪ make a promise ▪ profit ▪ take a risk ▪ trend

Teenage entrepreneurs

Mikaila Ulmer

Ulmer [1] ________________ when she was stung by a bee at four years old. As a way of overcoming her fear of them, she decided to learn about the creatures. This lead to her product, Me & the Bees Lemonade, and Ulmer herself appears on the bottle's [2] ________________. In 2016, at the age of 11, a [3] ________________ deal with Whole Foods Market worth $11 million was struck. 10% of the [4] ________________ is now given to bee charities, and she hopes to set a [5] ________________ among people to set up their own business without letting their age, gender or race get in the way.

have / get something done

5 Match problems 1–6 to actions a–f. Then complete a–h with the correct form of the verbs in brackets.

1 'I'm not sure how to advertise the festival.'
2 'We don't have the money to provide snacks.'
3 'Maria can't DJ anymore because she's ill.'
4 'Bob's camera is still broken and he's meant to be taking photos.'
5 'My van has broken down!'
6 'Those lights look a bit unsafe.'

a 'You could ________ some posters ________ (have / print) for the local area.'
b 'You really need ________ that ________ (get / organized) or we won't have music.'
c 'Maybe you should ________ them ________ (get / check) by an electrician.'
d 'Why don't you ________ some ________ by the local supermarket? (have / donate)'
e 'I'm sure you can ________ it ________ (have / repair) before Saturday'
f 'He really needs ________ it ________ (get / fix) before the event!

6 TASK You are going to plan a school fair. Discuss the following things with your partner.

- how to advertise the event
- what will need to be done before the event
- what to sell and how much to sell it for

Kenan Pala

Pala wanted to help out in the community in San Diego. He [6] ________________ and found out that most voluntary organizations didn't allow children under the age of 18 to volunteer. He decided to [7] ________________ in 2017, at the age of 13, by [8] ________________ his own non-profit company, Kids4Community. The organization allows people of any ages to support them and has [9] ________________ on the local community: raising $1 million for homeless people. He has even [10] ________________ to pass the organization onto his younger brother when he graduates.

Reading

1 Are these English words similar to words in your language? Which words are 'friends' (with the same meaning)? Which are 'false friends' (with different meanings)?

chef ■ communication ■ global ■ pension ■ receipt ■ status

2 What do you think can be the biggest problem when a product name is used in a different country? Choose the correct answer. Then read the article and check.

- **a** People don't understand the name.
- **b** The name has a negative meaning in another language.
- **c** People see the product as 'foreign' and don't want to buy it.

3 Match headings A–E to paragraphs 1–4. There is one heading that you do not need.

- **A** Errors in the East
- **B** Foreign is fashionable
- **C** Ask around
- **D** Successful slogans
- **E** Failures on four wheels

4 Read the article again and answer the questions.

1. Why are English words often seen as cool?
2. How can it be costly for companies in English-speaking countries not to know other languages?
3. Was the Rolls-Royce car name a disaster in Germany? Why / why not?
4. Why is it strange that Germans used a new English word for 'rucksack'?
5. Which languages cause the biggest problems for English translators?
6. What do marketing people need to accept?
7. When do marketing teams want to reuse advertising campaigns?

5 Match words and phrases from the article to definitions a–g.

1. executive
2. costly
3. be in a rush
4. lick
5. abroad
6. concept
7. embarrassing

- **a** idea
- **b** to touch with your tongue
- **c** making you feel stupid in public
- **d** expensive
- **e** to have to do something very quickly
- **f** a senior person in a company
- **g** in a different country

False friends

People learning a foreign language often recognize words that are similar to words in their own language. Sometimes these are helpful 'friends' – a Dutch, German or Flemish speaker learning English can relax when it comes to learning *hand* – it's exactly the same in their language. When Germans see the English word *handy* they might think they've found another 'friend', but this is a 'false friend' – the English adjective *handy* means 'convenient', whereas the German noun *Handy* is a word they use for 'mobile phone'!

1 ________

The German *Handy* is a good example of words being borrowed from another language in order to make something sound cool. In countries around the world, marketing and advertising executives often reach for the English dictionary, not because they really need to borrow a word, but because they want to borrow some of the status of English as the language of international communication. The message is: 'Hey, look, I'm using English, I'm part of the modern global community.'

So, when it comes to British, Australian and American companies selling their products abroad, you might think that they only have to keep the English names and everyone will be happy. Unfortunately it isn't as simple as that, and if English-speaking marketing departments don't do enough research into what their product names and slogans mean in other cultures, false friends can turn into costly enemies!

2 ________

Car names are a good example of the problem. Ford's *Fiera* wasn't as popular with Spanish speakers as the company had hoped, possibly because *fiera* can mean 'ugly' in Spanish. It's said that the well-known story that their *Nova* car suffered for a similar reason

– MARKETING ENEMIES

(*No va* in Spanish would mean 'doesn't go') is not actually true, but it appears nevertheless in many books about marketing. Rolls-Royce™ fortunately realized that their *Silver Mist* needed a name change before being launched in Germany (in German *Mist* means 'manure', the waste that comes out after a horse or cow has eaten!), where it became the *Silver Shadow*.

The German marketing people seemed to do well with *Handy*, but the English term they borrowed for a certain type of rucksack – which is actually a German word! – wasn't such a good idea. *Body bags* are actually what dead bodies are put in when they are moved from the scene of a crime.

3 ________

Having names and slogans translated into other languages isn't always an effective solution, especially with languages that are very different to English. In the rush to enter the growing Chinese market, the slogan 'Come alive with the Pepsi™ Generation' was translated into Chinese as 'Pepsi brings your ancestors back from the dead'! Kentucky Fried Chicken™ also had to do some more work on their idiomatic slogan 'finger-lickin' good', which was first translated to mean 'eat your fingers off'!

4 ________

Most problems can be avoided by checking product names and translations with enough local people in the target market. However, it's unusual for the result to be a perfect translation of the original marketing concept. 'The concept will never translate perfectly into another culture,' warns one marketing expert. It seems that the most embarrassing mistakes have been made by marketing teams who refuse to accept this. If a campaign has been very successful in one market, they will try their hardest to reuse it in a very different one, often failing to listen to what the locals say.

6 Complete the sentences with the correct form of the words and phrases in exercise 5.

1. Three-quarters of British people say they would like to live ________________. The majority would choose English-speaking countries.
2. The phrase 'more haste, less speed' means that when you're ________________ you make mistakes and end up taking longer to do things.
3. It seems wrong when the top ________________ of some charities earn more than $1 million a year.
4. Scientists still cannot find an explanation for why people's faces turn red when they do something ________________.
5. Buying college textbooks can be ________________, so look for used copies in second-hand bookshops.
6. Saving for the future is a strange ________________ for many teenagers – money is for spending!
7. Dogs often ________________ their wounds, but bacteria from their tongues can cause infections.

7 TASK Make a list of products with English names that you know. Would they be better if they had other names in your language? What would be a better name in your opinion?

Writing A formal email of complaint

1 Read the email below. Is it formal or informal? Complete the text with the words and phrases below.

- although
- dissatisfied with
- I am writing to complain about
- I still have not received
- what is more
- while

From: Oscar Hooper

Subject: Television problems

Dear Sir / Madam,

[1] ________________ the problems I have had with the latest smart television I bought from your company. I am extremely [2] ________________ both the television and your service.

First of all, the television came with a six-month loan, which promised to be interest-free. [3] ________________ I signed up in store to qualify for this deal, [4] ________________ details on how to pay for the television two months later!

To add to this, the television has developed several faults. The remote control's Netflix button is frequently stuck so we need to go onto the app, which takes time. Furthermore, the quality of the picture isn't good compared to the price we paid for it.

I have repeatedly tried to contact someone to discuss these problems by phone, but it is constantly busy. One day I waited for over half an hour and gave up. [5] ________________, when I try to contact you via your live chat online, I find that I am talking to a computer, rather than a real person. This is incredibly annoying. [6] ________________ I understand that you may find this method quicker than a human, a computer is terribly bad at answering my specific questions!

I would like to return the television and also cancel the loan I had for it. If you do not reply to this email or phone me within 14 days, I will contact the regulatory government department.

I look forward to receiving a reply from you soon.

Yours faithfully,

Oscar Hooper

2 Match the formal words and phrases in the email to these informal ways of saying the same thing.

1 really ____________
2 unhappy ____________
3 got some problems ____________
4 often ____________
5 talk about ____________
6 getting ____________

3 Read the email below. Is it formal or informal? Rewrite five parts of the email that use the wrong register.

Dear Suzie,

I am writing to inform you that your birthday present was received today. It's fantastic and I'm over the moon about it! A new backpack is just what was needed, and furthermore its size is ideal, so I will be able to use it for school and for weekend excursions. Thanks a lot!

I look forward to speaking to you soon.

Yours sincerely,

Jamal

____
____
____
____
____

4 Choose the correct words and phrases.

1 The trousers you sent me are not the size I ordered. **However, / Besides this,** they are the wrong colour.
2 **Although / However,** the assistant promised to call me back, I never heard from him.
3 **What's more, / While** the helpline advisor was pleasant and polite, she was unable to help me.
4 The food in your restaurant was rather tasteless. **Although / To add to this,** it was cold.
5 The new download service is pretty expensive. **However, / Furthermore,** it is extremely fast.

Writing guide

TASK **Write a formal email of complaint about something you've bought recently.**

PLAN 1 **Make notes about the following.**
- the product and the problems with it
- how you tried to solve the problems, without success
- what you want to happen now

PLAN 2 **Decide which ideas you are going to use and match them to these paragraphs.**

Paragraph 1: Explain why you are writing an email of complaint.
Paragraph 2: Describe the problems with the product and/or service.
Paragraph 3: Say why you are unhappy with the company's response to your complaints so far.
Paragraph 4: Say what you expect the company to do now, and what you will do if they don't do this.

WRITE **Write your formal email of complaint.**

REVIEW **Check the following points.**
- Have you included all the necessary information?
- Have you used polite language?
- Have you checked grammar, vocabulary, spelling and punctuation?

Assess your progress

Give yourself a mark 1–3 for each Learning Objective from the lesson.
1 I found this difficult. **2** This was OK. **3** I can do this well.

Lesson 6A

	Mark
I can infer information that the writer does not directly state in a text.	
I can recognize and understand paraphrasing / rephrasing.	
I can use words and phrases relating to advertising.	

How can I improve?

Lesson 6B

	Mark
I can use the passive with and without *by*.	
I can understand the key points in a radio programme.	

How can I improve?

Lesson 6C

	Mark
I can listen for specific information.	
I can use language to describe amounts.	
I can use language to express contrast.	

How can I improve?

Lesson 6D

	Mark
I can identify relevant words in a text to find specific information.	
I can use words relating to trade.	
I can use *have / get something done* to talk about things other people do to us or for us.	

How can I improve?

Lesson 6E

	Mark
I can write a formal email of complaint.	
I can use polite language for formal emails.	
I can distinguish between language for adding information and expressing contrast.	

How can I improve?

Action plan

Make a plan for what you can do next to improve. Discuss your ideas with your classmates / teacher.

7 It makes sense

Vocabulary

V Insight Perception and observation

1 Choose the correct words to complete the sentences.

1 I've only just __________ that the i in iPhone stands for 'internet, individual, instruct, inform and inspire'.
a detected b distinguished c realized
2 Many British people __________ London as being a cosmopolitan city.
a notice b realize c view
3 Japanese speakers of English find it difficult to __________ between the sounds 'l' and 'r'.
a distinguish b notice c detect
4 I'd never __________ that the @ sign is in a different place on American and British keyboards.
a detected b viewed c noticed
5 Arsenic is the poison often used to kill people in murder mysteries because it's difficult to __________.
a realize b detect c consider
6 People who are colour-blind find it most difficult to __________ between red and green, which makes traffic lights a challenge.
a differentiate b realize c notice
7 Have you __________ learning to drive now that you're 17?
a realized b considered c differentiated

V Insight Adverb–adjective collocations

2 Complete the sentences with the adjectives.

accepted ■ beneficial ■ careful ■ convinced ■ difficult ■ repulsive ■ spread ■ tasteless

1 I don't understand how people can eat oysters. I find them utterly __________ .
2 Many people are somewhat __________ to read and so it's hard to know what they're actually thinking.
3 I'm exceptionally __________ about what I post on LinkedIn – I want my future employers to know I'm professional.
4 Broccoli is highly __________ to your health – it contains a lot of fibre.
5 Poverty is more widely __________ in developed countries than people might think.
6 A I think Liang's telling the truth about what happened to the picture.
B Mm. I'm not entirely __________ .
7 It's strange to think that there isn't a universally __________ definition of what a mountain is.
8 I bought lots of special herbs and spices but, in the end, the meal was fairly __________ .

Vocabulary extra Food texture

3 Choose the correct words.

1 Mmm! How do you get this cake to be so **smooth** / **soft** and **moist** / **runny**? It's hard and dry when I make it.
2 I love mashed potato when it's really **smooth** / **crumbly**. It's horrible when it's **lumpy** / **chewy**.
3 I only like apples when they're really **crumbly** / **crunchy**. There's nothing worse than a soft apple.
4 These peaches are incredibly **chewy** / **juicy**. Be careful that it doesn't all run onto your shirt!
5 The steak was so **crunchy** / **chewy** that it took me about a minute to eat every mouthful.
6 These brownies are too **moist** / **crumbly**. When you take a bite, most of it falls on the floor.

4 Complete the recipe with the words and collocations.

consider ■ creamy ■ exceptionally careful ■ notice ■ oily ■ realize ■ runny ■ smooth ■ thick

Home-made tomato ketchup

It's easy to pick up a bottle of tomato ketchup in a shop, so why bother making your own? Well, I'm here to say you should [1] __________ doing just that. Everyone will be impressed and [2] __________ the difference! You might be surprised when you [3] __________ just how easy it is.

Ingredients

2 tins tomatoes (800g)
1 onion
2 tablespoons of oil
80g brown sugar
120ml vinegar
1 tablespoon tomato paste
1 teaspoon of cinnamon powder
1 teaspoon of black pepper
salt (to taste).

Method

Heat the oil (don't use too much or it will be [4] __________) and chopped onion in a pan for a few minutes. When the onion is soft, add the tomatoes. Next, add the tomato paste, vinegar and spices and mix well. Cook for 40 minutes, but be [5] __________ not to put it on a high heat. It should cook on a very low heat. Stir regularly. If it is too [6] __________, add some more tomato paste and if it is too [7] __________, add a little water.

Then put all the ingredients in a blender and the tomato ketchup will be nice and [8] __________ – and ready to eat.

5 TASK Write about your favourite thing to eat or cook. How do you make it? Why do you like it?

I like cooking fish pie. It takes a long time to cook but it's worth it. First, boil some potatoes until they are soft. Then add salt and pepper and mash them with milk and butter.

Reported speech

1 Rewrite the sentences in direct speech.

1 Megan said that she'd never been there before.
'I've never been there before,' Megan said.

2 The teacher pointed out that they were travelling past his old school.
We are travelling past his old school

3 Dimitre promised that he would call his mum soon.
I promise I will call my mum soon

4 The twins admitted that they were late that day, but said they had been early the day before.
We are late today, but we 've been early yestarday

5 Lucas explained that he'd already left the university by the time I'd arrived.
I've already left the university by the t arrived

6 Mrs Williams told me she could help me with my science homework if I was having problems with it.
I can help you with your scienle homework if you're having problems with it

2 Complete the email. Use the correct form of the verbs in brackets.

Hi Noah,

I went to the insurance company's office this afternoon and spoke to them about your snowboarding accident. I told them that you 1 were still waiting (still / wait) to hear from them, and they admitted that they 2 had lost (lose) your claim. They said that they 3 sent (send) you another form to complete. I pointed out that you 4 didn't want (not want) to have to contact them again by phone because you 5 had already speent (already / spend) so much time waiting. They explained that 6 had been (be) short-staffed last week and that they 7 could not (cannot) call you because they didn't have your details. I gave your number and they promised that they 8 would ask (ask) a manager to contact you. The woman I spoke to said that she was very sorry about the trouble, and said that she 9 wanted (want) to give you a discount.

Hope this helps.

Love

Ahmed

3 Rewrite the sentences in reported speech. Use the reporting verbs in brackets.

1 'I'll take you to the concert if I manage to get tickets.'
He promised he would take me to the concert if he managed to get the tickets (promised)

2 'Yes, we think the clock is running slow too.'
We agreed that the clock was running slow. (agreed)

3 'OK, it's true – we've charged you both too much.'
They admitted that it was true and that they ~~had charged us both to much~~. (admitted)

4 'You can't call Akito. Your phone doesn't have a signal.'
She pointed out that I couldn't call Akito ~~because my phone didn't have a signal~~ (pointed out)

5 'Your password didn't work because you didn't use any capital letters.'
He explained that my password hadn't worked because ~~I hadn't used any~~ capital letters. (explained)

6 'Oh, your aunt called to ask if you're going to her house.'
She added that my aunt had called to ask if I was going to her house. (added)

4 Complete the magazine article with the correct form of the verbs in brackets.

Article

Twin telepathy

It is a subject that has interested people for many years – can twins communicate telepathically? That is, without any of the usual communication methods. There are stories of twins having the same dreams, thinking the same things or sensing when the other twin was in danger.

Sally Keeble shares a similar story. She told the Guardian newspaper that 1 SHE HAD NEVER BELIVED (never / believe) in twin telepathy before. She said she 2 DIDN'T HAVE (not / have) time for those stories and the familiar questions her and her sister heard about being twins. She explained that people always 3 HAD ASKED (ask) if their parents got confused and things like that.

Then something happened to change her mind. She said that she 4 FELT (feel) sick when her sister, Helen, was pregnant. Then at 7.51 p.m. one day, the most amazing thing happened. She said that she 5 HAS FINISHED (finish) work when she felt a terrible pain in her stomach and buckled back in her chair. 'When I got home, there was a message from my mum,' she said. 'She told me Helen 6 GAVE (give) birth to a boy ... at 7.51.'

Sally added that she 7 WENT (go) through the same trauma and pain as her sister. She also felt guilty when she was told that the baby 8 WAS (be) healthy while her sister 9 WAS STILL BEING RECOVERED (still / recover) from the operation and didn't yet have this information.

After that experience she 10 COULD NOT (can / not) believe that it was just a coincidence. There must have been some kind of twin telepathy.

5 TASK Think of a conversation that you have had recently with a friend or family member. Use lots of different reporting verbs.

Listening, vocabulary and speaking

V Insight Noun suffixes: *-tion*, *-sion*

1 Are the words in bold in the correct form in each sentence? Correct seven mistakes.

1 A I was surprised by Lucy's **react** when I told her we were moving house. ___
  B So was I! I couldn't believe the **expression** on her face. ___
2 We would like to **conclude** this meeting by asking if anyone has any questions. ___
3 The **divide** of any number by zero is actually impossible. ___
4 My grandma made a big **impress** on me as a kid – that's why I'll always miss her. ___
5 What's the **connect** between Winnie the Pooh and Attila the Hun? They have the same middle name! ___
6 The criminal made a full **confession** in prison about what he'd done. ___
7 A I heard about your sister's **decide** not to talk to the local newspaper. ___
  B Yeah, she said she wanted to **protection** our family from any unnecessary attention. ___
8 The town council has agreed to **situate** the new factory away from the housing estate. ___

Complaining and asking people to do things

2 7.01 Look at the pictures. Then listen to the dialogues. Choose the picture (A or B) which shows the problem in each dialogue.

1
A 

B 

2
A 

B 

3
A 

B 

3 7.01 Listen again and choose the correct answers.

1 Why is the train late?
  a Because of the cold.
  b Because the information screen was wrong.
  c Because it's raining a lot.
2 Why is the customer able to exchange the trainers?
  a Because they were in the sale.
  b Because the shop has some in stock.
  c Because the boy chooses them in blue.
3 Why does Eva keep getting letters for Mrs Jenkins's daughter?
  a Because they are neighbours.
  b Because she's out when the post comes.
  c Because they have the same name.

4 7.01 Complete the lines from the dialogues. Then listen and check.

1 ___, but when is the 9.15 train to Oxford coming?
2 Fine, but ___ please put on a replacement bus service when this happens?
3 I'm afraid ___. I bought these trainers here …
4 A lot were sold in the sale yesterday. ___ a different colour or a refund?
5 ___ exchange them for red? I really like the design.
6 ___ while I see if we've got them in stock?
7 Hi Mrs Jenkins. ___, but I'm afraid …
8 But if you see the postman, ___ ask him again to be more careful?

5 TASK Read Adam's note to Sally. Write the dialogue when Sally phones Broadfast to complain.

Sally – call Broadfast about Wi-Fi problems:
- slow speed – ask them to check
- lose connection sometimes – ask why
- charged too much for last month – ask for refund

Vocabulary and grammar

V Insight Sight and sound

1 Complete the text with the correct form of the verbs below.

blink ▪ peer ▪ snore ▪ stare ▪ whisper

I went to the cinema with my mum once. It was a children's film so I imagine she was bored. But then she started [1]__________ loudly. I tried [2]__________, 'Mum, wake up!' but she didn't wake up properly. She just [3]__________ a bit and closed her eyes again. People were starting to [4]__________ from the row in front to see what the noise was. Then someone threw an empty ice cream tub. It landed right on her head. Suddenly, she was awake and [5]__________ straight ahead, in shock.

That was the last time I went to the cinema with my mum!

Vocabulary extra Ways of speaking

2 Choose the ways of speaking which go with the sentences.

1 You do this when you are angry.
   a cheer **b** shout **c** snuffle
2 You have difficulty saying some sounds.
   a stammer **b** sigh **c** whine
3 You do this when you complain about something.
   a exclaim **b** argue **c** stammer
4 You speak quietly when you do this.
   a exclaim **b** whisper **c** cheer
5 You do this when you are happy about something.
   a whine **b** sigh **c** cheer
6 You can do this without using words.
   a shout **b** argue **c** sigh

3 🔊7.02 Listen and choose the correct words.

1 'Shhh! Don't let my dad hear that we've come outside!' she **sighed** / **whispered**.
2 'I'm never going to get all this work done by tomorrow!', he **exclaimed** / **sighed**.
3 'I'm really sorry that I'm late. It won't happen again,' he **exclaimed** / **stammered**.
4 'It's not fair! Why should I have to clean my room on a Saturday!' she **whined** / **sighed**.
5 'Keep out of my bedroom!' he **shouted** / **cheered**.
6 'Come on Simon, you can do it!' she **cheered** / **argued**.

Reported questions and commands

4 Put the words in the correct order to make reported questions.

1 time / had / she / me / left / bus / the / asked / what / .
____
2 there / were / why / asked / we / Toby / waiting / us / .
____
3 if / refund / me / the / wanted / I / assistant / a / asked / .
____
4 need / Helen / whether / him / she / a / asked / would / password / .
____
5 could / asked / I / drive / me / if / Loui / .
____
6 reporter / mum / said / us / what / had / the / asked / my / .
____

5 Complete the reported questions and commands.

1 'What film are you watching?'
   He asked me __________.
2 'Don't go out alone when it's dark!'
   He told us __________.
3 'Where is the nearest bank?'
   She asked him __________.
4 'Eat fewer sweet things!'
   My doctor told __________.
5 'Can you go to Tom and Sachiko's wedding?'
   She asked Jill __________.
6 'Don't spend too much! Save for the holiday!'
   Mum told Dad __________.
7 'Have you seen Mr Matharu this morning?'
   He asked me __________.
8 'Forget about it!'
   My best friend __________.

6 TASK Find an interview with someone you admire. Report some of the questions that the interviewer asked, and what the answers were.

The interviewer asked Lionel Messi whether he'd always wanted to be a footballer. Messi answered that ...

Reading

1 **Read the first paragraph of the article. What do you think the article will be about?**

2 **Read the whole article. Match headings A–F to paragraphs 1–6.**

A Getting you to tell them about you!
B Being very general
C An audience who wants to believe
D Finding visual clues
E Research your audience before the event
F Reading your reactions

3 **Answer the questions.**

1 Where do the most loyal fans sit?
2 How does the volunteer help the mind reader in paragraph two?
3 What information would the writer want to know about the pizza?
4 Why do performers speak slowly?
5 What example does the writer give about jewellery?
6 Why isn't it enough to limit what other people can see on your social media?

4 **Study the highlighted words and phrases in the article. Then choose the correct meaning for each word or phrase.**

1 extra-sensory
  a beyond normal senses
  b unusually sensible
2 entire
  a complete
  b personal
3 spot on
  a nearly correct
  b exactly correct
4 bound
  a certain
  b unlikely
5 intense
  a strong or extreme
  b looking closely
6 on the right track
  a in the right direction
  b taking a long route
7 subconsciously
  a on purpose
  b without being aware
8 passer-by
  a shopper
  b someone walking past
9 revealing
  a showing
  b hiding
10 vigilant
  a thoughtful
  b careful

A mind reader or the tricks of the trade?

I'm sure most of us have seen YouTube™ clips or been to shows where the person on screen or on stage can 'mind-read'. Then they come out with information that they couldn't possibly know. They must have extra-sensory abilities. It's amazing! Or is it? See what you think after reading a few tricks of the trade …

1 ________

Chances are if you decide to get tickets for a show, you're already a fan of the performer. What would be the point if you weren't? You'd be unlikely to want to sit down and hear stuff you don't think is true. The same is true for mind-reading performances. The performer is well aware that the entire crowd wants them to succeed and the biggest fans will have managed to get the best seats, near the front. More often than not this is, therefore, where they take their volunteers from for various tricks.

2 ________

This is almost too good to be true, but it works! The mind reader might say, 'I'm sensing you're close to a person whose name starts with the letter C …' to which the volunteer thinks hard. After a while they come up with 'It might be Kerry.' 'Oh yes, Kerry, C and K can sound the same. Thank you.' Then they'll say something like, 'This person is a close family member or knows a relative …' Again, the volunteer will focus on this and say, 'It's my old school friend. She knows my family well.' Before long, the information is spot on without the volunteer being aware that they actually gave the mind reader the details.

3 ________

Another trick that is bound to work. It's almost like saying that the person they've selected likes pizza. Most people like pizza! Wouldn't it be far more impressive if they could tell you your preferred pizza topping and your favourite Italian restaurant? In this way, the performer will make a statement like, 'Sometimes you feel shy in different social situations.' I don't know a single person this wouldn't refer to, especially by using the word 'sometimes'.

4 ________

Mind readers will often talk slowly with an intense look on their faces. This is no accident. What they're actually doing is looking for how you respond to the information coming out of their mouths. It's about the facial expressions and the body language. A nod or a smile will tell the mind reader that they are on the right track. As they do more shows and get a bigger following, they're clearly going to become pretty good body language readers.

5 ________

This is something everyone does subconsciously on a daily basis. When we see a passer-by they are revealing unspoken things to us. Have you sat in a café and just people-watched? It's actually a lot of fun. Look at their clothes, their behaviour and their jewellery. If they're wearing a wedding ring, we can see they are in a relationship and might have kids. On stage, if they're dressed in a suit with a smart haircut the mind reader might say, 'I'm sensing you work in a professional job.'

6 ________

In my opinion, this is the biggest cheat of all. And it's largely thanks to the internet. An audience member is often picked out before the event. Even if you are vigilant and set your privacy setting to something like 'friends only' on social media accounts, there is usually enough out there to wow the audience when the performance day comes. Just one photo can tell you a lot about the person. For example, a picture of you and your family skiing will tell the mind reader about your free time and who you spend it with.

5 Write what the people actually said. Change the direct speech into reported speech using the verb in brackets.

1 The mind reader told the audience that he'd been doing shows for 30 years.

____

____

2 The mind reader asked the volunteer if he knew anyone called David.

____

____

3 The volunteer told him that David was a friend from university.

____

____

4 The mind reader told the audience to be silent while he thought.

____

____

5 The volunteer asked his mother how she could have known his password.

____

____

6 TASK Imagine that you and your friend are planning a day trip, but you disagree on your choice and reasons for going there. Explain the conversation to a brother or sister using reported speech.

Writing A report on survey findings

1 Look at information from a report on a survey. What was the survey about? Write the questions that were asked.

1 … just over half of students asked their friends questions about their project work.
Did you ask your friends questions about project work?

2 … approximately two thirds of students did their project work in their bedrooms.

____

3 … nearly all students did research online for their project work.

____

4 Around a quarter of students waited until the day before the deadline to do their project work.

____

5 … well over three quarters of students enjoyed the topic of their project work.

____

2 Match the percentages to the sentences in exercise 1.

a 24% **b** 82% **c** 52% **d** 97% **e** 67%

3 Read the report. Match sentences 1–5 in exercise 1 to gaps a–e in the report.

A survey on students and their project work

1 _______

The purpose of this report is to present the findings of a survey into project work done by students. The survey was carried out among the students of Class 13A and Class 13B in Year 13.

2 _______

The first question was about where students usually did their project work. It was thought that nearly all students did their project work in their own rooms, but in fact [a]_______ There were a variety of other places mentioned in the survey: second place was the dining room, and some did it in front of the television in the living room.

3 _______

Moving on to when project work was done, the main difference was between students who were organized and those who were not. [b]_______ just over a half did it the weekend before, and some did it the week before. A small minority started it on the day they got it and finished it early. With regard to their interest in the task, [c]_______ The rest admitted that they found it boring and would have liked to choose another topic.

4 _______

As far as getting help is concerned, [d]_______ 43% said that they asked a family member. Regarding the internet, [e]_______

5 _______

In conclusion, it appears that there was not just one method regarding where and when the project work was done in this group of students. There was, however, a clear preference for doing the research online, and most students worked in their bedrooms. It also seems clear that a significant majority enjoyed the work set.

4 Match phrases 1–3 to percentages a–c.

1 a small minority — **a** 85%
2 a significant majority — **b** 70%
3 a clear preference — **c** 5%

5 Match headings A–F to paragraphs 1–5 in the report. There is one heading that you do not need.

A Help **D** Aim
B Time **E** Conclusion
C Subjects **F** Place

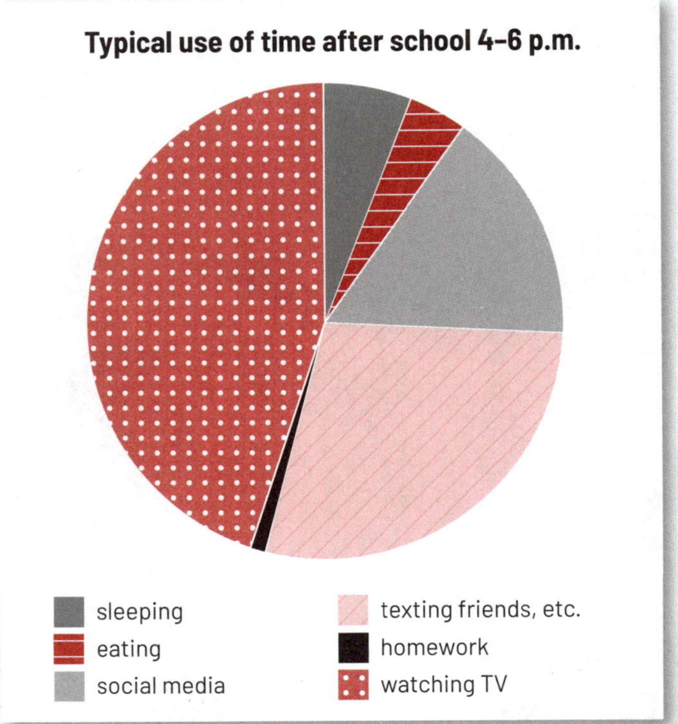

Writing guide

■ **TASK Write a report on the findings of a survey from your school on how students spend their time after school.**

■ **PLAN Make notes for each paragraph.**

Paragraph 1: Describe the purpose of the report, including the aim of making recommendations to start a new school club.
Paragraph 2: Analyse the most popular uses of time.
Paragraph 3: Analyse the other uses of time.
Paragraph 4: Draw conclusions about the most popular after-school activity and make recommendations for a new after-school club.

■ **WRITE Write your report.**

■ **REVIEW Check the following points.**

- Have you given each paragraph a heading?
- Have you used approximations and fractions as well as percentages?
- Have you used phrases to show you are moving from one point to another?
- Have you checked grammar, vocabulary, spelling and punctuation?

U7 Assess your progress

Give yourself a mark 1–3 for each Learning Objective from the lesson.
1 I found this difficult. **2** This was OK. **3** I can do this well.

Lesson 7A

	Mark
I can understand the purpose of different paragraphs in a text.	
I can use words relating to perception and observation.	
I can use adverb–adjective collocations.	
How can I improve?	

Lesson 7B

	Mark
I can identify incorrect information in a reported text.	
I can use reported speech to report what people have said.	
How can I improve?	

Lesson 7C

	Mark
I can identify relevant information in a listening text.	
I can form nouns using the suffixes *-tion* and *-sion*.	
I can use appropriate language to make complaints and requests.	
How can I improve?	

Lesson 7D

	Mark
I can form and test predictions about a text.	
I can use words relating to sight and sound.	
I can form and use reported questions and commands.	
How can I improve?	

Lesson 7E

	Mark
I can write a report on survey findings.	
I can use phrases to make my writing flow.	
I can use approximation language to describe statistics.	
How can I improve?	

Action plan

Make a plan for what you can do next to improve. Discuss your ideas with your classmates / teacher.

8 Decisions, decisions

Vocabulary

V Insight Describing jobs

1 Complete the sentences with the adjectives below.

▪ challenging ▪ dead-end ▪ highly skilled ▪ repetitive ▪ stressful ▪ varied ▪ worthwhile

1. I'd like to be a youth worker so that I can feel that I'm doing something ____________ by helping others.
2. Many countries only allow foreigners who are ____________ to come and work there.
3. I think Suhybe is finding his university course too easy. He needs something more ____________.
4. I get bored quickly, so I'd need a job where every day is different; it needs to be ____________.
5. Some people don't mind having ____________ jobs if they can do the things they want at weekends and during holidays.
6. Before the use of robots, people had to do the really boring, ____________ work in factories.
7. Nurses have very ____________ jobs because hospitals are often understaffed.

V Insight Idioms: work

2 Choose the correct words.

1. Robbie rose to the challenge and **managed to fix the car himself** / **took the car to a garage**.
2. To get the ball rolling, I'll **offer my own suggestions** / **show you another example**.
3. Elena will show you the ropes – she's been working here for three **days** / **years**.
4. They've thrown me in at the deep end, so **any help would be welcome** / **I'll show you how to do it**.
5. Bob has got a lot on his plate at the moment, so give this work to **him** / **Stacey**.
6. Why don't you put your feet up and **have a nice cup of coffee** / **finish your homework**?

Vocabulary extra Gender-neutral job titles

3 Use gender-neutral words. What do you call:

1. someone in charge of a school? ____________
2. someone who puts out fires? ____________
3. someone who brings you your meal on a plane? ____________
4. someone who tries to stop people breaking the law? ____________
5. someone who speaks publicly for an organization? ____________
6. someone who serves customers in a department store? ____________
7. someone who is in a play in the theatre? ____________
8. someone who does a sport professionally? ____________

4 Complete the text with the words below.

▪ glamorous ▪ high-flying ▪ put your feet up ▪ rise to the challenge ▪ show you the ropes ▪ stressful ▪ the bottom line ▪ thrown in at the deep end ▪ varied ▪ worthwhile

Working as a production runner

For many young people starting out, the film industry isn't as 1 ____________ as it looks on screen. There are no awards ceremonies or fancy parties.

If you come straight out of education, being a production runner is usually the only way in. As the name suggests, you'll have to run around doing things: making tea, cleaning things, driving to pick up equipment, getting food for the cast, etc. 2 ____________ is you'll have to be prepared to do anything and everything you're told to do. On top of this, the work can be very 3 ____________ – it's a fast-paced environment in which you have to work very hard for very little pay. There will be no time to 4 ____________. And don't expect anyone to 5 ____________. They'll be far too busy with their own jobs.

So, why would anyone do it? Well, for one, you can see how 6 ____________ the jobs on set are: directors, producers, set designers and make-up artists all require different skills. This should help you to decide which career path would be 7 ____________ for you to follow. Secondly by being 8 ____________, you can see how well you work under pressure. If you can't, the film industry probably isn't for you. Finally, if you manage to 9 ____________ and work hard each day, you will have valuable experience and contacts when you apply for your next job in the industry. The next thing you know, you could end up as a 10 ____________ director!

5 TASK Your friend is trying to decide between working for a company and starting their own business. Think about the advantages and disadvantages of each career path using the ideas below.

▪ opportunity ▪ responsibility ▪ salary ▪ security ▪ staff ▪ working hours

Third conditional

1 Choose the correct words.

1 If we'd left earlier, we wouldn't have missed the bus. (We left **early** / **late**. We **missed** / **didn't miss** the bus.)
2 You'd have watched a really good film if you'd stayed. (You **watched** / **didn't watch** the film. You **stayed** / **didn't stay**.)
3 If I hadn't listened to you, I'd have made a big mistake. (I **listened** / **didn't listen**. I **made** / **didn't make** a big mistake.)
4 She wouldn't have bought the car if she hadn't had the money. (She **bought** / **didn't buy** the car. She **had** / **didn't have** the money.)
5 If they'd had time, they would have gone for a walk. (They **had** / **didn't have** time. They **went** / **didn't go** for a walk.)

2 Complete the sentences using the third conditional and the correct form of the verbs in brackets.

1 'I ________________ (stay) if we ________________ (not win) the Champions League.' (*Didier Drogba on leaving Chelsea FC.*)
2 'If I ________________ (not make) the mistakes I'm ashamed of, I ________________ (never / make) the decisions I'm proud of.' (*Author Mark Amend, on why mistakes can be helpful.*)
3 'If I ________________ (ask) my customers what they wanted, they ________________ (say) "a faster horse".' (*Henry Ford, on why the invention of the motor car wasn't a result of customer research.*)
4 'If I ________________ (have) more time, I ________________ (write) a shorter letter.' (*From a letter by the author Mark Twain, on the difficulty of using as few words as possible.*)
5 'If I ________________ (not do) *Harry Potter*™, I ________________ (go) and done years of art.' (*Actor Emma Watson who plays Hermione Granger.*)
6 'If I ________________ (observe) all the rules, I ________________ (never / get) anywhere.' (*Actor Marilyn Monroe, on her dramatic life.*)

I wish and *if only*

3 Complete the second sentence so it has got a similar meaning to the first sentence.

1 It was silly of me to stay up so late. I am so tired.
If only ________________________________.
2 It was a bad idea to buy a cheap camera. The picture quality is terrible.
I wish ________________________________.
3 Duncan's phone has broken. It doesn't make any calls.
If only Duncan ________________________________.
4 Samira forgot to bring her ID card. She can't go inside.
Samira wishes ________________________________.
5 I was wrong to say that to Enya. She won't forgive me.
If only ________________________________.

4 Complete the text. Use the correct form of the verbs below.

be ▪ book ▪ check ▪ feel ▪ get ▪ not ask ▪ not miss ▪ regret

Subject: Coffee?
From: Paola
To: Maria

Hi Paola,

Just a quick message to say that I've just checked the dates and realized I can't come to Jackie's wedding. I know it's bad. If I [1] ________________ the date sooner, I would have been able to change my work trip. If only I [2] ________________ more organized like you. Things have been so busy lately. It's my fault.

The thing is, the arrangements have been made and I can't change them now. I wish I [3] ________________ the previous conference in Paris. If I had gone, I [4] ________________ someone else to go to this one. It's really annoying. Anyway, there's not much I can do about it I'm afraid.

I'm happy I can go on the weekend away beforehand though. That's better than nothing, isn't it? Good job we booked our tickets to Barcelona ages ago. It's going to be great. I [5] ________________ worse if we hadn't got this sorted.

I spoke to Ann the other day and I think she wishes she [6] ________________ when we all did. I told her she can probably still get a flight. There's room for her at the villa.

And I'm so pleased Mary is going to be there. If she [7] ________________ her mum to look after her kids for the weekend, she [8] ________________ it, I'm sure!

Anyway, are you still OK to meet for a coffee on Friday?

Maria

5 TASK Write about something that happened in the past that did not turn out the way you wanted it to. How would you change this event? Use the third conditional and *I wish* or *if only*. Use the ideas below to help you.

- a holiday
- a test
- a school friend
- a family member

Listening, vocabulary and speaking

V Insight Decisions and ideas

1 Study the phrases. Which action comes first in each pair? Write 1 or 2 to show the order.

1 a ______ change your mind
b ______ conceive an idea
2 a ______ come up with a scheme
b ______ have second thoughts
3 a ______ make a decision
b ______ reconsider a decision
4 a ______ go ahead with a plan
b ______ dream up an idea
5 a ______ reconsider a decision
b ______ finally make up your mind

Giving presentations

2 Complete the sentences about addressing an audience when giving a presentation with the words below. There are two words that you do not need.

allow ■ appropriate ■ make ■ project ■ read ■ remind ■ visuals

1 Make sure your presentation is ______ for your audience.
2 Remember to ______ your voice so that people can hear you.
3 Use some relevant ______ to get your point across and maintain interest.
4 Look up from your notes. Don't just ______ your notes with your head down.
5 ______ eye contact. It will show your audience that you are confident and friendly.

3 Complete the lines from a presentation about film. Use the phrases below.

finally, to sum up, ■ I'm going to look briefly at ■ in this presentation, my subject will be ■ let's begin by ■ moving on to ■ to illustrate this point,

1 ______ the history of film.

2 ______ the early history of film and then talk about recent developments in more detail.

3 ______ learning how the first films were produced.

4 ______ here's a picture of a cinematograph, invented by the Lumière brothers in 1895.

5 ______ the modern film industry, which uses digital editing. This obviously makes the process of making films much faster.

6 ______ the film industry has only been around for 100 years or so, but it has become an important part of our culture.

① Anyone who has never made a mistake in life has never tried anything new.
Albert Einstein

② 

③ Penicillin
X-rays
Chocolate chip cookies
Potato crisps

4 🔊8.01 Look at slides 1–3 from a presentation about making mistakes. Match them to summaries A–D of each part of the talk. There is one summary that you do not need. Then listen and check.

A Mistakes can be funny.
B How to avoid making mistakes.
C Mistakes can lead to inventions and discoveries.
D Mistakes are necessary in life.

5 🔊8.01 Put the words in the correct order to make sentences from the presentation. Then listen and check.

1 like / about / you / talk / today, / to / mistakes / I'd / to / !
2 impossible / making / it's / look / to / going / why / avoid / them / to / I'm / at / .
3 why / start / making / by / afraid / explaining / I'll / we're / mistakes / of / .
4 some / mistakes / end / I'll / examples / successful / with / of / .
5 quote / with / a / Einstein / begin / let's / from / .
6 mistakes / look / successful / now, / let's / some / at / .
7 being / wrong / things / to / afraid / stop / conclude, / so, / of / getting / !

6 TASK Choose one of the questions below and prepare your own presentation.

- What has been the most important invention of the last 100 years?
- Why is travel to other countries important?
- What is the best way to learn a language?

Vocabulary and grammar

V Insight Conflict

1 Complete the sentences with the words below.

boycotting ■ discrimination ■ injustice ■ marching ■ opposition ■ struggle

In countries around the world, young people:

1 are refusing to accept the ________ of laws against peaceful public protests.
2 are protesting against ________ by top universities against students from state schools.
3 are ________ through the streets to protest against billions of euros being given to failing banks.
4 complain about the ________ to manage the cost of living while being a university student.
5 have shown their ________ to cuts in education.
6 are ________ shops if their products are made by workers who don't receive a fair wage.

Vocabulary extra Conflict: phrasal verbs

2 Complete the placards with the verbs below.

BACK ■ FIGHT ■ GIVE ■ STAND ■ STEP ■ TAKE

1 ________ BACK AGAINST CUTS TO LOCAL SERVICES!

2 ________ UP FOR GENDER EQUALITY AT WORK!

3 LET'S ________ ON RACISM – THERE'S NO PLACE FOR IT IN SOCIETY!

4 DON'T ________ DOWN ON PROMISES TO REDUCE POLLUTION IN OUR CITIES!

5 MORE TO DO! ________ UP THE CAMPAIGN AGAINST USING PLASTIC!

6 DON'T ________ IN TO ANTISOCIAL BEHAVIOUR

Speculating about the past

3 Complete B's replies to A. Use *must / can't / might* or *could* and the correct form of the verbs in brackets.

1 A My sister looked disappointed after the exam.
B She ________ (do) very well.
2 A I can't see anyone out there with an umbrella.
B It ________ (stop) raining.
3 A No one knows where Charlie is.
B I saw him waiting at the train station earlier. He ________ (go) home.
4 A My dad never enjoyed my kick-boxing competitions.
B Yes, it ________ (be) easy for him.
5 A Where's Kim? She's very late for the lesson.
B You're right – she's normally here on time. She ________ (forget) about it.

4 Choose the correct words to complete the text.

One of the strangest mysteries is what happened at Dyatlov Pass on 1 February 1959. Nine experienced hikers disappeared in the Russian mountains where they had set up camp for the night.

Later that month, the discovery of their bodies only added to the mystery. Their tent had been ripped apart from the inside and they [1]**must / can't** have left the area in a hurry: some were wearing shoes, others were barefoot and most were found wearing light clothing that wasn't suited to cold weather.

The Russian government stated that the cause of death was hypothermia, but it [2]**can't / might** have been this because it didn't make sense. Some of the severe injuries they had weren't the sort you'd get from staying in the cold.

Theories include: the deaths [3]**must / could** have been due to UFOs, or [4]**can't / may** have been caused by secret government testing of radioactive weapons, or maybe there was an attack by a kind of yeti. Some people believe it was a natural disaster, but it [5]**may / can't** have been an avalanche – there was no tree damage and no history of avalanches ever in the area.

People only agree that it [6]**could / must** have been something powerful to make the hikers leave the relative warmth of their tent in the middle of the night. It remains a mystery to this day.

5 Complete the text using the correct form of the verbs in brackets.

The famous pilot Amelia Earhart disappeared mysteriously on 2 July 1937, while trying to become the first woman to fly around the world.

During her flight to the tiny Howland Island in the Pacific Ocean, Earhart disappeared. It was thought that the plane [1]________ (must / run out of) fuel and crashed into the sea. However, a search mission found no signs of a crash.

Some people claim that the plane [2]________ (can't / crash), and there have been some imaginative theories to explain the mystery. Some people say she [3]________ (may / work) as an American spy against the Japanese, who [4]________ (must / catch and kill) her. Others think she [5]________ (might / return) to the US to live a secret life as an ordinary housewife! And of course, there will always be people who believe that she [6]________ (must / take) by aliens. However, recent discoveries suggested that Earhart [7]________ (could / crash) and [8]________ (may / survived) there for a short time before dying. Locals found bones which [9]________ (could / be) Earhart's, and many insist that parts of a 1930s American shoe found there [10]________ (must / belong) to Amelia.

6 TASK Think of an unsolved mystery in history. Speculate about the situation.

The Mary Celeste left New York in 1872. Its destination was Genoa, in Italy. But it never arrived ...

Reading

1 **Many surnames used to tell us what jobs people did. What did people with the surnames below do in the past?**

Baker ▪ Carpenter ▪ Cook ▪ Gardner ▪ Miller ▪ Smith

2 **Read statements 1–3. Which do you think are true? Read the article and check.**

1 There is no connection between surnames and careers in modern times.
2 It can be helpful if your surname begins with a letter near the beginning of the alphabet.
3 People sometimes choose jobs that have some connection with their names.

3 **Match sentences A–E to gaps 1–5 in the article.**

A a surprisingly high number of dentists are called Dennis or Denise
B 'Lightning Bolt' was the most popular one
C and the teachers admitted that this encouraged discrimination
D in her and Romeo's cases, rich and important ones
E those with names early in the alphabet might have got more attention by being at the front of the class

4 **Read the article again. Are the sentences true (T), false (F) or not given (NG)? Correct the false ones.**

1 Names always used to tell you what jobs people did.
2 Newspaper headline writers enjoy playing with words and names.
3 People only make connections between names and careers in their own language.
4 More women than men live in Georgia.
5 The people at the bottom of a list are always less important.
6 In the past, a student called Zappa would have sat at the back of the class.
7 Teachers sometimes form opinions about their new students before the school year begins.
8 It isn't easy for women to be taken seriously as scientists.

The name game

Do our names affect our career choices?

1 'What's in a name?' Juliet asks Romeo in Shakespeare's play. She soon discovers the answer – quite a lot.

2 Juliet's problem was that surnames tell us which family someone comes from and [1] ______. Lower down in society, the family name would often tell us about people's jobs, for example, Baker, Cook, Gardner, Taylor and Smith. These are all names that still exist today. But these days there's clearly no connection between someone's name and their career ... is there?

3 The media certainly notice any connection between a name and what a famous person does. Usain Bolt is a gift for headline writers – [2] ______ – and Belgian footballer, Mark de Man, is another favourite with sports journalists. And as that example shows, these connections often work across languages – English-speakers think Koolhaas is a great name for the top Dutch architect! We see these, and examples such as the poet Wordsworth, as amusing coincidences.

4 Nevertheless, the editor of *New Scientist* magazine recently decided to study these coincidences after noticing how many of the books and scientific papers in the magazine were on topics connected with the author's name. He'd just been thinking about this when he turned to the next book on his desk, a work on the North and South Poles by ... Daniel Snowman.

5 Recent research has confirmed that people are more likely to choose careers that mirror their own names. The researchers suggest that it happens because we are attracted to things that remind us of ourselves, which explains why women called Georgia are more likely to move to the state of Georgia in the USA, and a larger than average proportion of men called Louis live in Louisiana. We're more likely to focus on things even if they only begin with the same letter as our own names, including first names – [3]______! It's more difficult to understand why people choose careers which you'd think they would have reconsidered if they'd thought about their surnames – there really are dentists called Dr Pain, and doctors called Dr Death (interestingly, they usually pronounce it 'Deeth').

6 Surnames can influence your life in other ways, too. A survey of American universities showed that academics whose surnames began with a letter at the beginning of the alphabet were likely to have had more success. This could have happened because the authors of some academic papers are listed in alphabetical order. The people at the top of the list therefore got noticed more, and we can't avoid thinking that those at the top of a list are more important. It's possible that this had an even stronger influence in the past, when classrooms ordered students alphabetically – [4]______.

7 In a survey of UK teachers, half said that they imagined what some of their new students would be like before they had met them, just from seeing their names on the class list. Whereas some first names were seen as 'trouble' – [5]______ – others suggested good behaviour, especially more 'feminine-sounding' names in the case of girls. And again, there is a strong connection with decisions about career. Girls with more 'feminine-sounding' names are much less likely to choose a career in science.

5 Find words in the article which match definitions 1–6.

1 the title of a newspaper article printed in large letters at the top ______ (paragraph 3)
2 examples of when two things happen at the same time by chance ______ (paragraph 3)
3 the most northern or southern part of the world ______ (paragraph 4)
4 the person you go to when you have problems with your teeth ______ (paragraph 5)
5 people who teach or do research at a university ______ (paragraph 6)
6 connected with or typical of girls and women ______ (paragraph 7)

6 Complete the sentences with the correct form of the words in exercise 5.

1 The South ______ in Antarctica is much colder than the North ______. In fact, the highest ever temperature recorded there was only -12.3°C.
2 I met an old school friend from Bristol when I was travelling through India – what an amazing ______!
3 I'm starting to get toothache – I need to see the ______.
4 What is considered to be ______ has changed a lot over the years. Now there's more of a sense of freedom and equality for women.
5 My colleague often reads the ______ in the morning before he starts work.
6 My cousin is an ______ in space travel – her work sounds fascinating.

7 TASK Do you know what your surname means? Are there any surnames in your country that come from jobs? Which are the most common?

Writing A covering email

1 Match jobs 1–6 to sentences a–f from covering emails.

1 gardener
2 dentist's assistant
3 cook
4 fitness trainer
5 tour guide
6 au pair

a I have shown people around various towns.
b I have been doing the Top Teen Health programme at my local gym for three years.
c I often help my parents in the garden, growing both flowers and vegetables.
d I have looked after several children before.
e I have always looked after my own teeth well.
f I often make different kinds of food.

2 Which of the statements in exercise 1 are too general? Rewrite them so they include some more detailed information.

3 Complete the email with the phrases below.

- all this experience has confirmed that
- as you will see from my CV
- I am writing to apply for
- I believe that this will provide
- I have co-ordinated
- please find attached
- would be available for interview

From: B Evans
To: srogers@grandtour.com
Subject: Re: Tour Guide position

Dear Mrs Rogers,

1 ______________ the Tour Guide post, as advertised in *The Daily Record* on 14th October.

I am currently studying for a degree in French and Spanish at Leeds University. I am keen to get into the tourist industry and use my language skills.

2 ______________, I got As in A level French, Spanish and tourism. I also enjoy meeting people and have assisted in the local Tourist Information Office on Saturdays for the past year. 3 ______________ a good foundation for any questions tourists might ask me. As well as this, 4 ______________ tours and developed visitor's guides of my local town for visiting groups of students from France and Italy. I have done this in university holidays since I was 18.

5 ______________ I would like to have a career in the tourist industry and I feel that this position would be a very good way to start. I am hard-working, friendly and work well in a team. 6 ______________ my CV and certificates.

I look forward to hearing from you soon, and I 7 ______________ on Tuesday and Friday afternoons.

Yours sincerely,

Beatrice Evans

4 Find three of the action verbs below in the email in exercise 3. Which of the other verbs below could be used to replace them?

- advise
- arrange
- assist
- co-ordinate
- design
- develop

5 Which of the verbs cannot be used in the sentences?

1 During the holidays I **helped** / **assisted** / **designed** at the local language school.
2 I have **organized** / **advised** / **co-ordinated** a series of photography workshops for young people.
3 I have **assisted** / **helped** / **developed** with setting up a campaign group on young workers' rights.
4 My team **assisted** / **developed** / **created** a programme to arrange visits to old people living alone.
5 We are hoping to **design** / **co-ordinate** / **arrange** further exchanges between our two schools.

Writing guide

TASK Write a covering email to apply for one of these jobs.

Summer Camp Activity Leaders needed!
A good Summer Camp Activity Leader will ...
- have good knowledge of different sports.
- have experience of working with teenagers.
- be lively and enthusiastic.

Training provided.

TUTOR WANTED
Two children, 11 and 13. Are you:
- experienced in secondary school English?
- able to teach in a fun and interesting way?
- able to explain things simply?

PLAN 1 Think about the qualifications you have, the experience you can offer and why you want this job.

PLAN 2 Make notes for each paragraph.
Paragraph 1: Explain where you saw the job advert and mention that you are attaching your CV.
Paragraph 2: Give reasons for your interest in this job.
Paragraph 3: Refer them to specific information on your CV and show how this relates to the job.
Paragraph 4: Mention any other experience from school, part-time work or voluntary work which might be relevant to the job.
Paragraph 5: Request an interview and say when you are available.

WRITE Write your covering email.

REVIEW Check the following points.
- Have you included all the necessary information?
- Have you used formal language?
- Have you checked grammar, vocabulary, spelling and punctuation?

U8 Assess your progress

Give yourself a mark 1–3 for each Learning Objective from the lesson.
1 I found this difficult. **2** This was OK. **3** I can do this well.

Lesson		Mark
Lesson 8A	I can identify relevant information in a reading text.	
	I can use adjectives to describe jobs.	
	I can use idioms relating to work.	
	How can I improve?	
Lesson 8B	I can use the third conditional to talk about unreal situations in the past.	
	I can use *wish* + past perfect to express regret about the past and *if only* to emphasize regret.	
	How can I improve?	
Lesson 8C	I can use a range of strategies to understand new words while listening.	
	I can use phrases relating to decisions and ideas.	
	I can structure and give a presentation.	
	How can I improve?	
Lesson 8D	I can understand and identify paraphrasing in an article.	
	I can use words and phrases relating to conflict.	
	I can use modal verbs to speculate about the past.	
	How can I improve?	
Lesson 8E	I can write a covering email for a job application.	
	I can use detail and specific examples to avoid generalizing in a job application.	
	I can use synonyms for action verbs.	
	How can I improve?	

Action plan

Make a plan for what you can do next to improve. Discuss your ideas with your classmates / teacher.

9 Born digital

Vocabulary

Insight Phrasal verbs: relationships

1 Choose the correct phrasal verbs to replace the words in italics.

1 I usually use social media to *bring myself up-to-date* with my family who live abroad.
 a catch up with **b** catch up to **c** catch up for
2 It took my dad ages to *get back to his usual self after* his accident.
 a get past **b** get round **c** get over
3 I *unexpectedly met* my old neighbour at the gym last week. It was a nice surprise.
 a ran across **b** ran over **c** ran into
4 Chris never says much at work but he seemed to really *talk freely* when we went for a coffee.
 a open out **b** open up **c** open over
5 I think it's a positive thing to see men who can *lose control of their feelings* when they feel emotional.
 a break up **b** break down **c** break out
6 *Supporting and defending* people who are being bullied is the right thing to do.
 a sticking out for
 b sticking behind for
 c sticking up for
7 My housemate and I *liked each other* from the start. We like doing the same things.
 a hit it up **b** hit it off **c** hit it on
8 I don't know why Meera *is horrible to* me. What did I ever do to her?
 a picks on **b** picks at **c** picks into

Insight Words often confused

2 Choose one word from the pairs of words below to complete the sentences.

actually / currently ■ eventually / possibly ■ friendly / sympathetic ■ last / latest

1 I'm getting the ____________ smartphone for Christmas!
2 Abdu asked Luke four times, and he ____________ agreed to go to the cinema with him.
3 This product is ____________ unavailable on our website. Please try again later.
4 My laptop battery keeps saying it's full, but it's ____________ at 50%.
5 The ____________ time someone stood on the moon was in 1972.
6 Don't tell my sister any of your problems. She's never very ____________ and will just tell you to not worry about it.
7 Everyone likes Mr Harrison because he's so ____________ to everyone he meets.
8 I haven't made any decisions about university. I'll ____________ study Politics because that interests me.

Vocabulary extra Technology

3 Put the actions in the correct order 1–9.

____ **a** Upload the photos on your phone.
____ **b** Download a photo editing program.
____ **c** Undo some of the changes to one of the photos.
____ **d** Log out of your computer.
____ **e** Install the program.
____ **f** Delete some of the photos and edit the others.
____ **g** Log into your computer.
____ **h** Post some photos on social media.
____ **i** Click on the icon to open the program.

4 Complete the article with the words below.

actually ■ clicking on ■ consequently ■ consistently ■ deleted ■ eventually ■ hit it off ■ open up ■ picked on ■ sympathetic ■ undo

Why people get scammed

Ever since the early days of the internet, people have [1] ____________ fallen for online scams. But why do we do it? There appears to be a number of reasons to do with human psychology.

One thing is greed. We all want to get rich quick and [2] ____________ we want to believe in a great new offer. And as soon as we've input some personal details we realize there's no [3] ____________ button.

Another, which is common in online dating, is trust. We may appear to [4] ____________ with a person who is really interested in us and keeps us chatting. By gaining our trust we may even [5] ____________ to this complete stranger about our life relatively quickly. Then they'll take the opportunity to ask for money and we'll be [6] ____________ to their situation. The next thing we know, they've [7] ____________ their fake profile picture and we never hear from them again.

Then there's giving back: the feeling that if someone does something for us, we need to repay them in some way. [8] ____________, this quite a common method scammers use. They do something free for us because they are looking at the bigger picture and [9] ____________ they'll get far more from us than we got from them. This could be as little as [10] ____________ a link to agree to some financial obligation.

So, if you don't want to feel [11] ____________ by the scammers, make it difficult for them and be careful not to fall into the usual traps!

5 TASK Imagine you could write to someone who lived years ago. How would you show them to do some basic things on a laptop? Write an explanation for them. Use one of the following ideas or your own.

- send a document
- join a website
- email a photo to someone

Defining relative clauses

1 **Write the correct relative pronouns. Then match 1–6 to a–f to make sentences.**

when ■ where ■ which (×2) ■ who ■ whose

1 I'm looking for one of those things __________
2 Excuse me, is this the room __________
3 I need to find someone __________
4 Next Saturday is the day __________
5 This is a public announcement. Could the person __________ van
6 Can you show me the phone __________

a is parked in front of the exit please move it?
b you're going to buy?
c the new supermarket opens.
d you use to put holes in paper. Ah, yes, a hole punch.
e knows how to speak Cantonese.
f the science exam is taking place?

2 **Complete the sentences with a relative pronoun and essential information. Use the verbs in brackets.**

1 Emily Brontë is the woman __________________.
(write / *Wuthering Heights*)
2 Mumbai is the place __________________.
(most Bollywood films / make)
3 Michelangelo is the artist __________________.
(paint / the Sistine Chapel ceiling)
4 31st October is the date __________________.
(Halloween / celebrate)
5 Converse is the brand __________ logo __________.
(look like / a star in a circle)
6 Loch Ness is the lake __________________.
(Loch Ness monster / see)

3 **Study the words in italics in each sentence and write S (subject) or O (object).**

1 ________ Where's the *button* that switches this thing off?
2 ________ Barbara is *the person* who you should ask.
3 ________ Gaelic is *a language* that few people speak.
4 ________ I'm not normally *someone* who forgets people's names.
5 ________ Paella is *a dish* which is very popular in Spain.
6 ________ The kuna is *the currency* that people use in Croatia.
7 ________ Binary code is the *language* which computers use.
8 ________ A baggage handler is *the person* who puts your luggage on an aeroplane.

4 **Look at the sentences in exercise 3 again. In the sentences with an object, underline the subject which follows it. Then cross out the relative pronouns in the sentences where you can leave them out.**

5 **Complete the text with relative pronouns. Use a pronoun only where necessary. Cross out the gap where you do not need the pronoun.**

UNFRIEND PHOBIA

Have you experienced times [1] __________ you hold your finger over 'Unfriend' on someone's Facebook™ profile, but just can't make the tap [2] __________ will remove them from your friends list? If the answer is 'yes', you might be someone [3] __________ suffers from 'unfriend phobia'. So, what is it [4] __________ makes us avoid unfriending people? Well, we often try to do it at a time [5] __________ we know that someone is very busy and might not notice, and that shows what we're afraid of. If the person [6] __________ you unfriend notices, what will they do about it? Will they be angry?

But why do we care? These are people [7] __________ we don't want to be friends with anymore! They're often people [8] __________ you should never have added as a friend in the first place! They're the people [9] __________ status updates appear every few minutes, telling you things [10] __________ you really don't want to know. With some of them, it's difficult to imagine ever being in a place [11] __________ you'll see them again, so what are you worried about? Perhaps you feel it's better to know about everything [12] __________ happens to all the people you know, even if they're your enemies rather than friends. And it's easy to ignore the things [13] __________ they post, except all those photos! As one boy said, 'I keep seeing photos of my sister [14] __________ show her kissing her boyfriend. Ugh! I sometimes want to unfriend and unfamily her!'

6 **TASK** **Complete the sentences below with the correct relative pronouns.**

1 Maths is a subject / study / school.
2 Tokyo is a place / watch / sumo.
3 Christmas is a time / give / presents.
4 A laptop is a thing / help / schoolwork.
5 A best friend is a person / rely on / any time.
6 A politician is a person / works / government.

Listening, vocabulary and speaking

V Insight Describing gadgets

1 Complete the extracts from adverts for gadgets with the adjectives.

convenient ▪ expensive ▪ fragile ▪ inexpensive ▪ out-of-date ▪ reliable ▪ waterproof

1 Wind-up and solar-powered radio – no more __________ batteries!

2 Does your TV seem old and __________? Click here for the latest range of home cinemas.

3 A powerful tablet that's small and __________ to put in your bag to go to and from the office.

4 Uses solar power, making it an __________ way light up your garden.

5 Other models on the market are often __________ and break easily, whereas this is both __________ for use when diving and strong.

6 If you don't believe how __________ our phones are, check out the reviews!

Asking for instructions and explanations

2 Read the instructions on how to do something with a gadget. Which gadget are they for – A, B or C?

- You need to check it really is out of ink before you actually change the cartridge.
- First, lift the lid and the scanner.
- Then, open the lid of the box and you'll see the cartridges.
- Now find the cartridge you need to replace.
- You need to pull the tabs on the side of the cartridge together as you pull it out.
- Now put the new cartridge in, but first take off the yellow tape which is stuck over a hole in the bottom of the cartridge.
- Just push and you'll hear a click when it's in properly.
- Close the scanner and lid and press OK.

3 🔊9.01 Listen and complete the lines from the dialogue between Lara and Bobby.

1 What __________ do?
2 __________ it needs replacing?
3 How __________ that?
4 __________ lift the lid and the scanner.
5 Do you see __________?
6 Right, __________ that.
7 Yep. What do __________?
8 Is everything __________?
9 Are you __________?
10 __________?
11 Yes, __________ ... so I need to take the black one out.

4 Put the instructions for replacing a laptop battery in the correct order 1–6.

____ a Slide the battery out of the body of the laptop.
____ b Find the battery pack on the bottom. There's a switch next to it.
____ c Turn the laptop off.
____ d Push the replacement battery into the compartment until it clicks into place.
____ e Move the switch to the right to unlock the battery.
____ f Close the screen and turn the laptop over.

5 TASK Write a dialogue similar to the one in exercise 3, in which you give instructions to a friend on how to do one of the following:

- join and create a meeting in Zoom
- upload and share documents from the cloud
- transfer files from an old laptop to a new one

Vocabulary and grammar

V Insight Words with more than one meaning

1 Complete the sentences with the words below. Use each word twice.

appear ▪ manage ▪ share ▪ status

1 The police failed to __________ the excited crowd.
2 Why don't you check her __________ on social media to see what she's up to?
3 Dan and Max __________ the same political beliefs.
4 You __________ to have got the wrong date.
5 I didn't __________ to complete the project on time.
6 The criminal will __________ in court tomorrow.
7 My mum has received celebrity __________ in the local area.
8 I __________ my story on Instagram™ every day.

Vocabulary extra Poetry

2 Match the words below to the sentences.

metaphor ▪ personification ▪ prose ▪ rhyme ▪ rhythm ▪ simile

1 She sang like an angel. __________
2 When the rain comes, and the storm clouds grow, the thickening sky goes dark. __________
3 The dark windows of the house stared out angrily. __________
4 You are the harbour my ship sails towards. __________
5 In your eyes, I will rise, into the deep blue skies. __________
6 This poem was written for my grandmother, who taught me the value of learning poems by heart. __________

Non-defining relative clauses

3 Rewrite the two sentences as one sentence. Put the extra information in a relative clause.

1 Apple continues to make the most popular smartphones. Its profits make it one of the richest companies in the world.
____
2 Northern Ireland is actually part of the United Kingdom. I was born there.
____
3 Drinking coffee has been found to reduce your risk of cancer and Alzheimer's. A lot of people think it's unhealthy.
____
4 Japan opened its borders to foreign trade in 1854. The country had been isolated for 200 years.
____
5 RJ Palacio wrote the successful novel *Wonder*. Her real name is Raquel Jaramillo.
____
6 Chinese New Year is at the end of January or the start of February. Many children receive money on that day.
____

4 Tick (✓) the sentences which need more information to understand what the person is talking about.

1 My brother's gone to see the man ☐
2 At the weekend we're going to my uncle's farm in the country ☐
3 Gold is the only metal ☐
4 14th February is St Valentine's Day ☐
5 My bedroom is one of the few places ☐
6 Next Friday is the day ☐
7 We usually go swimming at the local leisure centre ☐

5 Match 1–7 in exercise 4 to a–g to make sentences. Use a relative pronoun (*which*, *where*, *when*, *who* or *whose*) and a comma where necessary.

a stays shiny forever.
b I can be completely alone with my thoughts.
c lovers give each other cards and gifts.
d offered him a Saturday job in his shop.
e has a 50 m pool.
f he keeps lots of horses.
g we get our exam results!

6 Complete the text with clauses a–g, adding a relative pronoun. What do you think the device is?

a are fixed together in numbered order
b electronic gadgets aren't advised
c finger can be used to swipe to it
d find the reading without a screen exciting
e has been proved by the fact that it doesn't break when dropped from a great height
f it is opened with the human hand
g doesn't appear to need any batteries

A LOW-TECH READING DEVICE

It's the year 2030, and many teenagers have rediscovered an amazing reading device [1]__________. It consists of a number of sheets of paper, [2]__________. It does not need switching on – a page appears instantly [3]__________. Any other page can be accessed immediately by the user, [4]__________. It's very portable, and can even be used for reading in the bath, [5]__________. It's simple to use and can be operated even by very small children, [6]__________. It's also extremely durable, [7]__________.

The device is completely reliable, and never crashes. Some people say that the devices can last for over 100 years!

7 TASK Write a short biography about an author, songwriter or poet you like. Use non-defining relative clauses.

Reading

1 What does the word *cheat* mean?

a win a game because you are intelligent
b play a game together as a team
c break rules to beat other players

2 The teenage gamer in the photo was banned from playing *Fortnite*. How do you think he felt when he got the ban?

a he didn't care
b he felt sad
c he got angry

3 Read the article and choose the correct answers.

1 In the first paragraph, the writer suggests that
  a cheating gives people more enjoyment when it is done online.
  b most people get pleasure from winning.
  c she didn't expect people to cheat online.
  d people cheat less in the virtual world.

2 People who cheat in games believe
  a they become friends with their opponents.
  b the loser will be really upset.
  c it shows that you are a good player.
  d they can code parts of the game.

3 What is griefing?
  a Trying to destroy the game completely.
  b Changing the rules for everyone.
  c Working with the developer to improve the game.
  d Playing the online game with one of the game-makers.

4 Why was FaZe Jarvis banned?
  a for cheating during a competition
  b for not knowing the punishment for cheating
  c for showing it to his subscribers on YouTube
  d for using aimbots when he was playing

4 Study the highlighted words in the article. Then write the meaning of the words in English. Use the context within the article to help you.

1 widespread
It must mean something like 'global, happening everywhere' or 'found in a large area'
2 participated __________
3 hacks __________
4 acceptable __________
5 impact __________
6 limits __________
7 tackle __________
8 severe __________

Knowing how to play the game

(1) Most people like to win. That feeling when we cross the finish line in first place, win a tennis match or beat someone at a board game. It's part of what makes us human. It comes as no surprise, then, that online multiplayer games are going to give us the same sense of happiness. But, just as people cheat in real life, they cheat in the virtual world, too. In fact, it would seem that online, even when there is often nothing tangible to win, cheating is even more widespread.

(2) If you've participated in anything with multiple players online, chances are that a significant percentage of players have used hacks to get what they want in the game. This could be by using wall hacks, which make walls invisible so that you can see where the enemy is hiding; speed hacks, which allow them to move more quickly; or aimbots, which mean that you cannot fail to hit your target. Obviously, there are rewards in the form of reaching the next level or gaining access to different areas or tools. However, even in games like *Fall Guys*, which is a kind of race with colourful animal characters, people use speed hacks. And yet there are no real rewards.

(3) So why do it? For some, cheating is a completely acceptable part of the whole experience. It actually adds a skilful element to the game and everyone does. Plus, the virtual world isn't the real world, so no real harm is done to the loser. When you add to this the faceless nature of being online, not knowing or even caring about your opponents, you can see the attraction. Even some game developers – the people who make the games – have often coded cheat elements into their games.

(4) However, others do care. They want to play an online game where the only win worth having is one in which you play fairly. In a study by Irdeto, a cybersecurity company, while 37% of gamers say they had cheated, around 90% of the 9,436 people surveyed said that their game had had a negative impact because of other players cheating.

(5) Then there are those who see a difference based on how far people go with regards to cheating. If you cheat within the limits of the game, this is fine. It's more like bending the rules to have an advantage over someone. But griefing

is another thing altogether. This is when your opponent deliberately tries to spoil your game by stealing things, firing on teammates and provoking players. The aim is to ruin it for everyone involved and this isn't enjoyable for anyone. It's just annoying!

(6) Whatever view someone might have, the game developers are trying to tackle it. In 2019, a YouTube gamer with over 2 million subscribers received a lifetime ban from *Fortnite* by Epic Games for cheating in a live online game. FaZe Jarvis used aimbots during an online match. The 17-year-old, who said he was sorry that he had used cheat software in the match, said he had been unaware of how severe the punishment would be, especially as it hadn't been a competitive match with rules and cash prizes. At a time when cheating is so common, it's important for developers to make sure that cheating doesn't put people off playing the game completely. For the future of game design, this is going to be one of their greatest challenges.

5 Complete the sentences with the highlighted words in the article.

1 Don't ask your brother to do too much for you. Everyone has their ___________.
2 Governments don't seem to want to ___________ the problem of climate change.
3 Use of English in the world is ___________ because it's the international language.
4 The ___________ of the storm could be seen in the town.
5 Everyone ___________ in the football match – even the parents.
6 She had a ___________ headache and had to go home.
7 I don't think it's ___________ for children under ten to work.

6 Cover the article. Read sentences 1–5 from the text. Add a comma where necessary before the relative clauses. Then check your answers.

1 This could be by using wall hacks which make walls invisible so that you can see where the enemy is hiding.
2 However, even in games like *Fall Guys* which is a kind of race with colourful animal characters people use speed hacks.
3 They want to play an online game where the only win worth having is one in which you play fairly.
4 Then there are those who see a difference according to how far people go with regards to cheating.
5 The 17-year-old who said he was sorry that he had used cheat software in the match said he had been unaware how severe the punishment would be …

7 TASK How would you cope if you were banned from the internet? What would you do with your extra time? Do you think your life would be better or worse?

Writing A for and against essay

1 Look at some points from an essay. What is the essay about? Which points are for and which are against?

A ... a lot of unnecessary pressure is put on the wearer
B ... they'll remind you to get off the sofa
C ... at best they are usually an approximate number of steps
D ... they can really help your motivation
E ... they are extremely easy to use regardless of technical knowledge
F ... you can post your progress online and discuss routes
G ... it would probably be better to invest in some expensive trainers

2 Match points A–G in exercise 1 to gaps 1–7 in the essay. Then complete the title.

The **ADVANTAGES** and **DISADVANTAGES** of ________

Some people argue that using fitness trackers in our daily lives is beneficial. Others would say that they are a fashionable gadget you don't really need. In this essay, I will discuss the advantages and disadvantages of using these gadgets to get fit.

The obvious advantage is that [1]________. They help you to get up and get going with step and calorie counts. And if you have stopped being as active as usual, [2]________. Another argument for using fitness trackers is the social element: [3]________. In this way, exercise becomes a challenge for a group of people who help each other to better themselves. If this technology is available, why wouldn't you use it? It may also be argued that [4]________. I thought I'd have to help my grandmother set hers up, but she could do it by herself.

However, it may also be argued that using these devices is bad because they put [5]________. The focus should really be on feeling healthy and strong rather than feeling bad because you didn't beat your last step count or meet your target. On top of this, fitness trackers aren't always accurate; [6]________. Finally, there are also those who say that these gadgets are expensive, especially if you don't use them very often. [7]________.

In conclusion, I believe that fitness trackers can be a good way to monitor your progress when you are trying to get fit. They have also become a must-have fashionable accessory for many. Nevertheless, the main thing is to get out and do some exercise to feel good about yourself and become stronger. Whether you have a fitness tracker or not shouldn't change this.

3 Underline examples of sentences in the essay which express points in a neutral way.

4 Find words in the text or in points A–G which mean:

1 correct.
2 to spend money on.
3 enthusiasm to do something.
4 however.
5 useful or good for you.

Writing guide

- **TASK** Write a for and against essay about the advantages and disadvantages of having e-readers.
- **PLAN 1** Make notes on the advantages (e.g. easy to carry, reading in the dark) and disadvantages (e.g. not the same experience as a book, you need to charge them) of e-readers.
- **PLAN 2** Decide which ideas you are going to use and match them to these paragraphs.
  Paragraph 1: Introduce the topic and the purpose of your essay.
  Paragraph 2: Present the advantages of having e-readers.
  Paragraph 3: Present the disadvantages.
  Paragraph 4: Write a conclusion, including your own opinion of whether the advantages are more important than the disadvantages.
- **WRITE** Write your for and against essay.
- **REVIEW** Check the following points.
  - Have you followed the paragraph structure?
  - Have you used neutral language?
  - Have you used words that show you are adding or contrasting points?
  - Have you checked grammar, vocabulary, spelling and punctuation?

U9 Assess your progress

Give yourself a mark 1–3 for each Learning Objective from the lesson.
1 I found this difficult. **2** This was OK. **3** I can do this well.

Lesson 9A

	Mark
I can identify and evaluate opinions and ideas in a text.	
I can use phrasal verbs relating to relationships.	
I can distinguish easily confused words.	

How can I improve?

Lesson 9B

	Mark
I can use defining relative clauses to identify who or what I am talking about.	
I can find specific information in a text.	

How can I improve?

Lesson 9C

	Mark
I can listen for specific information.	
I can use adjectives to describe gadgets.	
I can use ask for and give instructions, and check and confirm understanding.	

How can I improve?

Lesson 9D

	Mark
I can understand factual information in a text.	
I can distinguish meaning between words with more than one meaning.	
I can use non-defining relative clauses to give additional information.	

How can I improve?

Lesson 9E

	Mark
I can write a for and against essay.	
I can use neutral language in a for and against essay.	

How can I improve?

Action plan

Make a plan for what you can do next to improve. Discuss your ideas with your classmates / teacher.

10 Getting creative

Vocabulary

V Insight Abstract nouns: talent

1 Complete the text with the words below.

beauty ■ dedication ■ genius ■ maturity ■ originality ■ style ■ success ■ vision

Antony Gormley is a British sculptor who has enjoyed an incredible amount of [1]________ for his artistic creations. After studying Fine Art in London, he travelled for three years. During that time, he became interested in representing the [2]________ of the human body. His [3]________ was to explore the relationship between humans and nature.

Testing a World View shows five identical bent figures, based on his own body, which were placed in a room to represent different emotions. The [4]________ of this work earned him the Turner Prize in 1994.

Another Place is an example of his [5]________ to his art: no less than 100 sculptures stretch along the beach looking out to sea. When the sea comes in, some of the figures are covered in water. They were also designed with their lungs full. This makes them look both tense and relaxed. Again, the [6]________ of the figures was based on his own body.

Anyone who has travelled to the north of England has probably seen one of Gormley's most famous works. The *Angel of the North* is almost the same size as a jumbo jet! The [7]________ of its positioning, above the A1 motorway, means that the sculpture is the most viewed work of art in Britain. As it is made from steel, it represents the industrial history of the area.

Gormley's [8]________ as an artist means he no longer does the hard physical labour of his sculptures. However, he is still very much involved in their design.

V Insight Phrases with *and*

2 Complete the phrases below. Then use them to complete the sentences.

- above and ________
- up and ________
- trial and ________
- pick and ________
- ups and ________
- far and ________

1 You can ________________ your friends, and change them whenever you want, but family is yours for life.
2 She's an ________________ young writer. It's worth reading her novels.
3 I had to search ________________ to find shoes that go with these trousers, but I finally found a great pair.
4 Jack goes ________________ what is expected of him. He is such a hard worker.
5 'I am NOT moody! It's true I have my ________________, but that's perfectly normal!'
6 You have to just try to communicate when you learn a foreign language, and learn by ________________.

Vocabulary extra The arts

3 Write the words below in the correct category. You can use some words in more than one category.

actor ■ aria ■ biographer ■ carve ■ composer ■ draw ■ fiction novelist ■ painter ■ playwright ■ poet ■ portrait ■ recital ■ sculptor ■ sketch ■ singer

Writing	Music

Theatre	Art

4 Match some of the people in exercise 3 to the critics' quotes about their work.

1 'A modern masterpiece of theatre with some truly memorable quotes.' ________
2 'A disappointing read about the life of one of our best-loved comedians.' ________
3 'The way the stone has been carved to show clothing is pure talent.' ________
4 'An instantly forgettable piece of music with little originality.' ________
5 'Her voice is perfect for soprano parts.' ________

5 TASK Write about the most memorable piece of work by one of the people below. Why was it memorable for you?

actor ■ musician ■ poet ■ singer ■ writer

Grammar

Participle clauses

1 Complete the sentences using the correct form of the verbs in brackets.

1 *The Lord of the Rings* and *The Hobbit* series, ____________ (film) in New Zealand, have increased tourism to the country.
2 The *Young Bond* series, ____________ (write) by Charlie Higson, are successful books about 007's schooldays. The first book which tried to do this, ____________ (call) *The Adventures of James Bond Junior 003½*, was a failure in the 1960s.
3 The longest ever work of 3D street art, ____________ (paint) in London, measured 106.5 metres long.
4 Daniel Barenboim conducts the West-Eastern Divan orchestra, ____________ (work) with young Arab and Israeli musicians.
5 *To Kill a Mockingbird* is about a girl ____________ (live) in Alabama in the 1930s, and the racism she sees there.
6 *Whenever, Wherever*, ____________ (sing) by Shakira at the 2020 Super Bowl, was the song that helped the Colombian singer to become famous in the United States almost 20 years earlier.

2 Rewrite the parts of the participle clauses in italics as full relative clauses.

1 The giant painting was created by two artists *working* together for six months. who worked
2 The young singer, *obviously encouraged* by the reaction to his first concert, decided to turn professional. ____________
3 The biography, *clearly written* by a ghostwriter, was very disappointing to read. ____________
4 You can tell that this poem was written by someone *living* in the 19th century. ____________
5 This short film has been made by a student *studying* at the local art college. ____________
6 Please take a look at some of my recent photographs, *enclosed* with this letter. ____________
7 The conductor, *speaking* on behalf of the whole orchestra, thanked everyone for their support. ____________
8 The scriptwriter, *often criticized* for being over-sentimental, has done a fantastic job with this film. ____________

3 Complete the text with the correct participle form of the verbs in brackets.

Dancing on Ice

Dancing on Ice is a popular television series, 1 ____________ (present) by famous faces of British daytime TV Holly Willoughby and Phillip Schofield. In the show, 12 celebrities, 2 ____________ (pair) with professional ice skaters, compete in front of a panel of judges. Each week, a dance couple gets voted off, 3 ____________ (end) with one pair picking up the trophy after the eight-week run.

But the series, 4 ____________ (show) in 2006 for the first time, is like no other on British TV because of the number of injuries competitors pick up.

The popular programme, 5 ____________ (force) to end a week early in 2021 because of the number of contestants who were hurt, hasn't had much luck over the years.

David Seaman, 6 ____________ (swing) the professional skater Pam O'Connor by her feet, famously dropped her and she was left with a cut on her chin. Not something you'd expect of a former England goalkeeper!

Another injury involved Brandee Malto landing on her partner, soap star Antony Cotton, 7 ____________ (injure) two of his ribs in the process.

Perhaps the worst was when Jennifer Ellison, also a soap star, managed to cut her head with her own skate! The ambitious 'scorpion kick', 8 ____________ (perform) successfully in training, didn't go so well in the live performance.

So why on earth would anyone want to take part in such a show? It would seem that, even 9 ____________ (know) the obvious dangers, the opportunity for a new challenge is what makes it an attractive offer.

4 TASK Find out as much new information as you can about a TV programme you enjoy watching. Write a summary for a review website. Use participle clauses to add interesting facts.

Listening, vocabulary and speaking

V Insight Describing art

1 Match quotes 1–6 to adjectives a–f.

1 'This is like nothing I've ever seen before!'
2 'There's a lot going on in his photography; there's a sense of colour, movement and action.'
3 'I couldn't hold back my tears at the end of the film.'
4 'The level of detail in these complex images is incredible.'
5 'Her paintings really make me laugh out loud!'
6 'It's almost as if you can't tell who is an actual person and what is a sculpture!'

a dramatic c lifelike e elaborate
b comical d moving f original

Debating

2 Read the definitions of two types of art. Write the words below in the correct category based on the type of art they are usually associated with.

Figurative art contains images of things from the real world, including objects, landscapes and human figures. **Abstract art** does not contain images which recognizably show things from the real world. It often expresses emotions or attitudes.

■ colours ■ lines ■ objects ■ original ■ people ■ real ■ recognizable ■ shapes

Figurative art	Abstract art

3 🔊10.01 Listen to four students debating about abstract and figurative art and check your ideas from exercise 2. Which type of art does each person argue for in the debate?

	Ela	Jo	Ben	Dan
Figurative art				
Abstract art				

4 Put phrases 1–8 into the correct category a–c.

1 I think you're absolutely right.
2 Sorry to interrupt …
3 I feel quite strongly about this and I totally disagree with Ela.
4 Yes. I agree with Jo.
5 Can I add something to that?
6 I wanted to say that that's not always the case, …
7 That's a good point, Dan.
8 I'd say the exact opposite.

a Agreeing ________, ________, ________
b Disagreeing ________, ________, ________
c Interrupting ________, ________

5 Read the dialogue from the same debate. Choose the correct options.

Alex I think that abstract artists aren't as good at painting.
Dan [1] **That's so true. / Not necessarily.** Figurative painters need more technique to paint real objects in a lifelike way.
Bianca Abstract artists have more imagination.
Dan [2] **I'd say the exact opposite. / That's so true.** You need more imagination to show everyday things in a new and different way.
Alex Some people pretend to like abstract art because they think it makes them seem intelligent.
Dan [3] **That's not always the case. / I think you're absolutely right.** I know people who talk endlessly about abstract art because they think they sound really intellectual.
Bianca The point about abstract art is that it's expressing a deeper part of ourselves, a part which isn't about everyday things, and it does that in a way that has to be more symbolic. That's because—
Dan [4] **That's a good point. / Could I just interrupt here?** I think that …

6 TASK Write a short dialogue of a debate. Choose one of the topics below.

■ We should spend money on health, not art.
■ Graffiti is not an art form.

Vocabulary and grammar

Insight Compound adjectives: describing events

1 Complete the compound adjectives using the words below. Then match 1–8 to comments a–h.

air ■ awaited ■ edge ■ famous ■ length ■ oriented ■ provoking ■ time

1 eagerly-__________ second album
2 world-__________ singer
3 cutting-__________ design
4 family-__________ concert
5 open-__________ show
6 thought-__________ documentary
7 first-__________ opera-goer
8 feature-__________ film

a 'We shouldn't need a babysitter because we can take the kids.'
b 'I've been waiting for it to come out for months!'
c 'We'd never been to one before, but the aria was familiar.'
d 'It really made me reconsider why I eat fish.'
e 'Wear some sun cream. The forecast is good.'
f 'I'm going to need some snacks because it's almost three hours long!'
g 'The new aircraft looks like something from a science-fiction film.'
h 'Wherever you go, people have heard of Harry Styles.'

Vocabulary extra Organizing a festival

2 Choose the correct words.

1 If you think we're ready to give our first concert, then we'll need to find a **stall** / **venue**.
2 The cafés near the venue will be closed, so I'm sure they'll provide a **stall** / **catering service**.
3 I don't think my parents would like his act. It appeals to a much younger **stage** / **audience**.
4 We can't afford to pay all the helpers we need – we'll have to recruit some **volunteers** / **audience**.
5 We didn't get to see many of the bands playing because we were so busy running the food **stall** / **event**.
6 I'm happy my brother's heavy metal band is successful, but I don't attend many of their **performances** / **venues**.
7 I'm not very tall, so I try to get to festivals early and get a good vantage **place** / **point**.
8 We've sold so many tickets! I think we should hold this **performance** / **event** every year.

Determiners

3 Choose which of the words or phrases from each pair go together.

1 **a** a little / a few **b** artists / success
a little success, a few artists
2 **a** few / little **b** vision / paintings
__________, __________
3 **a** all / each **b** poet / writers
__________, __________
4 **a** each / many **b** venue / events
__________, __________
5 **a** all / every **b** play / actors
__________, __________
6 **a** few / little **b** originality / designers
__________, __________
7 **a** most / most of **b** the audience / volunteers
__________, __________
8 **a** each / many **b** time / performances
__________, __________

4 Complete the text with the words and phrases below.

a few ■ a little ■ appeal to ■ attend ■ catering service ■ eagerly awaited ■ managed ■ most of ■ open-air ■ place ■ recruit ■ run ■ venue

VOLUNTEERS NEEDED!

Preparations for our [1]__________ One Love music event are now underway. We are now looking to [2]__________ volunteers to help us at the three-day reggae and dub festival. [3]__________ these will be for various positions around the [4]__________. There will be an external [5]__________ providing food for festival-goers, but we will still require volunteers to [6]__________ the merchandise stall, take tickets on the gates and collect rubbish.

As the event is on an [7]__________ site, we need to leave it as we found it. For this reason, some volunteers will be needed for [8]__________ days after the festival has taken [9]__________.

In exchange you'll get great experience in how a festival of this size is [10]__________ and you might even be allowed backstage! You'll also get the chance to [11]__________ performances outside your working hours with your free three-day pass. For [12]__________ hard work, this has to be a good deal!

If rock, ska, dub and reggae would [13]__________ your musical taste, please apply using the email address below.

5 TASK You are going to organize a party for a friend or family member. Write about how you would need to prepare and how other people could help you.

- I'd need to find some ...
- I'd get a few ...
- I wouldn't need many ...

Reading

1 Choose the correct answers. Then read the article and check.

1 Perspective is
  a the use of modern plastic materials in art.
  b a critic's opinion of a painting.
  c the technique of drawing things to look closer or further away.

2 The mathematical rules about making drawings realistic were first developed in
  a Ancient Greece.
  b 15th century Italy.
  c the 20th century.

2 Match sentences a–f to the paragraph 1–6 in which the information is stated.

a Street art can make you feel as if you are in danger. ______

b Many works of art from the past look badly drawn to us now. ______

c Street art uses more artistic skill than graffiti. ______

d 3D art works because your eye misunderstands where light is coming from. ______

e You need to stay in the same position when you make a 3D drawing. ______

f Street art is often welcomed and encouraged by the local population. ______

Street art

1 In the past, murals on public buildings and frescoes in churches were the only way most people ever saw a work of art. Artists are still sometimes sponsored to paint murals, but paintings on modern public buildings are often done by artists who are paid nothing. Street art, also referred to as 'urban art', is sometimes even carried out without permission, something it can have in common with graffiti. It's less controversial than graffiti because of a greater use of artistic vision and technique. Street art can be thought-provoking and political, but more often, the aim is to inspire people by making a dull public space more interesting and attractive.

2 Street art is found in many cities and large towns, but receives more public support in some than others. In Łódź, in Poland, the mayor has created a permanent urban art exhibition in the city centre called the Urban Forms Gallery, inviting artists to paint on the sides of the apartment blocks there. Street Art Belgium is a website documenting all the 'street installations' which aim to beautify the country's towns and cities. It encourages the community to engage with the works by sharing their views on them, and has the inspiring slogan, 'Making Belgium beautiful one piece at a time'.

3 A stunning development in the urban art movement is 3D street art. 3D paintings are an elaborate application of perspective, which was first developed in Ancient Greece, but only fully understood by 15th century Renaissance artists in Italy. Before that, similar figures in the foreground and background of a picture were painted exactly the same size, which looks completely wrong to the modern eye. We now know that objects further away need to be drawn smaller, and that railway lines need to get closer to each other as they move further away in a drawing. 3D art takes the laws of perspective even further, and makes the eye believe that a flat object has three dimensions.

4 Walking towards some 3D street art, you might think you are about to walk into something or fall into a deep hole. As you get nearer to the drawing and see it from above, you will see the distortion of all the shapes in it, which creating the 3D illusion from a certain viewpoint.

How to make a 3D drawing

5 The trick is to make the viewer think that light coming from different parts of the painting is coming from points nearer or further away than they actually are. To make the viewer think that light is coming from point A, the street artist draws it at point B on the ground. Point C is drawn at point D. The distance between B and D on the ground is much greater than the distance between A and C, so the painting which looks like a circle is a long oval when seen from above.

6 Put a ball on a piece of paper. Close one eye and don't move your head as you draw around the outside of the ball. Don't touch the ball, and draw your line on the paper where it appears to be next to the outside of the ball. If you look at your drawing from above, it is an oval. Look at it from the same viewpoint you drew it from with one eye, and it will look like a circle. Add shading as if light is falling on the ball from one side, and it will start to look 3D.

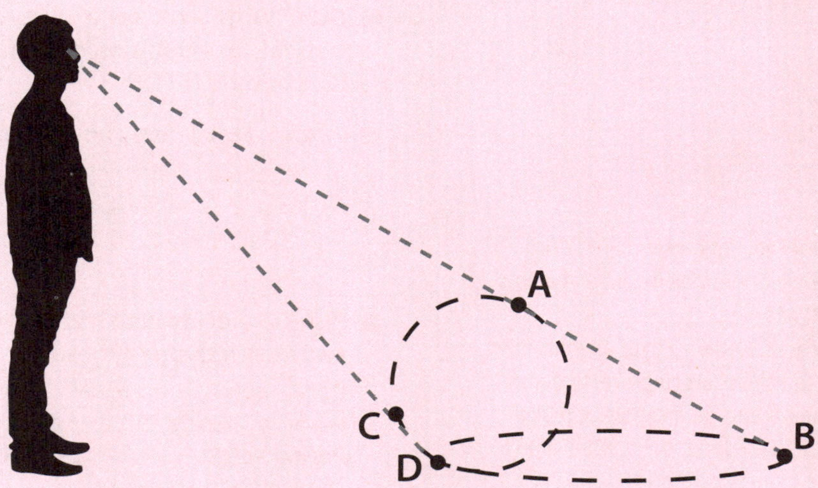

3 Find words in the article which end in *-ion*. Then match them to definitions 1–8.

1 length, width or depth / height ____________
2 something which seems to be real, but isn't ____________
3 a picture in your imagination; the ability to plan with imagination ____________
4 the practical use of something ____________
5 a statement that you are allowed to do something ____________
6 a collection of art shown to the public ____________
7 changing of the shape of something ____________
8 a large piece of artwork which changes the way a place is experienced ____________

4 Complete the summary of the article with the words below.

beauty ■ boring ■ comment ■ development ■ encourage ■ free majority ■ modern ■ near ■ realistic ■ totally

Public murals were once the only art the [1]____________ of people ever saw. Similarly, street art is a popular form of public art today. Artists often do it for [2]____________, to bring interest and [3]____________ to public spaces which are [4]____________. Furthermore, in some countries, the local authorities actually [5]____________ artists to paint on public buildings, and ask the public to [6]____________ on the artworks.

3D art is a [7]____________ form of traditional street art. It uses a further [8]____________ of the idea of perspective, which was only truly understood in the 15th century. The 3D effects are very [9]____________ from a certain viewpoint, although the shapes appear [10]____________ distorted when you get [11]____________ to the drawings.

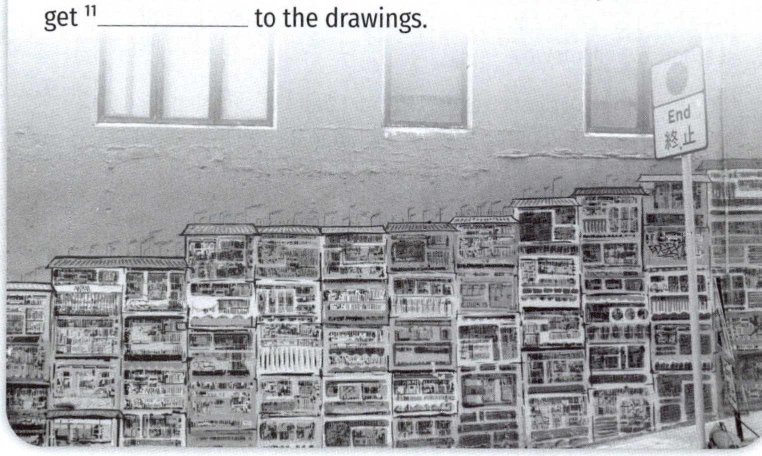

5 TASK **What type of art do you like? What type of art do you dislike? Give reasons for your answers.**

Writing A review of an event

1 Complete the sentences using *so* or *such* and the words in brackets. Add *that* where possible.

1 They're both ____________ (talented) pianists – it's brilliant when they play together.
2 The film was ____________ (depressing) I had to leave the cinema.
3 It was ____________ (interesting / book) I wanted to read it again.
4 These are ____________ (fascinating) paintings – you should enter a competition.
5 That is ____________ (incredible / sculpture) it looks completely lifelike!
6 The gallery was ____________ (crowded) I decided to come back another day.

2 Read the review of an event. Complete it with *so*, *such* or *what*.

On Sunday, I went to the Ashmolean Museum in Oxford. It's [1]____________ a lovely place to visit if you're ever in the city. The museum itself has [2]____________ a fascinating range of collections to see – Egyptian mummies, pre-Raphaelite paintings and classical sculpture, to name a few. Every year, the museum puts on a couple of really interesting exhibitions and 'Last Supper in Pompeii' didn't disappoint.

It included 400 objects found at the site of Pompeii after the volcanic eruption of Mount Vesuvius in 79 CE. The event has been [3]____________ well documented that it's hard to put a new angle on it. But that's exactly what the museum did by focusing on food and drink.

I liked how it didn't focus on the tragedy of the event, but the aspects of Roman life that are [4]____________ relatable to people today. Both rich and poor enjoyed eating, drinking and being sociable. The exhibition itself is set in a typical Italian villa. There's carbonized (completely burnt) food and kitchen equipment on display as well as a 2,000-year-old bottle of olive oil which has survived. My personal favourite piece is a mosaic which shows [5]____________ a beautiful composition of marine life. Most of the creatures in it will have been eaten, of course, as the people of Pompeii's love of seafood is well known.

[6]____________ I didn't like was the fact that the exhibition organizer chose to put the body of a woman, frozen in time, at the end of the exhibition. It stands out after the relatively fun food and drink focus. It seems [7]____________ awful to record at what must have been the last moments of her life. However, it does remind the visitor of the remarkable power of nature. I would recommend it to anyone who has an interest in art, history and food!

3 Rewrite the second sentence in each pair so it has a similar meaning to the first sentence.

1 I love the way the painting looks real.
What ____________________.
2 The speech she gave at the end impressed me the most.
What ____________________.
3 The photographs strike everybody first when they see this exhibition.
What ____________________.
4 Most people will remember the final performance of that actress.
What ____________________.

Writing guide

TASK **Write a review of an event you went to: a festival, an exhibition or a theatre performance, for example.**

PLAN 1 **Make notes about the following.**
- the details of the event: what, where, when and who?
- the purpose of the event
- the things you liked most about it
- the things you didn't like

PLAN 2 **Decide which ideas you are going to use and match them to these paragraphs.**

Paragraph 1: Give the background details of the event.
Paragraph 2: Describe what the event was trying to do.
Paragraph 3: Say what you liked most about it – use some evaluative adjectives.
Paragraph 4: Say what you didn't like about it – use some evaluative adjectives.
Paragraph 5: Summarize your view of the event and say whether you would recommend it.

WRITE **Write your review.**

REVIEW **Check the following points.**
- Have you kept all the information in the correct paragraphs?
- Have you used a variety of evaluative adjectives?
- Have you checked grammar, vocabulary, spelling and punctuation?

U10 Assess your progress

Give yourself a mark 1–3 for each Learning Objective from the lesson.
1 I found this difficult. **2** This was OK. **3** I can do this well.

Lesson 10A

	Mark
I can summarize a text.	
I can scan a text for specific information.	
I can use abstract nouns to talk about talent.	
How can I improve?	

Lesson 10B

	Mark
I can use participle clauses to replace relative clauses.	
I can recognize and understand paraphrasing.	
How can I improve?	

Lesson 10C

	Mark
I can identify specific information in a listening text.	
I can use adjectives to describe art.	
I can use a range of language in a debate.	
How can I improve?	

Lesson 10D

	Mark
I can identify specific information in a text.	
I can use compound adjectives to describe events.	
I can use determiners to talk about quantities.	
How can I improve?	

Lesson 10E

	Mark
I can write a review.	
I can use a range of evaluative adjectives.	
I can use emphasis to highlight important points in a review.	
How can I improve?	

Action plan

Make a plan for what you can do next to improve. Discuss your ideas with your classmates / teacher.

1.1 Present simple and present continuous

Present simple

Affirmative	base form of verb (+ *-s* / *-es* for third person singular)
Negative	*don't* / *doesn't* + infinitive
Questions	*do* / *does* + subject + infinitive

He always wears designer clothes.
Fashions and customs don't always stay the same.
Do you like tattoos? Yes, I do. / No, I don't.

Use

We use the present simple to talk about:

- habits and everyday routines.
- facts and general truths.
- states. Some verbs that describe states are *believe*, *hate*, *have*, *know*, *like*, *need*, *prefer*, *see*, *seem*, *think*, *understand*, *want*.

We use the following time expressions with the present simple: *always*, *every day*, *often*, *regularly*, *usually*, *sometimes*, *hardly ever*, *never*.

1 Choose the correct answers.

1 At what temperature **is** / **does** water freeze?
2 I **'m not** / **don't** like the idea of cosmetic surgery.
3 Paul **don't** / **doesn't** always do his homework.
4 Helen and Amira **watch** / **watches** a lot of television.
5 My mum **goes** / **go** to the gym every Friday.
6 We hardly **never** / **ever** take the train.

Present continuous

Affirmative	*is* / *are* + *-ing* form
Negative	*isn't* / *aren't* + *-ing* form
Questions	*is* / *are* + subject + *-ing* form

The grass in the garden is getting very long.
I'm not wearing my hair in a ponytail today.
Are you looking for a particular type of jacket?
Yes, I am. / No, I'm not.

Use

We use the present continuous to talk about:

- actions that are happening now, or around now.
  I'm looking for a vintage dress.
- temporary situations.
  I'm staying with my aunt and uncle at the moment.
- changing or developing situations.
  More and more people are becoming overweight.
- irritating habits, often with *always*.
  He's always playing that awful music.

We use the following time expressions with the present continuous: *right now*, *at the moment*, *nowadays*, *today*.

2 Complete the sentences. Use the present continuous form of the verb in brackets.

1 Right now, I ________________ in the Clock Café. (sit)
2 Some wild animals ________________ more used to people. (become)
3 Ollie ________________ about his girlfriend. It's really annoying. (always / talk)
4 What music ________________ to on your phone? (you / listen)
5 I ________________ anything important right now. (not do)
6 We ________________ with our grandparents this week because of the bad weather. (not stay)
7 It ________________ very hot in here, isn't it? (get)
8 Magazines ________________ us with images of beautiful young people. (always / bombard)

3 Choose the correct sentence endings.

1 He annoys me because he
   a is always looking at his mobile.
   b always looks at his mobile.
2 The text is in German, so I
   a don't understand it.
   b am not understanding it.
3 Julie loves make-up. In fact, she
   a is wearing it every day.
   b wears it every day.
4 I'd love to help you, but
   a I'm making lunch at the moment.
   b I make lunch at the moment.
5 When wild animals are ill or injured, they
   a always look for a hidden place to rest.
   b are always looking for a hidden place to rest.
6 The summer is nearly finished and
   a it's getting dark earlier.
   b it gets dark earlier.

4 Rewrite the sentences that are incorrect.

1 Good morning. I look for a chic scarf as a present for my sister.
____
2 School finishes early on the last day of term.
____
3 Jack and Senyo are always playing that silly computer game.
____
4 We plan a party at the moment.
____
5 They don't think that it's a very good idea.
____
6 Right now, I watch a really interesting programme about teenagers in Nigeria.
____
7 Why are you buying two skirts that are the same?
____
8 He's usually seeming very friendly and confident.
____

1.2 ■ Verb patterns

When two verbs appear together in a sentence, the first one can be followed by the infinitive (with or without *to*) or the *-ing* form of the second.

It is important to remember the pattern for each verb. Below are some of the most common ones.

- Verb + infinitive with *to* (*decide, expect, promise, choose, seem, need, want*)
  We decided to meet outside the Clock Café.
- Verb + infinitive without *to* (*shall, must, could, will, should*)
  You should eat less junk food.
- Verb + *-ing* (*suggest, consider, admit, enjoy, avoid, imagine*)
  I enjoyed listening to Dan's music.
- Verb + infinitive or *-ing* (*like, love, prefer*)
  Paula doesn't like staying up late.
  Paula doesn't like to stay up late.

Some verbs change their meaning depending on whether they are followed by infinitive + *to* or verb + *-ing*. These include: *remember, forget, stop, try, regret*.

- *remember* + infinitive with *to*: to remember that you need to do something.
  I remembered to buy milk.
- *remember* + *-ing*: to have a memory of doing something.
  I remember buying milk, but I don't remember picking up my purse in the shop.
- *forget* + infinitive with *to*: we forget before the action.
  We forgot to buy a cake for Martha's birthday.
- *forget* + *-ing*: often in the phrase *will never forget*, to talk about a memorable experience.
  I'll never forget spending that week in Rome.
- *stop* + infinitive with *to*: to stop in order to do something.
  She stopped to look in the shop window.
- *stop* + *-ing*: to end an action.
  She stopped looking in the window and walked off towards the station.
- *try* + infinitive with *to*: to do your best.
  I'm trying to do my homework, so can you please make less noise?
- *try* + *-ing*: to do something that might solve a problem.
  We've tried putting oil in the lock, but we still can't open the door.
- *regret* + infinitive with *to*: a formal way of giving bad news.
  We regret to inform you that the 14.05 train to York is cancelled.
- *regret* + *-ing*: to feel sorry about something that you did in the past.
  Ayesha really regrets saying those things to Suzy.

1 Complete the sentences. Use the infinitive form of the verbs in brackets, either with or without *to*.

1 We couldn't WAIT for very long. (wait)
2 When I left, I promised TO STAY in touch. (stay)
3 What will we DO without a goalkeeper in our team? (do)
4 Has Sam decided TO JOIN our club? (join)
5 You must FIND time to exercise every day. (find)
6 Charles didn't expect TO SEE so many wild animals in one place. (see)

2 Complete the sentences. Use either the infinitive + *to* or the *-ing* form of the verbs in brackets. If both the infinitive and the *-ing* form are possible, write both forms.

1 They always avoid TO TRAV by train if possible. (travel)
2 I suggested GOING for a walk, but then it started to rain. (go)
3 Eddie loves MAKING dinner for everyone. (make)
4 Don't forget TO BUY some milk later, will you? (buy)
5 He admitted TO TAKE the money, but not the jewellery. (take)
6 I can't imagine HAVING dinner in an expensive restaurant. (have)
7 Soraya doesn't remember MEETING me all those years ago. (meet)
8 Do you catch the bus into town, or do you prefer TO WALK? (walk)

3 Complete the sentences. Use either the *-ing* form or the infinitive form of the verbs below.

■ have ■ work ■ take ■ spend ■ mention ■ wear ■ lock ■ sleep

1 I immediately regretted ______________ her mistake, and I apologized.
2 Dad sometimes forgets ______________ the door at night, so Mum always checks it.
3 Please try ______________. You'll be very tired tomorrow if you don't.
4 At five o'clock exactly, everyone at the factory stops ______________ and goes home.
5 I hope Fiona remembered ______________ the meat out of the freezer last night.
6 We worked in the garden all morning, and stopped ______________ lunch at one o'clock.
7 I'll never forget ______________ such a wonderful summer at Ryan's house in Canada.
8 If your feet are hurting, you should try ______________ different shoes.

Grammar reference and practice 2

2.1 Narrative tenses

Past simple

Affirmative	verb + *-ed* / *-d*
Negative	*didn't* + infinitive
Questions	*did* + subject + infinitive

She described the holiday in detail.
They didn't see the sights.
Did you go backpacking? Yes, we did. / No, we didn't.

Many verbs have irregular past simple forms, e.g. *have* → *had*, *see* → *saw*, *buy* → *bought*.

Use

We use the past simple to talk about:

- completed past actions or past states.
  We visited several important sites during the week.
- a sequence of actions in the past.
  I tried to ask the man for directions in French. He smiled at me and replied in perfect English.
- past habits.
  Before he bought a car, John travelled everywhere by bike.

We use *when* + past simple + past simple to talk about two connected actions that happen at around the same time.
When Rosa read Rachel's note, she started laughing.

When can appear in the middle of the sentence, without a comma.
Rosa started laughing when she read Rachel's note.

Past continuous

Affirmative	*was* / *were* + *-ing* form
Negative	*wasn't* / *weren't* + *-ing* form
Questions	*was* / *were* + subject + *-ing* form

It was raining when we arrived.
We weren't cycling very fast.
Were you waiting very long for the coach?
Yes, we were. / No, we weren't.

Use

We use the past continuous to talk about:

- background descriptions.
  The sun was shining and everyone was smiling and laughing.
- actions in progress at a specific time in the past.
  I was talking to a very interesting person this afternoon.
- longer actions interrupted by shorter actions.
  I was putting my bag in the luggage rack when I dropped my phone.

We use *while* to introduce an action in the past continuous. *While* isn't followed by the past simple.
While you were talking to Denise, Jack phoned.

We don't use the past continuous with state verbs, e.g. *believe*, *need*, etc.

Past perfect

Affirmative	*had* + past participle
Negative	*hadn't* + past participle
Questions	*had* + subject + past participle

Geeta had remembered to bring a torch.
I hadn't been on a coach tour before.
Had you tried a house-swap before this summer?
Yes, I had. / No, I hadn't.

Use

We use the past perfect to talk about:

- an action or event that happened before another action in the past.
  They had saved up a lot of money before they went on the cruise.
- to talk about two completed past actions, introduced by *when* or *after*. The past perfect always refers to the action that happened first.
  When / After we had checked into the hotel, we found our room and went to bed.

This is quite similar to *when* + past simple + past simple, but the use of the past perfect generally suggests a longer period of time between the two actions.
When / After Rosa had read Rachel's note, she started laughing.

1 Choose the correct sentence in each pair.

1 a Were you finding your watch when you tidied up?
  b Did you find your watch while you were tidying up?
2 a I saw a big spider in my sleeping bag when I opened it.
  b I was seeing a big spider in my sleeping bag when I opened it.
3 a It was eight o'clock. The sun was setting and people were enjoying the warm evening air.
  b It was eight o'clock. The sun set and people enjoyed the warm evening air.
4 a While you were putting your bag in the overhead locker, something fell out.
  b While you put your bag in the overhead locker, something fell out.
5 a We discussed our holiday destination when Kaya had a great idea.
  b We were discussing our holiday destination when Kaya had a great idea.
6 a Matilda's shoe broke while she was walking around town, so she bought a new pair.
  b Matilda's shoe was breaking while she was walking around town, so she bought a new pair.
7 a Once the plane was starting its engines, Kieran realized that he was very nervous.
  b Once the plane started its engines, Kieran realized that he was very nervous.

2 One of the verbs in each sentence is wrong. Rewrite one of the verbs in each sentence in the correct form. Use the past simple, past continuous or past perfect.

1 Dina felt disappointed with the result because she never failed an exam in her life.
SHE Had never failed

2 The driver stopped the bus and had opened a map. Someone asked him if he was lost.
and opened

3 The trip went really well and everyone was having a good time. Suddenly, the tour guide announced that there was a problem.
was going

4 While Emma had taken Sammy back to the campsite, we stayed on the beach and played volleyball.
was taking

5 When we arrived at the hotel, we'd decided not to stay there.
we decided

6 When I came into the bedroom last night, you talked in your sleep.
were talking

3 Complete the sentences with the correct form of the verbs in brackets. Use the past simple, past continuous or past perfect. If two tenses are possible, write both forms.

1 Jane KNEW (knew) the area well because she HAD GONE (go) the year before.
2 Everyone TURNED AROUND (turn round) when she WALKED (walk) into the room.
3 While you WERE ENJOYED (enjoy) your holiday, we HAD TO (have to) look after the house.
4 She SPOKE (speak) Spanish very well considering she HAND'T ever HAD (not have) any classes.
5 When Pete GOT (get) to know the town, he FELT (feel) much safer there.
6 Tania WAS LEAVING (leave) but we MANAGED (manage) to persuade her to stay.
7 When the traffic HAD MOVED (move), our taxi SPEEDED UP (speed up).
8 We DECIDED (decide) to go for a walk after we HAD EATEN (eat).

2.2 *used to* and *would*

We use *used to* + infinitive to talk about:

- past habits that do not happen now.
  When I was young, I used to walk 8 km to school every day.
  My family used to stay at the same campsite every year.

We don't use *used to* for single actions.
My family used to stay at the same campsite every year.
NOT ~~*My family used to stay at the same campsite last July.*~~

Mum used to work as a tour guide.
It didn't use to be obligatory to wear a seat belt.
Did your grandparents use to go on a working holiday every year? Yes, they did. / No, they didn't.

We can use *would* + infinitive in the same way as *used to* to talk about past habits and repeated actions.
As children, they used to play together for hours.
As children, they would play together for hours.

However, *would* is not used to describe past states.
NOT ~~*Grandad would be a postman when he was younger.*~~

When we are talking about past habits, we generally use *would* only in the affirmative.
NOT ~~*We wouldn't go on holiday to the same place every year when I was little.*~~
NOT ~~*Would you go on holiday to the same place every year when you were little?*~~

Although *would* and *used to* are very similar, *used to* simply expresses a fact, while *would* emphasizes that the action is typical of a person or a situation.
When we were little, it used to rain on the first day of the holidays.
When we were little, it would always rain on the first day of the holidays.

1 Complete the sentences with the correct form of *used to* or *would*. If both *used to* and *would* are correct, write both forms.

1 My granny says that people ______ be happier in the past.
2 I ______ like seafood, but I eat it all the time now.
3 I remember the way that Dad ______ pretend to be a tour guide whenever we visited London.
4 ______ you ______ share a bedroom with both your sisters?
5 Every evening at exactly seven o'clock, we ______ find our cat sitting on our doorstep.
6 In the past, many families ______ spend every summer holiday in the same small hotel.

2 Rewrite the sentences in the past. Use the correct form of *used to* or *would*. If both *used to* and *would* are possible, write both forms.

1 Fiona has four pairs of sunglasses.
______
2 Leo doesn't use his mobile much.
______
3 Bukayo gets really scared when boarding a plane.
______
4 On long car journeys, my little sister always says 'Are we nearly there yet?'
______
5 Jack and Kim live in the same street.
______
6 Do you and Lisa know each other?
______

3.1 Past simple and present perfect

Past simple	Present perfect
For actions that happened at a specific point in the past, usually with a time expression. Lee went to Portugal last year.	For actions that happened at some point in the past; the time is unknown or unimportant. Carrie has stayed at that hotel twice.
For situations that happened in a period of time that has ended. I lived in Germany from 2002 to 2006.	For actions or states that began in the past and that continue up to the present, usually with *for* or *since*. Freda has worked here for several years. Marek has been a teacher since 2010.
With past time references, such as *yesterday*, *last …* and *… ago*. We finished our exams last week. Karen started her new school a few days ago.	With *ever*, *never*, *already*, *just* and *yet*. Have you ever been here before? No, I've never been here in my life. Have the girls arrived yet? Isabel has already arrived. Kirsty has just got here, but Maryam hasn't arrived yet.
With time references such as *this morning*, *today* and *this week* to talk about something that happened in a part of that period that is finished. I saw Fred this morning. (The morning is finished.) Did Laura phone today? (It is now the evening, so the main part of 'today' is finished.)	With time references such as *this morning*, *today* and *this week* to talk about the whole of that period of time up to now. I haven't seen Fred this morning. (It is still the morning.) Has Laura phoned today? (It is still the daytime.)
With the question form *How long ago … ?* How long ago did Darius break his leg? He broke it two years ago.	With the question form *How long … ?* and with *for* or *since*. How long have you had that rash? I've had it for a month / since February.

Note that it is possible to use *How long* with a past simple verb and *for*, but we can't use *since* in the past simple answer.
How long did Tom have the rash for? (Tom no longer has the rash.)
He had it for a month.
NOT ~~He had it since February.~~

The verb *go* has two past participle forms: *been* and *gone*. We use *been* when we know that someone has returned from a trip. We use *gone* when they have not returned.
Josh has been to India. (= He is back now.)
Josh has gone to India. (= He is still in India.)

In the past simple, there is only one form for the past of *go*: *went*.
Josh went to India last year. (We don't know if he came back, or if he is still there.)

We can use the past simple or the present perfect with time expressions, such as: *today*, *this morning*, *this evening*, *this week*, *this year*, etc. Compare the sentences:
I wrote three emails this morning. (The speaker is talking in the evening, so the period of time has ended.)
I've written three emails this morning. (The speaker is talking in the morning, so the period of time continues.)

1 Choose the correct sentence endings.

1 It's two o'clock in the afternoon. Leo usually phones at ten o'clock
  a but he didn't phone me this morning.
  b but he hasn't phoned me this morning.
2 I'm trying to contact my old penfriend but
  a she moved to a new city.
  b she has moved to a new city.
3 They keep getting lost because
  a they haven't been here before.
  b they didn't go here before.
4 I've stopped going skating because
  a I've broken my leg the last time I went.
  b I broke my leg the last time I went.
5 She didn't buy a coat in the market because
  a she didn't find anything suitable there.
  b she hasn't found anything suitable there.
6 It's strange. I can't find Simon, but he
  a was here a few minutes ago.
  b has been here a few minutes ago.

2 **Complete the sentences. Use the present perfect or past simple form of the verbs below.**

be ▪ come ▪ get ▪ go ▪ live ▪ not eat ▪ own ▪ run

1 I know you live in England now, but how long ___________ you ___________ in Ireland for?
2 The Romans ___________ to Britain over 2,000 years ago.
3 Grandad ___________ in hospital since last week.
4 Aziz ___________ every morning for a year, and he isn't going to stop now.
5 How long ago ___________ your parents ___________ married?
6 My aunt and uncle ___________ to India for six months. They gave me this lovely souvenir.
7 How long ___________ you ___________ your pet snake?
8 We had a sandwich last night but we ___________ since then.

3.2 ▪ Present perfect simple and present perfect continuous

Affirmative and negative		
I You We They	have been haven't been	watching TV.
He She It	has been hasn't been	

Questions and short answers			
Have	I you we they	been watching TV?	Yes, I have. No, I haven't.
Has	he she it		Yes, he has. No, she hasn't.

Use

We use the present perfect continuous to talk about:

- a situation or action that began in the past and is still in progress. The emphasis is on the duration of the activity. We can use *for* and *since* to show how long.
  You've been writing that letter for three hours.
- an action that has happened repeatedly in the past and that is still happening now.
  Dan's been taking guitar lessons.
- a very recent action which has either just finished or which has just been interrupted; the present perfect continuous often introduces a reason or explanation.
  Kate and Lucy have been playing tennis.
  I'm tired because I've been working all day.

The present perfect and the present perfect continuous can sometimes be used with little difference in meaning, especially with verbs that express a continuous action such as *wait*, *live*, *work* + *for* or *since*.
He's waited a long time for this moment.
He's been waiting a long time for this moment.

However, the present perfect can tell us that an action finished recently, while the present perfect continuous emphasizes the activity itself.
I've done my homework. (I recently finished my homework.)
I've been doing my homework. (That is how I've spent my time until just now.)

The present perfect continuous can't be used with state verbs, e.g. *be*, *like*, *believe*, *have*.
I've been a teacher since 2008.
NOT ~~I've been being a teacher since 2008.~~

The present perfect continuous isn't used to say how often something happened.
They've visited us many times.
NOT ~~They've been visiting us many times.~~

1 **Complete the sentences using the present perfect continuous form of the verbs below.**

chat ▪ do ▪ get ▪ not study ▪ take ▪ wait

1 I ___________ at this bus stop for half an hour.
2 You're soaking wet! What ___________ you ___________?
3 Marcia ___________ to her friend on the phone since 5.30.
4 Mark ___________ very hard for his exam.
5 We ___________ extra lessons to help us with our maths.
6 The population ___________ taller over the past few decades.

2 **Choose the correct sentence. Sometimes both are correct.**

1 a We're late because we've been helping Dad clean the garage.
  b We're late because we've helped Dad clean the garage.
2 a The Fielding family have lived in this area for at least a century.
  b The Fielding family have been living in this area for at least a century.
3 a I've had a headache since lunchtime.
  b I've been having a headache since lunchtime.
4 a Ben's been writing a science fiction story. In fact, he's nearly finished it.
  b Ben's written a science fiction story. In fact, he's nearly finished it.
5 a It's been raining, so the grass is quite wet.
  b It's rained, so the grass is quite wet.
6 a The reason I'm covered in flour is because I've made biscuits.
  b The reason I'm covered in flour is because I've been making biscuits.

4.1 ■ Expressing the future

Present simple

We use the present simple to talk about future events that are fixed because they are based on a schedule, calendar or timetable.

Pete's flight lands at 11.00 tomorrow morning.

What time does the film start?

Present continuous

We use the present continuous to talk about personal arrangements for a future day or date.

I'm meeting up with Olivia tonight.

I'm not doing anything later.

1 Choose the correct words.

1 We **have** / **are having** a meeting tomorrow to discuss how to raise funds.
2 According to the timetable, the drama group **rehearses** / **is rehearsing** at six o'clock.
3 What **do you do** / **are you doing** later?
4 **Does everyone go** / **Is everyone going** to Luke's party on Saturday?
5 They **don't hold** / **aren't holding** a meeting this week.
6 The football match **ends** / **is ending** at 7.00, so we can watch the film afterwards.

2 Rewrite the sentences. Use the present simple or the present continuous form of the verbs in brackets.

1 Jan and Kim have decided to go to Amy's party on Saturday. (go)

____

2 Fatima has just bought a plane ticket for a flight to Madrid next Tuesday. (fly)

____

3 The plane's departure time is 9.20. (leave)

____

4 The summer lecture programme is scheduled to begin on 15th June. (start)

____

5 Matt and Jamie have booked a badminton court for later. (play)

____

will

We use *will* and *won't* to talk about:

- promises and hopes for the future, often with verbs like *hope*, *expect* or *promise* + *that* (you can omit *that*).
  I hope (that) you'll be very happy here.
  We can also use the infinitive with *to* after these verbs.
  We hope to arrange another meeting soon.
- predictions, often after *I think* or *I don't think*, or future facts that we are certain about.
  I don't think it will be difficult to pass this exam.
  That plant won't survive for long without water.
- future facts that we are less certain about, with *probably*.
  We will probably go to the park, but it depends on the weather.

going to

We use *be* + *going to* to talk about:

- intentions.
  Ben's going to join a gym.
- predictions about the future based on something we can see in the present.
  Look at the sky. It's going to be a beautiful day.

Compare:

going to	*They aren't going to stay very long.* (That is their intention.)
will / won't	*They won't stay very long.* (I predict this.)

Sometimes there is little difference between *going to* and the present continuous when talking about the future.

We're going to have a party next weekend.

We're having a party next weekend.

We use the present continuous to talk about a definite plan for which the arrangements have been made. And we use *going to* to show that the plan is only an intention.

may / *might*

We use *may* or *might* when we are less certain about the future. Although *may* is considered to be more definite than *might*, there is, in fact, very little difference in meaning between the two words.

3 Complete the sentences with the correct form of *will* or *be going to* and one of the verbs below.

cause ■ fall ■ make ■ not go ■ not take ■ start

1 I hope this _______ a long time. I'm very busy.
2 It is clear that further drought _______ very serious problems in the area.
3 Look at that man! He _______ off the roof!
4 We _______ to the meeting. We've got too much work to do.
5 Clean water _______ probably _______ the biggest difference to the people in the village.
6 They _______ a campaign to help to promote the message.

4 Match 1–8 to a–h to make sentences.

1 I've got a cold, so I probably
2 Sarah and I won't be at the picnic, but we
3 It's great news. We're
4 Good luck. I hope I
5 Mike isn't sure, but he thinks
6 The temperature is dropping. It
7 Carla isn't certain, but she
8 They intended to join us on the protest, but they

a might meet us later.
b aren't going to come now.
c won't go swimming later.
d the journey will take about three hours.
e going to get a dog, at last.
f may see you at Jack's party.
g 'll see you again soon.
h 's going to be very cold tonight.

4.2 Future continuous and future perfect

Future perfect

Affirmative and negative		
I You He / She / It We You They	will have won't have	helped many people.

Questions and short answers			
Will	I you he / she / it we you they	have helped many people?	Yes, you will. No, they won't.

Use

We use the future perfect to talk about:

- an action that will be completed before a definite time in the future.

We often use *by* + a time expression to say when the action will be finished.
The traffic situation will have improved by eleven o'clock.
Call Chris tomorrow. He'll have had more time to think about the idea by then.

We can also use *before* + time expression.
Chris won't have made his decision before tomorrow.

A time expression is not always necessary, however.
I hope that we won't have done all that hard work for nothing.
The campaign will raise awareness of the issue, but in the end, what will it have achieved?

1 Complete the sentences with the future perfect form of the verbs in brackets.

1 By four o'clock this afternoon, Priyanka ________________ her driving test. (take)
2 Wait until tomorrow to speak to Mark. He ________________ his mind up before then. (not make up)
3 By this time tomorrow, Mr Reed ________________ across the English Channel. (swim)
4 By the end of this essay, I ________________ over 2,000 words. (write)
5 ________________ you ________________ your exam results by this time tomorrow? (receive)
6 By this time on Friday, I ________________ this film six times. (see)

Future continuous

Affirmative and negative		
I You He / She / It We You They	will be won't be	helping many people.

Questions and short answers			
Will	I you he / she / it we you they	be helping many people?	Yes, you will. No, they won't.

Use

We use the future continuous with a future time expression to talk about actions that will be in progress at a definite time in the future.
I'll be travelling to Africa this time next week.

It is not always necessary to use a future time expression, particularly if the time frame is clear from the context.
Will you be helping out at the event? (some time between the start and the end of the event)

2 Complete sentence b so that it has a similar meaning to sentence a. Use the future perfect or future continuous tense.

1 **a** The concert finishes at 9.00.
b At 8.59, the concert ________________.
2 **a** We leave school at 3.45.
b By 4.00, I ________________ school.
3 **a** Nick is going to arrive home later than 12.00.
b Nick ________________ home by 11.55.
4 **a** It's eleven o'clock. At eleven o'clock tomorrow, she's flying to Lisbon.
b This time tomorrow she ________________ to Lisbon.
5 **a** The package will take several weeks to arrive.
b The package ________________ by tomorrow.
6 **a** The protest begins tomorrow morning at 9 a.m. and continues all day.
b By 9.30 tomorrow, the protest ________________ ________________.

5.1 First and second conditionals

First conditional

We use the first conditional to talk about a real or very likely action or situation and its probable result in the present or future.

If you lie a lot,	he will never believe you.
CONDITION	RESULT
If + present simple,	*will* + infinitive

We can put the condition clause first. There is no comma.

He will never believe you	if you lie a lot.
RESULT	CONDITION
will + infinitive	*if* + present simple

Remember: in the condition clause, *if* is followed by the present simple, even though the verb can refer to the future.
If we miss the train, we'll be late for school.
NOT ~~If we'll miss the train ...~~

In the result clause, we can use other modal verbs apart from *will*.
If you tell the truth all the time, you might offend people.

It is possible to use a negative verb in either or both parts of a conditional sentence.
If you don't arrive on time, I won't wait for you.

Instead of *if*, we can use *unless*. *Unless* means *if something does not happen*.
Compare:
If shops don't do something to stop shoplifting, we will all have to pay higher prices.
Unless shops do something to stop shoplifting, we will all have to pay higher prices.

1 Choose the correct sentence endings.

1 If we leave now,
 a we be in time for the bus.
 b we'll be in time for the bus.
2 If you don't study for these exams,
 a you might pass them.
 b you might not pass them.
3 You'll need to have a good reason
 a if you accuse someone of something.
 b if you'd accuse someone of something.
4 Unless we do something,
 a the thief will get away with it.
 b the thief won't get away with it.
5 I'll call Lucy at three o'clock
 a unless she'll call me before then.
 b unless she calls me before then.
6 If he continues to behave like this,
 a his friends won't put up with it.
 b his friends wouldn't put up with it.

Second conditional

We use the second conditional to talk about an imaginary or unlikely situation and its imagined result. They can describe present and future situations. The past forms are used to show the situation is different from reality.

If you apologized to Laura,	she would forgive you.
CONDITION	RESULT
If + past simple,	*would* (or *'d*) + infinitive
If I lived in Africa,	my life would be different.

In the same way as for first conditional sentences, the result can come first.

My life would be different	if I lived in Africa.
RESULT	CONDITION
would (or *'d*) + infinitive	*if* + past simple

It is possible to use other modals in the result clause.
If I said what I really thought, they might get offended.

We can also use *unless* in second conditional sentences.

We can use *were* instead of *was*, especially in formal style.
I wouldn't say that if it wasn't / weren't true.

2 Make second conditional sentences using the correct form of the verbs in brackets.

1 If they ________ (have) more money, they ________ (spend) more on the campaign.
2 Ted ________ (be) happier if he ________ (live) in a hot country.
3 If Claire ________ (work) harder, she ________ (do) better in her exams.
4 If I ________ (not want) to come, I ________ (tell) you.
5 Bako ________ (not accuse) her unless he ________ (have) a good reason.
6 We ________ (walk) there if it ________ (not be) so far.

3 Rewrite the first and second conditional sentences that are incorrect. In the incorrect sentences, only one verb is wrong.

1 If you told David the truth, he wouldn't believe it.
____
2 If we have time on our trip next week, we visit the famous castle.
____
3 You wouldn't like it if I tell you lies.
____
4 If you see Anita, you'll notice that there is something different about her.
____
5 It will be a great end to the event unless something will go wrong.
____

5.2 Modals of obligation, prohibition and permission

We use the modal verbs *can (can't)*, *may (may not)*, *must (mustn't)* and *have to (don't have to)* to talk about obligation, prohibition and permission.

can and *may*

We can use the modal verbs *can* and *may* to give someone permission to do something or to say what is allowed in general. *May* is more formal than *can*.
When you reach the age of 18, you can / may vote.

can't and *may not*

We use the negative forms *can't* and *may not* to refuse someone permission or to say what is not allowed.
In the UK, people may not / can't get married until the age of 16.

must and *mustn't*

We use *must* to talk about a rule, or something that is necessary to do.
You must be more careful with your things.

We use *mustn't* to talk about something that people are not allowed to do.
People mustn't park their cars here. There's a car park around the corner.

have to and *don't have to*

We can use *have to* in a similar way to *must*.
You have to ask permission to leave the room during lesson time.

We use *don't have to* to talk about something that isn't necessary for people to do. However, they can do it if they want to.
You don't have to carry your identity card everywhere you go. (But some people do.)

We normally use *must* when the speaker thinks that something is important, and *have to* when someone else thinks it is. However, it is fairly common to use *have to* instead of *must* when talking about an obligation that comes from the speaker.

1 Choose the correct words.

1 Nobody **can** / **must** borrow these books without permission.
2 Visitors **mustn't** / **don't have to** feed the animals in the zoo, as this may harm the animals.
3 Students **must** / **may** bring a small bottle of water into the exam, if they wish.
4 Drivers **may** / **must** stop at a red traffic light.
5 According to the map, we **have to** / **can** walk as far as the river, but not beyond that.
6 You **must not** / **don't have to** take any photos inside the art gallery. However, there are postcards available of all the paintings.

2 Rewrite the sentences. Use *must*, *mustn't*, *have to* or *don't have to*. If more than one answer is correct, write both forms.

1 I think it is necessary that you wait for Lizzie.
You ____________ wait for Lizzie.
2 It isn't necessary that you eat all your lunch.
You ____________ eat all your lunch.
3 Our teacher thinks it is necessary that we speak to the police officer.
We ____________ speak to the police officer.
4 It is against the law for people to cross the road here.
People ____________ cross the road here.
5 It is a rule that everyone is quiet in a library.
Everyone ____________ be quiet in a library.
6 It's OK if I don't go to bed early on a Friday.
I ____________ go to bed early on a Friday.
7 It's really important that I'm not late home today.
I ____________ be late home today.
8 It's compulsory for children to do sport three times a week at school.
Children ____________ do sport three times a week at school.

Grammar reference and practice 6

6.1 The passive

The passive is formed with the verb *be* + past participle of the main verb.

We use the passive:

- when we are more interested in the action than in the person who performs the action.
- when we don't know who performs the action, or when it is clear from the context who performs the action.

Passive verbs have the same tenses as active verbs, and the rules for tense usage are the same.
When we want to say who performs an action in a passive sentence, we use the preposition *by*.

ACTIVE Unemployed members of the community started the business.
PASSIVE The business was started by unemployed members of the community.

Present simple passive

= *am*, *is*, *are* + past participle
Some of the profit is spent on improving living conditions.
Cotton isn't grown in the UK.
Are farmers paid a fair price for their produce?

Present continuous passive

= *am* / *is* / *are being* + past participle
Stealth marketing is being used more and more as a way to sell products and services.
The profits aren't being passed on to the people who make these goods.
Are these measures being introduced in every country?

1 Complete the present simple passive and present continuous passive sentences.

1 I keep seeing the same person behind me. ___________ I ___________ followed?
2 Glossy magazines ___________ commonly used to promote luxury goods.
3 Brand image is very important, and ___________ usually developed by experts at a marketing agency.
4 The new advertising campaign ___________ launched yet.
5 Generally speaking, once the decision ___________ announced publicly, there is nothing anyone can do about it.
6 It is important to always take account of the consumer while the products ___________ designed.
7 The bread ___________ baked in the oven right now, and will be ready in about ten minutes.
8 During a marketing campaign, free samples of a product ___________ offered to people in the industry.

Past simple passive

= *was* / *were* + past participle
This commercial was created by a famous advertising agency.
The advertising campaign wasn't considered a success.
We weren't given anything to eat.
Was the school built on time?

Present perfect passive

= *has* / *have been* + past participle
A lot of articles have been published about this.
The campaign hasn't been seen as an overwhelming success, but we hope this will change.
Has the campaign been criticized?
Have the clothes been hung up?

2 Complete the sentences using the correct past simple passive or present perfect passive form of the verbs in brackets.

1 Max ___________ (ask) to speak in front of the whole school. He's really excited about it.
2 We ___________ (not invite) to the end-of-year party yet.
3 The railway station ___________ (build) ten years before the town hall.
4 ___________ our car ___________ (manufacture) in the UK?
5 When you asked about José, what ___________ you ___________ (tell)?
6 ___________ you ever ___________ (hurt) in an accident?

Past continuous passive

= *was* / *were being* + past participle
Several designs were being considered at one time.
There was confusion because people weren't being given the right information.
Was research being carried out at that time?

Past perfect passive

= *had been* + past participle
The sisters were happy because they'd been given the chance to set up their own business.
Many people were angry that they hadn't been given the chance to give their views.
Had you been promised a refund on a previous occasion?

3 **Complete the past continuous passive and past perfect passive sentences with *had* (or *hadn't*) *been*, *was* (or *wasn't*) *being*, *were* (or *weren't*) *being*.**

1 The man looked thin because he __________ held prisoner for several months.
2 When we came out of the shop, we realized that our bikes __________ stolen.
3 The workers didn't have any money because they __________ paid.
4 Kiara listened politely, but she had the feeling that she __________ told the truth.
5 It was obvious that the letter __________ written a long time ago.
6 What were you doing while Anna __________ chased by that dog?

Future passive

= *will be* + past participle

The campaign will be extended to other countries.
The report won't be finished until November.
Will the clothes be sold here?

4 **Complete the sentences using the future passive form of the verbs below.**

ask ▪ forget ▪ give ▪ keep ▪ not make ▪ not start ▪ spend ▪ take

1 Everyone who comes into this building __________ to show their identity card.
2 In a few days, this incident __________ and everything will carry on as normal.
3 Tomorrow afternoon, you __________ on a tour of the old town.
4 A decision on the school's future __________ until next year.
5 What __________ all the money we collected __________ on?
6 At the end of the competition, a prize __________ for the best design.
7 Work on the new building __________ for another six months.
8 Don't worry about the money. Once we count it, it __________ in a safe place.

5 **Rewrite the active sentences in the passive. Use *by* if necessary.**

1 Someone was ringing the church bells.
____
2 Has someone fed the cat today?
____
3 Charleston United have beaten Sunderland City.
____
4 First, you mix together the two paints.
____
5 Joe started the argument.
____
6 We had already introduced Kate and Archie.
____

6.2 ▪ *have / get something done*

The verb *have* can be used in the passive structure *have something done*, which means to arrange for another person to do something for you. *Have* can be used in any tense, but in this structure, it is always followed by an object + past participle.

I'm having my hair cut later. (Another person is cutting my hair.)
We've had our house professionally cleaned.

We can use *have something done* in the negative and in questions. In the present simple form, we use *don't / doesn't have* (not *haven't / hasn't got*).

She doesn't have her food delivered. She buys it at the supermarket herself.

In informal and spoken English it is possible to use *get* instead of *have* in this structure (*get something done*). *Get* can also be used in different tenses.

We'll get a key made for you.
I got my shoes repaired last week.

1 **Complete the sentences with the correct form of *have something done*.**

1 Kamili's at the optician at the moment.
She __________ her eyes tested.
2 Paul went to the garage yesterday.
He __________ his motorbike repaired there.
3 Jane and Liz have done something very patriotic.
They __________ their nails painted in red, white and blue.
4 Carla's partner had asked the hotel to put flowers and chocolates in the room before their arrival.
Carla's partner __________ flowers and chocolates put in the room before their arrival.
5 Someone will be painting our fence later.
We __________ our fence painted later on.
6 Is the house being professionally cleaned?
__________ we __________ the house professionally cleaned?

7.1 Reported speech

We use reported speech when we want to tell someone about something that another person said. Tenses and pronouns change in reported speech if the time and the speaker change. The tense of the main verb changes in the following ways:

Direct speech		Reported speech
Present simple She said: 'Ian snores very loudly.'	→	Past simple She said that Ian snored very loudly.
Present continuous 'May's listening to music,' I said.	→	Past continuous I said that May was listening to music.
Present perfect 'I've made my decision,' she said.	→	Past perfect She said that she had made her decision.
Past simple 'We waited a long time,' Giles said.	→	Past perfect Giles said that they had waited a long time.
Past perfect 'I'd already seen the film,' said Mari.	→	Past perfect Mari said she'd already seen the film.
can 'You can try again,' he said.	→	*could* He said that I could try again.
will They said: 'We'll think about it.'	→	*would* They said that they would think about it.

It is usually necessary to change pronouns and possessive adjectives, too:

'My dog isn't very well,' Harry said. → Harry said that his dog wasn't very well.

'I'm buying a present for my dad,' she said. → She said that she was buying a present for her dad.

We also change references to time and place.

Time		
now	→	then / at that moment
today	→	that day
this week	→	that week
last week	→	the week before
yesterday	→	the day before
tomorrow	→	the next / following day
a minute ago	→	a minute earlier / before
next week	→	the following week
Place		
here	→	there

We can use the verb *tell* instead of *say* to report what someone says.

If we use *tell*, we must follow it with a personal pronoun.
Theo told me that he had a plan.
NOT ~~Theo told that he had a plan.~~

However, we never use a personal pronoun after *say*.
NOT ~~Theo said me that ...~~

There are other reporting verbs that we can use apart from *say* and *tell*, e.g. *add*, *admit*, *agree*, *explain*, *point out*, *promise*, *reply*, *warn*. Of the verbs in this list, only *promise* and *warn* are followed by a personal pronoun.

1 Complete the sentences in reported speech.

1 'We can't go together,' said Kaheem.
Kaheem said that we ________________ together.
2 'Marina and Dan haven't eaten anything,' said Phil.
Phil said that Marina and Dan ________________ anything.
3 'I finished the crossword,' said Grandma.
Grandma said that she ________________ the crossword.
4 'They're always playing computer games,' said Mum.
Mum said that they ________________ computer games.
5 'The sunset will be beautiful,' said Ellen.
Ellen said that the sunset ________________ beautiful.
6 'Dad is a really good cook,' said David.
David said that Dad ________________ a really good cook.

2 Complete the sentences with the correct pronouns or possessive forms. Sometimes no change is needed.

1 'Colin can't find his dog,' said Ewan.
Ewan said that Colin couldn't find __________ dog.
2 'Mum is annoyed with both of you,' said Debbie.
Debbie said that Mum was annoyed with both of __________.
3 'We aren't going on the school trip today,' said Wendy.
Wendy said that __________ weren't going on the school trip that day.
4 'You will love your present,' my brothers told me.
My brothers told me that __________ would love __________ present.
5 'I know your sister,' Chidi said.
Chidi said that __________ knew __________ sister.
6 'I really like Carol and her brother,' said Steve.
Steve said that __________ really liked Carol and __________ brother.

3 **Choose the correct words.**

1 He **promised** / **warned** that I might be in a dangerous situation.
2 I thought we would be late, but Sarah **agreed** / **pointed out** that the train wasn't due to leave for another hour.
3 Abe **warned** / **explained** that he was at home because the school was closed.
4 Although she denied it at first, Thea eventually **admitted** / **promised** that she had lost the book.
5 Ken **explained** / **admitted** that he wouldn't tell anyone my secret.
6 At first, Diana said I was wrong, but in the end, she **promised** / **agreed** that it would be better to do things my way.

7.2 Reported questions and commands

We report questions with the verb *ask*. *Ask* can be followed by a personal pronoun, or can be used without one.

To report a *yes/no* question, we use the structure *ask* (+ object) + *if*. The word order is the same as in an affirmative sentence. This means that the subject comes before the verb.
John asked if I was feeling all right.
John asked me if I was feeling all right.
NOT ~~John asked me if was I feeling all right.~~

We can use *whether* instead of *if*. There is no difference in meaning.
Max asked if we wanted to go to the cinema.
OR Max asked whether we wanted to go to the cinema.

To report a *wh-* question, we use a *wh-* word followed by an affirmative word order.
She asked (Fiona) what the time was.
NOT ~~She asked (Fiona) what was the time.~~

We report orders and commands with the verb *tell*. We use the structure *tell* + personal pronoun + infinitive with *to*.
They told us to stand in the queue.

To report an order not to do something, we put *not* before the infinitive with *to*.
She told me not to worry.

Remember that it is still necessary to follow the rules about changing tenses, pronouns and possessive forms, as well as references to place and time.
'Come back here tomorrow evening,' he said. → He told me to go back there the next / following evening.

1 **Choose the correct sentence endings. Sometimes both are correct.**

1 The police officer asked me
  a what was I doing?
  b what I was doing.
2 Nina asked her mum
  a if she could go into town to meet a friend.
  b whether could she go into town to meet a friend.
3 I spotted Tim and asked him
  a if he wanted to play football in the park.
  b if he wants to play football in the park.
4 Our neighbours asked us
  a if we had seen their dog.
  b whether we had seen their dog.
5 The model plane that Grandad made was amazing, and I asked
  a him how he had made it.
  b did it take long to make it.
6 A tourist stopped us in the street and asked us
  a where was he.
  b where he was.
7 We asked our teacher
  a when would start the exams.
  b when the exams would start.
8 Guillaume came over and asked
  a me if the news was true.
  b if the news was true.

2 **Write the active questions and commands as reported questions and commands. Use the correct form of the reporting verbs *tell* and *ask*.**

1 'Wait here for me,' said Luke.
______
2 'Where does Paul live?' asked Mum.
______
3 'How's your toe?' asked Nancy.
______
4 'Give me the torch,' she said.
______
5 'Don't do anything until next week,' Mr Carr said.
______
6 'Have you been ill?' asked Soroush.
______
7 'Don't play your music so loud, you two,' said Dad.
______
8 'Are you Ted Fielding's nephew?' asked the man.
______

8.1 Third conditional

We use the third conditional to talk about unreal situations in the past. The condition is impossible, because we cannot change what happened. Consequently, the result is also impossible.

If you had studied,	you would have passed the exam.
CONDITION	RESULT
If + past perfect,	*would* (*'d*) *have* + past participle

In the same way as for other conditional sentences, the result can come first.

You would have passed the exam	if you had studied.
RESULT	CONDITION

It is possible to use other modals in the result clause.
If you'd mentioned it earlier, I might have been able to do something about it.
If we hadn't taken the wrong road, we could have got there sooner.

Unless is never used in third conditional sentences.

1 Choose the correct third conditional sentences.

1 a If he had known the risks, he would change his mind.
  b If he had known the risks, he would have changed his mind.

2 a We would have enjoyed ourselves more if our teacher hadn't been there.
  b We would enjoyed ourselves more if our teacher hadn't been there.

3 a Unless I had organized the demonstration, I would have done it differently.
  b If I had organized the demonstration, I would have done it differently.

4 a If she would understand the question, she might have got the answer right.
  b If she had understood the question, she might have got the answer right.

5 a I would have backed down if I had been in his position.
  b I would have backed down if I would have been in his position.

6 a If someone had shown us the ropes, we would have known what to do.
  b If someone would have shown us the ropes, we had known what to do.

7 a Gary didn't throw the papers out if he realized that they were important.
  b Gary wouldn't have thrown the papers out if he'd realized that they were important.

8 a We could have bought a nice souvenir if we had had more money.
  b We would have bought a nice souvenir if we could have more money.

2 Complete the third conditional sentences with the correct form of the verbs in brackets.

1 If you HAD LISTENED (listen) more closely, you WOULD HAVE KNOW (know) what to do.
2 I WOULD HAVE PLAYED (play) in the match if I HAD BOUGHT (bring) my football boots.
3 We WOULD'NT HAVE SAID (not say) anything if we HAD REILIZED (realize) the trouble it would cause.
4 If he HADN'T ASKED (not ask) for directions, he WOULDN'T HAVE ARRIVED (not arrive) on time.
5 If Jessica HAD BEEN (be) worried about us, she WOULD HAVE PHONED (phone) us.
6 My brother WOULD HAVE WON (win) the race if he HADN'T FELLEN (not fall).
7 If they HAD WANTED (want) to come along, WOULDN'T they HAVE TOLD (tell) us?
8 You WOULDN'T HAVE FAILED (not) fail your exams if you HAD DONE (do) more studying!

8.2 *I wish* and *if only*

I wish

We use *wish* + past simple to say that we would like a present situation to be different.
I wish we had a dog. (I would like to have a dog, but I haven't got one.)
Sam wishes he lived in the USA. (Sam would like to live in the USA, but he doesn't.)

We can use *wish* followed by a negative verb.
I wish I didn't have such a complicated life! (I would like my life to be easier, but it isn't.)

As with the second conditional, we can use *were* instead of *was*.
I wish Joe was / were here. Do you wish Joe were here?

We don't use *would* to express a wish about the present.
NOT ~~I wish Joe would be here.~~

To say that we regret something that happened in the past, we use *wish* + past perfect.
Karina wishes she had come on the trip with us. (She didn't come with us, and she now regrets that.)
I wish I hadn't said all those things.

If only

It is also possible to use *If only* + past perfect to express a regret about something that happened in the past.
If only we hadn't missed our bus.

If only + past simple is also used to express a wish for things to be different in the present. However, it is stronger than *wish*.
If only I was / were taller.
If only I didn't have such short legs!

1 **Complete the second sentences using *wish* + a negative or affirmative verb.**

1 James doesn't live in the countryside.
James ____________________ in the countryside.
2 Tamsin leads a stressful life.
Tamsin ____________________ a stressful life.
3 Daria isn't here with me.
I ____________________ here with me.
4 We gave away Dad's watch.
I ____________________ Dad's watch.
5 They didn't ask me to be in the team.
I ____________________ to be in the team.
6 You and Ian were late for the meal last night.
I ____________________ late for the meal last night.

2 **Choose the correct sentence endings.**

1 I've spent all my money. If only
a I saved it.
b I'd saved it.
2 Molly arrived late at school. If only
a she didn't miss her train.
b she hadn't missed her train.
3 I always speak to my French friend in English. If only
a I would speak French.
b I spoke French.
4 Julio didn't see his favourite band because they cancelled the concert. If only
a they hadn't cancelled the concert.
b they didn't cancel the concert.
5 Our two dogs wake me up early every day. If only
a they hadn't been so excitable.
b they weren't so excitable.
6 Caroline had a big lunch and couldn't go swimming. If only
a she hadn't had so much to eat.
b she didn't have so much to eat.

3 **Complete the sentences with *hadn't*, *didn't* or *wouldn't*.**

1 If we ____________________ told you about Nick, you ____________________ have found out.
2 I wish Mike ____________________ bought me such an expensive present. I feel a bit embarrassed.
3 Zoe sometimes wishes she ____________________ have a twin sister. It can be confusing for other people.
4 I'm thinking of buying this jacket, but I'm not sure. If only it ____________________ have those plastic buttons.
5 My dad ____________________ have met my mum if he ____________________ started learning German at evening classes.
6 If only you ____________________ told Clare about my problem. Now everyone knows.
7 If I ____________________ seen the evidence, I ____________________ have believed it.
8 Do you sometimes wish computers ____________________ exist?

8.3 Speculating about the past

We use the following forms to speculate about the past: *may have*, *could have*, *might have*, *must have*, *can't have*.

They are all followed by a past participle.

We use *may have*, *could have* and *might have* to talk about things that possibly happened in the past.
Paul's late. He may have / could have / might have got lost.

Must have and *can't have* have opposite meanings to each other. We use *must have* to speculate about things that we are certain were true or happened in the past. We use *can't have* to speculate about things that we are almost certain were not true or did not happen in the past.
Julie isn't here. She must have left early.
Jack has been at home all day. You can't have seen him in town.

Note that it is not possible to use *mustn't have* to speculate about the past.
NOT ~~You mustn't have seen him in town.~~

1 **Choose the correct words.**

1 Nobody has seen Jackie for about an hour. She **must** / **might** have left.
2 Paula always gets top marks in maths. She **mustn't** / **can't** have failed her maths exam.
3 Donna's been at home all morning. You **can't** / **could** have seen her in town earlier.
4 I **may** / **must** have spoken to your Aunt Jane, but I'm not sure.
5 It **might** / **must** have rained during the night, as all the roads are wet.
6 I don't know when Sam visited our house. It **can't** / **could** have been Tuesday, because Mum was at home for the whole day, and she didn't see him.

2 **Complete the sentences with *may have*, *might have*, *could have*, *must have* or *can't have*, and the past participle of the verbs in brackets. If more than one answer is possible, give all the answers.**

1 Our dog ran away only a minute ago, so he ____________________ (go) far.
2 I asked so many people to come to the party, I suppose I ____________________ (invite) Ben and Andy as well.
3 After Holly left David's house, she looked really upset. He ____________________ (say) something awful to her.
4 The eclipse happened earlier this morning. We ____________________ (miss) it.
5 Any pupils who were in or near the building at the time ____________________ (see) the burglars. If that's the case, please speak to a teacher.
6 When I heard that we'd won the lottery I thought that someone ____________________ (make) a mistake.

Grammar reference and practice 9

9.1 ■ Defining relative clauses

We use relative clauses to connect two ideas. A relative clause comes immediately after a noun.

Defining relative clauses give essential information about the noun. If we took out the relative clause, the sentence would not make sense. Relative clauses are introduced by relative pronouns and adverbs.

The relative pronoun *that* can refer back to a person or a thing. *Who* refers to a person, and *which* refers to a thing.
Tweeting is an activity which / that didn't exist ten years ago.
My sister is a person who / that is always sympathetic.

When combining two sentences, we do not repeat the subject or object of the relative pronoun.
There is the castle. I was telling you about it earlier.
→ There is the castle that I was telling you about earlier.
NOT ~~There is the castle that I was telling you about it earlier.~~

It is possible to leave out the relative pronoun *who*, *which* or *that* when it refers to the object of the relative clause, but not when it is the subject of the relative clause.
I need a laptop (which / that) I can carry around easily.
BUT I need a laptop which / that is light but durable.

The relative pronoun *whom* can be used instead of *who* in formal contexts to talk about a person when the person is the object of the relative clause.
The man who / whom they arrested is one of my neighbours.

We use the relative pronoun *whose* to refer back to a person or animal that possesses something, or for a relationship between two people.
I'd like to meet the man whose phone I found.
Is she the girl whose brother is a doctor?

It is possible to use the relative adverbs *when* and *where* to link ideas.

We use *when* to refer to a time at which something happened.
Do you remember the time when we all went on holiday together?

We use *where* to refer to a place in which something took place.
This is the shop where I bought my mobile.

Note that the relative pronoun *whose*, and the adverbs *when* and *where*, can't be followed directly by a verb.

1 Put the words in order to make sentences.

1 places / where / used to / several / There were / meet / we / .
______
2 has left / you / arrived with / boy / that / The / .
______
3 an animal / quite fast / is / which / elephant / can run / An / .
______
4 which / a town / cinemas / Bordley / is / two / has / .
______
5 recently / Is that / won / a prize / girl / who / the / ?
______
6 I'd / show you / like to / live / where we / the street / .
______

2 Complete the sentences with *which*, *who*, *where*, *when* or *whose*.

1 The people ______ we complained to were very sympathetic.
2 I wanted to buy a laptop ______ was reliable and inexpensive.
3 The man ______ door we first knocked on wasn't very helpful.
4 I need to find a shop ______ they sell gadgets and digital equipment.
5 He's really looking forward to the day ______ he learns to drive a car.
6 I'd like to introduce you to the man ______ life story I'm writing.

3 Choose the correct sentence in each pair. In two cases, both are correct.

1 **a** What did you do with the money that was in your bag?
b What did you do with the money which was in your bag?
2 **a** I can't remember the name of the boy whose idea it was.
b I can't remember the name of the boy that idea it was.
3 **a** Provincetown is the place where arrived the first ships from England.
b Provincetown is the place where the first ships from England arrived.
4 **a** This morning, I ran into someone I hadn't seen for a long time.
b This morning, I ran into someone that I hadn't seen for a long time.
5 **a** The file which was attached to Jody's email contained a virus.
b The file was attached to Jody's email contained a virus.
6 **a** Did you speak to the neighbour which took your ball?
b Did you speak to the neighbour who took your ball?

9.2 ▪ Non-defining relative clauses

Non-defining relative clauses also combine two ideas, but in a different way.

David and Chris have known each other since they started school. They are on the same course.
→ David and Chris, who have known each other since they started school, are on the same course.

Here, the relative clause, which is introduced by *who*, is between commas. The commas have a similar function to brackets. The non-defining relative clause gives additional information about the subject, rather than essential information. If the relative clause were taken out, the sentence would still make sense.

David and Chris [...] are on the same course.

We can use *which*, *when*, *where* and *whose* in non-defining relative clauses.

Just as for defining relative clauses, we do not repeat the subject or object when we combine two sentences.

I bought my mobile two years ago. It is already out of date.
→ My mobile, which I bought two years ago, is already out of date.

NOT ~~My mobile, which I bought it two years ago ...~~

We can't use *that* in non-defining relative clauses.

NOT ~~My mobile, that I bought two years ago, is already out-of-date.~~

A non-defining relative clause does not have to come between two other clauses. It can be followed simply by a full stop if it comes at the end of a sentence.

More details about the book are available from the publisher, whose website includes lots of interesting links.

Defining relative clauses are more common in spoken language, whilst non-defining relative clauses are more common in written language. When we speak, we usually pause before and after a non-defining relative clause.

My best friend, (pause) who moved to Canada last year, (pause) is coming over to visit me next month.

1 Choose the correct answers.

1 I've got a lot in common with Jed, ________
  a who he is a friend from Facebook.
  b who is a friend from Facebook.
2 We went to a market in Langton, ________
  a which isn't very far from Sam's home.
  b that isn't very far from Sam's home.
3 We're going to Joe's flat, ________
  a where is on the 15th floor.
  b which is on the 15th floor.
4 Dan's friend Rajesh, ________ wants to become an astronaut.
  a whose dad is a postman,
  b who his dad is a postman,
5 My great-grandmother, ________ was an amazing person.
  a who I met her only once,
  b who I met only once,
6 This football ground, ________ is being be sold.
  a where Darnholm United have played since 1901,
  b that Darnholm United have played since 1901,
7 Everyone had a fantastic time at Nick's party, ________
  a his parents paid for.
  b which his parents paid for.
8 Two hundred years ago, ________ this area was full of factories.
  a where this area was in the middle of the Industrial Revolution,
  b when this country was in the middle of the Industrial Revolution,

2 Combine both sentences to make a non-defining relative clause. Use a suitable relative pronoun or relative adverb.

1 David is a person you can trust completely. I've known him since we were at primary school.
____
2 That's Akari. She is in my class at school.
____
3 Mario got some new trainers. They were given to him for his birthday.
____
4 I'm meeting Charlotte Newton. Her brother Henry is the top scorer in the football team.
____
5 We went to Maynardale and had a picnic. There's a famous waterfall at Maynardale.
____
6 My mum recently bought herself an e-book reader. An e-book reader is more convenient than paper books.
____

10.1 ■ Participle clauses

Instead of using a full relative clause (defining or non-defining) to connect ideas, we can use a clause introduced by a participle. The participle can be an *-ing* form or an *-ed* form. These participles are known as present participles (*-ing* form) and past participles (*-ed* form).

A present participle replaces an active verb in the present.

I need to get a message to someone <u>who is getting</u> on the plane.
I need to get a message to someone <u>getting</u> on the plane.

We can also use the present participle to replace an active verb in the past.

Oliver, <u>who was worrying</u> about his exam results, didn't notice that his bus had just left.
Oliver, <u>worrying</u> about his exam results, didn't notice that his bus had just left.

The participle can only replace a relative pronoun when it refers to the subject of the relative clause, not the object.

Oliver, who I was worrying about, ...
NOT ~~Oliver, I worrying about, ...~~

The participle can replace *that, which* and *who*, but not *when*, *where* or *whose*.

The police stopped a small car that / which was carrying ten people.
The police stopped a small car carrying ten people.

A past participle replaces a passive verb, which can be in the present or past.

Bags of rubbish <u>which are left</u> on the pavement are causing problems.
Bags of rubbish <u>left</u> on the pavement are causing problems.
The book, <u>which was bought</u> online, was torn when I received it.
The book, <u>bought</u> online, was torn when I received it.

If the relative clause includes a negative verb, we simply put *not* in front of the participle, whether an active or a passive participle.

Oliver, who wasn't thinking about anything in particular, ...
→ Oliver, not thinking about anything in particular, ...
The book, which wasn't bought in a shop, ...
→ The book, not bought in a shop, ...

1 Choose the correct sentence. Sometimes both options are correct.

1 a My brother, appearing on stage for the first time with his band, looked nervous.
  b My brother, appeared on stage for the first time with his band, looked nervous.
2 a The cat, which looking very hungry, came to us.
  b The cat, looking very hungry, came to us.
3 a The people who attended the event arrived from far and wide.
  b The people attending the event arrived from far and wide.
4 a The event taking place on stage at the moment is really comical.
  b The event that is taking place on stage at the moment is really comical.
5 a David, not looking very interested, asked me if it was time to leave yet.
  b David, not looked very interested, asked me if it was time to leave yet.
6 a The clouds which were forming looked threatening.
  b The clouds formed looked threatening.

2 Replace the underlined words with the correct active or passive participle form.

1 The film, <u>which was described</u> by the director as a product of trial and error, was a huge success. ______
2 The person <u>who was chosen</u> to play the main role in the film was a little-known actor. ______
3 The catering service <u>which provided</u> the food was a local one. ______
4 People <u>that teach</u> very young children have a difficult and important job. ______
5 The words <u>that were spoken</u> by the actor were not the ones in the script. ______
6 Music festivals, <u>which are now held</u> all over the world, offer the chance to see world-famous performers on stage. ______

3 Rewrite the sentences using the correct participle form.

1 The man who is training my sister used to be a world-famous swimmer.
______
2 Some children who were standing nearby started laughing.
______
3 The event, which was attended by nearly 2,000 people, will be held again next year.
______
4 The drama company which is based in Shoreditch is called the Black Box Company.
______
5 The tree that was cut down by the council recently was over 200 years old.
______

10.2 ■ Determiners

We use the following determiners to talk about quantity: *(a) little, (a) few, some, any, much, many, a lot of, most, all, no, each.*

We use *some* and *any* before uncountable nouns or plural countable nouns to mean *a number of* or *an amount of.*

- We use *some* in affirmative sentences or in questions when making an offer.
  We've got some apples but we need some juice.
  Would you like some coffee?
- We use *any* in negative sentences and in questions.
  Did the supermarket have any chicken? No, and we haven't got any meat in the fridge either.

We use *much* and *many* in negatives and questions to talk about large quantities.

- We use *much* with uncountable nouns.
  'Have you got much rice?' 'No, and I haven't got much milk, either.'
- We use *many* with plural countable nouns.
  'Are there many glasses in the cupboard?' 'Yes, but there aren't many plates.'
- We generally use *a lot of* to talk about large quantities in affirmatives, for both uncountable and plural countable nouns. It is also possible to use *a lot of* in negatives and in questions.
  Ollie eats a lot of fruit and vegetables.

Most means *the majority of.* It can be used before uncountable and plural countable nouns.
Most meat is eaten on Sundays.
Most children prefer to start and finish school early.

We use *a little* and *a few* in negatives and questions to talk about very small quantities.

- We use *a little* with uncountable nouns.
  We only need a little pasta as we already have half a packet.
- We use *a few* with plural countable nouns.
  This meal would be healthier if you added a few vegetables.

When *little* and *few* are used without *a*, this often gives a negative impression.
The concert didn't go ahead because few people bought tickets. (few = not enough)
A few people asked me where they could buy tickets for the concert. (a few = several)
The meeting went on so long that there was little time for questions at the end. (little = not enough)
There was a little time at the end of the meeting for questions. (a little = some)

We use *all* and *no* before uncountable and plural countable verbs. We can use *all* before *the*, either with or without *of.*
All dancers have to look after their feet very carefully.
All (of) the dancers were very good.

No is followed by the noun, not by *the.*
No tea or coffee was available.

Each means *every single.* It is used before a singular noun.
She wore four earrings in each ear.

Every has a similar meaning to *each*, and is also used before a singular noun.
My brother's been to four festivals this year. He said that every festival was great.

Except for *a lot of* and *all*, the determiners listed above can't be used immediately before an article, pronoun or determiner such as: *a, an, the*; *my, your, his*; *this, these, those*; *you, it, them*, etc.

Instead, we add *of.* We use it to talk about a particular item or items.
Some of those people look younger than 16. (some people in a particular group)
Some people look younger than 16. (people in general)

No can't be followed by *of.* Instead, we use *none* (= *not one*) + *of.*
None of my friends wanted to go and see the band.
NOT ~~No of my friends ...~~
Every can't be followed by *of.*
NOT ~~Every of my brothers and sisters was born in May or June.~~

1 Choose the correct words.

1 It's very sad; **few / a few** people are interested in our particular charity.
2 We've got **few / a few** pounds between us, so we can buy a sandwich and a drink each.
3 The course was good but unfortunately there was **a little / little** opportunity to practise our new skills.
4 I think there's **little / a little** milk left in the fridge if you'd like a cup of tea.
5 For this trip, **all / each** student will receive a study pack.
6 The director said that **many / much** actors get nervous before they go on stage.

2 Complete the sentences with the determiners below. There are two words that you do not need.

■ all ■ a lot of ■ any ■ every ■ many ■ much ■ no ■ some

1 We haven't got ________ ice cream so Angela has gone out to the shop.
2 I'd like you to meet ________ friends from my school.
3 I phoned Cathy but there was ________ news about her sister's condition.
4 ________ time I try to call her, her phone is switched off.
5 Sorry, I didn't have ________ time so I couldn't get everything on the list.
6 Nadia said that ________ people didn't recognize her when she wore a hat.

Literature Insight 1 *Treasure Island* – Robert Louis Stevenson

Before you read

1 Read about Robert Louis Stevenson. How did he think of the idea for *Treasure Island*?
2 Read the background to the story on page 105. Where does Jim Hawkins live?

About the author

Robert Louis Stevenson
Born: 1850 in Edinburgh, Scotland
Died: 1894

Important works: *Treasure Island* (1883), *The Strange Case of Doctor Jekyll and Mr Hyde* (1886), *Kidnapped* (1886)

Did you know? From when he was a small child Robert Louis Stevenson's health was not good. His mother kept him inside during the damp Scottish winter, so Robert spent a lot of time watching other boys play and he made up stories about them. Robert's father wanted his son to study engineering, but Robert chose to study law. He passed his exams, but never practised as a lawyer. He had only gone to university to please his father – he really wanted to be a writer.

Robert married an American woman called Fanny, who was ten years older than him and had three children.

In 1881, the family went on holiday to Scotland. It rained for weeks. Fanny's son Lloyd got bored and so he drew a map of an imaginary island. Inspired by the map, Stevenson began to write *Treasure Island*.

Robert Louis Stevenson loved travelling. In 1887, the Stevensons moved to New York and then to San Francisco. In 1888, they sailed around the Pacific. The climate was so good for Robert's health that they decided to stay. In 1889, he and his family arrived in the Samoan Islands. He built a house in Western Samoa and though he spent the rest of his life there, he continued to feel a deep love for Scotland's traditions and history.

1 **Read the extract from *Treasure Island*. Why do Jim and his mother open the chest?**

2 **Read the extract again. Answer the questions.**
1 What sound can Jim and his mother hear on the frozen road?
2 What does Jim take from the Captain's chest?
3 Where do Jim and his mother hide?
4 What do the pirates do when they reach the door of the inn?
5 What are they looking for?
6 Who do they think has taken the papers?

3 **SPEAKING** **Work in pairs. Answer the questions.**
1 Imagine you have just found a chest. Are you going to open it or leave it? Why?
2 If you found treasure, would you keep it for yourself or would you share it? Who would you share it with? What would you buy with your treasure?
3 Can you think of any famous pirates from books or films? What do they look like?

4 **Read what happens next. In the papers there is a map. What will Jim do now?**

Read on

Jim realizes that it's the map to Treasure Island. The treasure on that island once belonged to a famous pirate called Captain Flint, who buried it in a secret place on the island before his death. Other pirates are searching for the treasure, including the most dangerous pirate of them all: Long John Silver.

Jim wants to look for the treasure.

He leaves England, with his friends Doctor Livesey and Squire Trelawney, in the ship *Hispaniola*. However, he soon learns that there are pirates on the ship. They plan to steal the treasure and kill Jim and his friends.

Finally, they reach the island where Jim meets a strange man.

5 **LI.01 Listen to the next part of the story. Do you think that the man is a friend or an enemy?**

6 **LI.01 Listen again. Complete the sentences.**
1 The man moved very ____________ like an animal.
2 Jim ____________ that he had a pistol.
3 His ____________ was black from the sun.
4 He has been ____________ on the island for three years.
5 Pirates often left a man alone on an island to ____________ him.
6 If Ben can help Jim, Jim will give him ____________.
7 Jim thinks Ben is crazy because he tells Jim he's ____________.
8 When Jim speaks about Silver, Ben seems ____________.

7 **SPEAKING** **Work in pairs. Answer the questions.**
1 Why do you think Ben was marooned? Who marooned him?
2 Do you think Ben is really rich? Why / why not?
3 Imagine a modern day Treasure Island. Where is it? How do you get there? What is it like?

Writing

8 **You are on a desert island and you want to tell people about your life there. Write a message in a bottle. The title of the message is *Life on a Desert Island*. Use your notes from the previous speaking exercise and include the following information:**
- how you arrived on the island.
- what food you are eating.
- where you can find fresh water.
- the house you are building.
- how you tried to escape.

Background to the story

Jim Hawkins is an ordinary young boy. He lives with his parents at their inn, the *Admiral Benbow*, which is near the sea. Jim's life is peaceful until an old sea captain called Billy Bones arrives. He stays for a long time but he doesn't pay the money he owes them for the room.

Visitors who come to the inn are afraid of the old sea captain, but Jim isn't. Bones asks Jim to tell him if other sailors arrive. One day, a pirate called Blind Pew arrives at the inn and gives Billy a black spot – a circular card that is black on one side. Among pirates, the spot means approaching death, and as soon as Billy Bones looks at it, he falls down dead.

When Jim and his mother open the sea captain's chest to take the money he owes them, they hear pirates approaching.

Treasure Island

We were half-way through when I heard a sound that filled my heart with fear; the tap-tapping of the blind man's stick on the frozen road. Then it knocked against the inn door and we did not breathe. But then the tapping started again and slowly died away.

'Mother,' I said, 'take it all, and let's go before the blind man comes back with his friends.'

But my mother went on counting until we heard a low shout coming from the hill outside. 'I'll take what I have,' she said, jumping to her feet.

'And I'll take this for what I'm owed,' I said, and picked up the cloth of papers.

We ran from the inn and along the road to the village. It was dark but there was a full moon. We heard running feet coming towards us.

'Take the money and run on,' my mother said breathlessly. But I refused to leave her. Quickly, I pulled her off the road and down under a small bridge. There we hid, trembling.

Not a moment too soon. Seven or eight men were running past us. Three men ran in front, and I saw that the one in the middle was the blind man. Silently, I climbed back up to the road and lay in the long grass to watch what happened.

'Down with the door!' the blind man shouted.

Four or five of them broke down the door of the *Admiral Benbow* and ran inside. There was a shout: 'Bill's dead!'

The blind man swore at them. 'Look upstairs and find the chest!' he cried.

I could hear their feet on the stairs, then a voice shouting down to the blind man in the road outside: 'Pew! They've been here before us. The money's here but Flint's papers have gone!'

'It's those people of the inn – it's that boy!' shouted the blind man Pew. 'Search and find 'em.'

Just then there came the sound of horses and riders thundering along the road. It was heard by the men in the inn, and in a second they were out in the road, running into the darkness of the fields. They did not wait for blind Pew, who tried to follow them, tapping wildly with his stick. 'Johnny, Black Dog! You won't leave your old friend Pew, boys – not old Pew!'

He was still in the middle of the road when the horses thundered up to the inn. Pew turned with a scream, but he turned the wrong way, and ran straight into the first of the horses. The rider tried to save him, but failed. Down went Pew, under the horse's feet, with a cry that rang high into the night. It was all over in a few seconds, and Pew didn't move again.

From Oxford Bookworms Library Level 4: *Treasure Island* by Robert Louis Stevenson, retold by John Escott, 9780194791908

Literature Insight 2 *Silas Marner* – George Eliot

Before you read

1 Read about George Eliot. Why did she choose the pen name 'George?'
2 Read the background to the story on page 107. How does Dunstan Cass waste the money he borrows?

About the author

George Eliot (real name Mary Anne Evans)
Born: 1819 in Warwickshire, England
Died: 1880 in London, England

Important works: *Adam Bede* (1859), *The Mill on the Floss* (1860), *Silas Marner* (1861), *Middlemarch* (1872)

Did you know? George Eliot, born Mary Anne Evans, grew up in a strict religious family but led an unusual life. Her first job in London was as assistant editor of *The Westminster Review* and it made her financially independent. In London, she met journalist George Henry Lewes – they fell in love and she took Lewes's first name as her pen name for writing, because she feared that people would not be interested in serious novels written by a woman. The problem came when her first book, *Adam Bede*, became a success. A number of men said that they had written it and George Eliot had to tell the truth about her name.

Eliot was an intellectual woman and a radical author. She wrote about rural life in 19th-century England. She was not interested in writing about heroes, but in analysing the complicated minds of everyday people. Eliot wrote about ordinary people and the difficult decisions they often have to make. *Silas Marner* also teaches us about life in Victorian England. As industry developed and new factories were built in the cities, many people in the countryside felt left behind.

1 Read the extract from *Silas Marner*. Why does Dunstan sit by the fire?

2 Read the extract again. Choose the correct answers.

1 Dunstan sees ____________ on his way back to Raveloe.
 a children b someone c no one
2 The cottage is ____________.
 a bright and warm b small and cold
 c cold and dusty
3 A piece of ____________ is hanging from a key over the fire.
 a wood b fish c meat
4 Dunstan thinks Silas could be ____________.
 a dead b collecting meat c chopping wood
5 Dunstan finds the gold ____________.
 a under the bed b under the floorboards
 c behind the loom

3 SPEAKING Work in pairs. Answer the questions.

1 Why does Dunstan knock at the door of the cottage?
2 What does Dunstan think has happened to Silas?
3 What do you think Dunstan will do with the money?

4 Read what happens next. What do you think Silas Marner will do when he finds out that someone has taken his gold?

Read on

Silas Marner is not far from home when Dunstan Cass leaves with his gold. At first, Silas does not notice that there is anything different in the cottage, but when he takes up the floorboards to count the gold, he realises it's gone. Silas runs to the pub to tell everyone. The next morning the whole village knows about the stolen gold.

The Squire's eldest son Godfrey is also worried, because his brother Dunstan has not returned home. Dunstan is the only one who knows Godfrey's secret. Years ago, Godfrey fell in love with Molly, a poor girl, and they got married in secret. Godfrey no longer loves his wife and wants to marry Nancy Lammeter, who is very rich.

On New Year's Eve, there is a dance at the Squire's house. Godfrey asks Nancy for the first dance and as they dance he forgets all his problems.

Godfrey does not know that at that moment his wife Molly is walking along the snow-covered road towards the village and the Squire's house. She is carrying her sleeping child in her arms and she no longer cares that Godfrey is ashamed of her. Molly has decided to tell everyone that she is Godfrey's wife and that this is his child.

5 LI.02 **Listen to the next part of the story. Who goes into Silas Marner's cottage on New Year's Eve?**

6 LI.02 **Listen again and complete the sentences.**

1 It is evening and the time is ____________.
2 Molly is tired and she lies down on the ____________.
3 The child sees a ____________ which comes from an open door.
4 The villagers told Silas to stay awake until ____________ to have good luck.
5 Later, Silas thinks he can see ____________ by the fire.
6 His hand touches soft curls and not ____________ coins.

7 SPEAKING Work in pairs. Answer the questions.

1 Silas hopes that staying awake until midnight on New Year's Eve will bring him good luck. Are you superstitious? Which superstitions do you believe in?
2 Money is a central theme in *Silas Marner*. Read the proverbs about money. Do you agree with them?
 - Health is better than wealth.
 - The love of money is the root of all evil.

Writing

8 ***Silas Marner*** **is a story with a moral message; good people are rewarded and bad people are punished. Write an ending to the story. Think about:**

- what happens to Dunstan and the gold.
- what happens to Silas Marner and the child.

Background to the story

The story is set in the quiet village of Raveloe in 19th-century England. Silas Marner is a cloth weaver, who lives alone and has no family. He works seven days a week and his only pleasure is counting the gold he has saved.
The Squire of Raveloe has two sons, Godfrey and Dunstan. The eldest son, Godfrey Cass, has a secret wife and child. The youngest son, Dunstan Cass, is a dishonest man who borrows money and never pays it back. He gambles a lot and often gets into trouble. One afternoon, when Dunstan is passing Silas Marner's cottage, he remembers how everyone talks about the weaver's hidden gold.

Silas Marner

It was four o'clock in the afternoon, and the whole countryside was covered by a thick mist. Dunstan did not see anyone on his way back to Raveloe. He knew he was getting close to the old quarry, although he could not see the road in front of him. At last, he saw light coming from the weaver's cottage, and he decided to knock at the door. 'Why not ask the man for money now?' he thought.

But when he knocked loudly, there was no reply. And when he pushed the door, it opened. Dunstan found himself in front of a bright fire which showed every corner of the small living room. Silas Marner was not there. Dunstan was tired and cold, so he went quickly to sit by the warm fire. As he sat down, he noticed a small piece of meat cooking over the fire. It was hanging from a large door key.

'So, the old man's cooking meat for his supper is he?' thought Dunstan. 'But where is he? Why is his door unlocked? Perhaps he went out to fetch some wood for the fire, and fell into the quarry! Perhaps he's dead!' This was an interesting new idea. 'And if he's dead, *who inherits his money? Who would know that anybody had come to take it away?*' And the most important question of all – *'Where is the money?'*

Dunstan's excitement made him forget that the weaver could still be alive. He wanted Silas to be dead, and he wanted Silas's money. He looked round the cottage again. There was very little furniture, just a bed, the loom, three chairs and a table. Dunstan looked under the bed, but the money was not there. Then he noticed a place on the floor, near the loom, where the floorboards looked different. By pulling up one of the boards, he discovered Silas's hiding place. He took out the two heavy bags filled with gold, put the boards back and hurried to the door.

From Oxford Bookworms Library Level 4: *Silas Marner* by George Elliot, retold by Clare West, 9780194791847

Before you read

1 Read about Wilkie Collins. Why do many people think that *The Moonstone* is important?
2 Read the background to the story on page 109. Where was the Moonstone stolen from?

About the author

Wilkie Collins
Born: 1824 in London, England
Died: 1889
Important works: *The Woman in White* (1860), *No Name* (1862), *The Moonstone* (1867)
Did you know? Wilkie Collins grew up with a famous father, William Collins, who was a talented artist and member of the Royal Academy. When Collins was 11, his family moved to Italy where they lived for two years. Collins said that he learned more in Italy from the scenery, paintings and people than he ever learned at school. Collins studied law, but he didn't become a lawyer, as he wanted to be a writer.
The Moonstone was published in serial form in the magazine *All the Year Round* and readers of every social class loved it from the beginning. People even made bets about who the thief was. Many think that *The Moonstone* is the first true detective novel. Collins adapted the crime story, adding a detective and an unsolvable mystery, strange clues and a surprising ending. He developed a new way of writing. Instead of a central narrator who tells the story, there are several narrators who know something about the disappearance of the diamond. Many of the main characters are servants, which is unusual for a Victorian novel as servants usually appeared only in the background.
Wilkie Collins was a good friend of Charles Dickens. They met in 1851, through a friend, the artist Augustus Egg, and they remained friends until Dickens' death.

1 Read the extract from *The Moonstone*. What kind of letter does Limping Lucy give Franklin?

2 Read the extract again. Match sentences A–G to gaps 1–7 in the extract.

A It was a page of instructions:
B The sea was very low now.
C Inside they found a letter and a man's nightgown.
D He quickly searched for the chain and put his hand into the low water.
E 'What *do* you mean?'
F 'So Rosanna *was* hiding something after all.'
G Take your letter.

3 SPEAKING Work in pairs. Answer the questions.

1 Why doesn't Limping Lucy like Franklin?
2 The Shivering Sand is dangerous. Do you think that Franklin is brave or stupid to go there?
3 Do you think Franklin is innocent or guilty? Why?
4 How do you think Rosanna knows about the Moonstone?
5 What do you think happens next? Do you think Betteredge, the servant, will go to the police?
6 Read what happens next. What does the letter say?

Read on

Rosanna explains in her letter that she bought cloth and made a new nightgown in order to replace the one with the smear of paint. Franklin doesn't remember taking the diamond and when Franklin asks Betteredge if he has ever seen him walking in his sleep, he says that he has not. Franklin takes the letter and the nightgown to Mr Bruff, the family lawyer. They both agree that this explains Rachel's behaviour towards Franklin. She must think that he stole the diamond. Rachel refuses to meet Franklin, so he asks Mr Bruff to invite her to his home. The next day, Franklin surprises Rachel at Mr Bruff's house. At first, she accepts Franklin's kisses, but then she pushes him angrily away.

4 LI.03 Listen to the next part of the story. Do you think Rachel will believe Franklin?

5 LI.03 Listen again. Are the sentences true (T) or false (F)? Correct the false ones.

1 Rachel saw Franklin take the Moonstone.
2 Franklin remembers when he took the Moonstone.
3 At about twelve o'clock, Rachel got up to get a candle.
4 Franklin held the Moonstone in his left hand.
5 Rachel says that she has never liked Franklin.
6 Rachel wrote a letter to the police.

6 SPEAKING Work in pairs. Answer the questions.

1 Why do you think Rachel cries when she sees Franklin again?
2 Why do you think Franklin took the Moonstone?
3 What do you think happens at the end of the story?

Writing

7 You are Rachel and you have just met Franklin again. Write a diary entry. Include the following and your own ideas:

- what you saw at midnight.
- why you like your cousin Franklin.
- why you think he is / isn't the thief.
- what you think will happen.

Background to the story

The story begins in 1791, when John Herncastle steals a beautiful yellow diamond, the Moonstone, from the statue of a Moon God in India. The diamond used to be owned by priests and it carries a curse. Terrible things happen to people who steal the Moonstone. John Herncastle dies in 1848, and he leaves the diamond to his niece, Rachel Verinder. Her cousin, Franklin Blake, gives it to her on her 18th birthday. That same night someone steals the diamond. Rosanna, the housemaid, knows something, but then she kills herself. Rachel, who once loved Franklin, is now angry with him, and Franklin wants to know why. Franklin's servant, Betteredge, tells him that before she died, Rosanna left a letter for Franklin with Limping Lucy, a fisherman's daughter. Franklin and Betteredge go to the sea, to the fisherman's cottage, to read the letter and talk to Limping Lucy.

The Moonstone

'So you are Rosanna's murderer!' she said to him boldly.

[1] __________ asked Franklin angrily.

'Rosanna told me, "There are men who are worth dying for and Franklin Blake is one of them!" She took care of you and worried about you, but you never even noticed her. She was my dearest friend and you took her away from me! [2] __________ I hope that I never see you again.'

She threw the letter at Franklin and limped away noisily. Franklin opened Rosanna's letter and read it at once. [3] __________

Go to the Shivering Sand when the sea is low. Walk out to sea along the low rocks on the far side of the beach. When you can see the Yollands' cottage at the other side of the Shivering Sand, then lie down on the rocks and feel in the sand at the edge of the rocks. You will find a chain that is tied to the rocks. Pull the chain out of the sand.

Franklin gave the message to Betteredge to read. [4] __________ said Betteredge, 'The sea is going out now. Let's go straight to the Shivering Sand.' They soon reached the lonely beach. It was a fine spring day and the wet sand shone in the sunlight. [5] __________ Carefully, Franklin walked along the rocks and followed Rosanna's instructions. He knelt down and carefully felt at the edge of the rocks for the chain. As Franklin looked across the beach, he thought he could see Rosanna's ghost coming out of the sand to help him. [6] __________ He felt the chain and pulled it; a small black box appeared.

Franklin ran back to Betteredge with the box and they opened it at once. [7] __________

When they examined the nightgown more carefully, they found some paint on it. They remembered Sergeant Cuff's words; 'When you find the clothes that made the paint smear, you can find the diamond.'

They looked inside the nightgown to find who it belonged to. They saw the letters 'F.B.' Franklin had indeed discovered the truth about the Moonstone; although he did not remember the fact, he himself seemed to be the thief!

From Oxford Dominoes Level 3: *The Moonstone* by Wilkie Collins, retold by Merinda Wilson, 9780194248211

Literature Insight 4 *The Secret Garden* – Frances Hodgson Burnett

Before you read

1 Read about Frances Hodgson Burnett. Where did she live when she was 16?
2 Read the background to the story on page 111. Who does Mary find in a large bedroom in the house?

About the author

Frances Hodgson Burnett (née Frances Eliza Hodgson)
Born: 1849 in Manchester, England
Died: 1924 in the USA
Important works: *Little Lord Fauntleroy* (1886), *A Little Princess* (1905), *The Secret Garden* (1910)
Did you know? Like her characters, Frances Hodgson Burnett had a difficult childhood. Her father died and the family lost their money. In 1865, when Frances was only 16, her mother took her five children to the USA and they lived in a log cabin in Tennessee. When her mother died, Frances wrote stories for magazines to earn money for her brothers and sisters. In 1873, Frances married and had two sons and because she wanted them to look like the character in her novel, *Little Lord Fauntleroy*, she dressed them in velvet suits and made their hair curly.
By the time *The Secret Garden* was published in 1910, Frances had two homes. One was in Long Island, USA, and the other was Great Maytham Hall in Kent, England. She lived in Great Maytham Hall from 1898 until 1907, and this house became her inspiration for *The Secret Garden*. It was there that a robin helped Frances find the door to the walled garden, which was hidden by ivy. Frances worked in the garden, planted roses and wrote her books there.

1 **Read the extract from *The Secret Garden*. What happened to the garden when Colin was born?**

2 **Read the extract again. Put sentences a–h in the correct order 1–8.**

_____ **a** Mary wants the garden to be their secret.
_____ **b** The doctor is poor.
_____ **c** Mary thinks that the house has many secrets.
_____ **d** They can help the garden come alive again.
_____ **e** They need a boy who can push Colin in his wheelchair.
_____ **f** The servants always do what Colin wants.
_____ **g** Her cousin, Colin, says he is going to die.
_____ **h** Both Colin and Mary are ten.

3 **SPEAKING** **Work in pairs. Answer the questions.**

1 Do you think Mary will help Colin to get better? How?
2 What do you think happens next? Why does Mary think that Colin will feel better outside? Who will push the wheelchair?

4 **Read what happens next. What does Mary say to Colin?**

Read on

The servants are surprised when they find Mary and Colin together, and Dr Craven doesn't look pleased. At Colin's request, Mary visits him every day and the servants soon realise that Mary is good for him. Then one night, Mary hears terrible screams and Martha, one of the servants, tells her it's Colin. Mary runs with Martha to his bedroom and she shouts at him and tells him to stop screaming. Colin is so shocked that he stops – no one ever speaks to him this way. Then he tells Mary that there's something wrong with his back and that he's going to die. Mary looks carefully at Colin's thin, white back and she tells him that it's straight and there's nothing wrong with it. Colin believes her. He isn't afraid anymore and from that moment his life changes. He asks Mary to take him into the garden. So, one day, Mary and her friend Dickon take Colin outside in his wheelchair and push him into the secret garden.

5 **LI.04 Listen to the next part of the story. What does Colin see when he opens his eyes in the secret garden?**

6 **LI.04 Listen again. Match characters a–d to statements 1–10.**

a Colin **b** Mary **c** Dickon **d** Ben (the gardener)

1 _____ likes the warm outdoor air.
2 _____ explains where the key was.
3 _____ wants to get better and live forever.
4 _____ wants to go to the garden every afternoon.
5 _____ knows the names of all the plants.
6 _____ worries that his legs aren't very strong.
7 _____ notices an angry face looking over the wall.
8 _____ asks why Mary is in the garden.
9 _____ followed a robin to the secret door.
10 _____ is surprised to see Colin.

7 **SPEAKING** **Work in pairs. Answer the questions.**

1 What does Colin do until he's inside the garden?
2 When Colin is outside he feels a lot better. Can fresh air really affect your health? Why / why not?
3 Ben finds the children in the secret garden. What do you think he will do now?

Writing

8 **Imagine that you have found a secret place. Write an email to a friend and share the secret. Tell them:**

- where this place is.
- how you found it.
- why you like it.
- what you do there.
- how it makes you feel when you are there.

Background to the story

Mary is a selfish, bad-tempered English girl who lives in India with her parents. They don't spend any time with her, and because of her behaviour, Mary doesn't have any friends. There are lots of servants in the house in India and she's used to giving them orders. When Mary's parents die suddenly of cholera, she's sent home to England to live with her uncle in Yorkshire. The house is large, but Mary has nothing to do and no one to talk to. She chats to Ben, the gardener, and one day, Martha, who is a servant, tells Mary about the secret garden. Mary's aunt loved this garden and when she died, Mary's uncle locked the door and buried the key. The garden has been locked for ten years. One day, Mary finds a key. She's sure it's the key to the garden, but there is something else bothering her.
She can often hear someone crying in the house. The housekeeper, Mrs Medlock, tells her it's the wind, but one night Mary opens a door and finds a boy in a large bedroom. He's Colin Craven, her uncle's son.

The Secret Garden

'What a strange house this is!' said Mary. 'So many secrets! Does your father come and see you often?'

'Not often. He doesn't like seeing me because it makes him remember my mother. She died when I was born, so he almost hates me, I think.'

'Why do you say you're going to die?' asked Mary.

'I've always been ill. I've nearly died several times, and my back's never been strong. My doctor feels sure that I'm going to die. But he's my father's cousin, and very poor, so he'd like me to die. Then he'd get all the money when my father dies. He gives me medicine and tells me to rest. We had a grand doctor from London once, who told me to go out in the fresh air and try to get well. But I hate fresh air. And another thing, all the servants have to do what I want, because if I'm angry, I become ill.'

Mary thought she liked this boy, although he seemed so strange. He asked her lots of questions, and she told him all about her life in India.

'How old are you?' he asked suddenly.

'I'm ten, and so are you,' replied Mary, forgetting to be careful, 'because when you were born, the garden door was locked and the key was buried. And I know that was ten years ago.'

Colin sat up in bed and looked very interested. 'What door? Who locked it? Where's the key? I want to see it. I'll make the servants tell me where it is. They'll take me there and you can come too.'

'Oh, please! Don't – don't do that!' cried Mary.

Colin stared at her. 'Don't you want to see it?'

'Yes, but if you make them open the door, it will never be a secret again. You see, if only *we* know about it, if we – if we can find the key, we can go and play there every day. We can help the garden come alive again. And no one will know about it – except us!'

'I see,' said Colin slowly. 'Yes, I'd like that. It'll be our secret. I've never had a secret before.'

'And perhaps,' added Mary cleverly, 'we can find a boy to push you in your wheelchair, if you can't walk, and we can go there together without any other people. You'll feel better outside. I know I do.'

'I'd like that,' he said dreamily. 'I think I'd like fresh air, in a secret garden.'

From Oxford Bookworms Level 3: *The Secret Garden* by Frances Hodgson Burnett, retold by Clare West, 9780194791298

Before you read

1 Read about Jane Austen. Why couldn't she marry Tom Lefroy? Did she ever marry?
2 Read the background to the story on page 113. Why was the family home given to the girls' half-brother when their father died?

About the author

Jane Austen
Born: 1775 in Hampshire, England
Died: 1817

Important works: *Sense and Sensibility* (1811), *Pride and Prejudice* (1813), *Mansfield Park* (1814), *Emma* (1815)
Did you know? Although she wrote about romance and her novels end with the marriage of the hero and heroine, Jane never married. Her first love was Tom Lefroy, the nephew of a close friend. Tom's family wanted him to marry a rich woman, so he was sent to London to study law – far away from Jane. Finally, at the age of 27, a family friend called Harris Bigg-Wither asked Jane to marry him. She accepted the marriage proposal but changed her mind the next day. At that time marriage was seen as a way for women to get security and people were shocked when Jane refused to marry him.
Jane was shy about her writing and did not want servants or visitors to know what she was doing. The door to the room where she worked made a noise when someone opened it and she could quickly hide her work. Jane became a well-known writer, but she never became a public figure.

1 **Read the extract from *Sense and Sensibility*. Where do Marianne and Margaret go?**

2 **Read the extract again. Are the sentences true (T), false (F) or not given (NG)? Correct the false ones.**
1 Mrs Dashwood thinks the weather will change.
2 At first, the sky is cloudy and grey.
3 It starts to rain, but they have an umbrella.
4 They run down a hill and Marianne falls.
5 A gentleman, who is fishing, comes to help them.
6 He carries Marianne to the cottage and puts her down in the kitchen.
7 Elinor and her mother do not like this stranger.
8 The man asks if he can visit them the next day.

3 **SPEAKING** **Work in pairs. Answer the questions.**
1 What do Marianne and Margaret enjoy at the start of their walk?
2 Why do they start running? What happens then?
3 What is Mrs Dashwood's first impression of Willoughby?
4 Willoughby asks if he can call again the next day. What do you think will happen?

4 **Read what happens next. What do you think Willoughby says when he sees Marianne again?**

Read on

Willoughby spends every day in Marianne's company and she soon believes that he is the perfect man. Willoughby has never spoken of engagement but when Marianne gives him a lock of her hair, Elinor is sure that they are engaged.
However, things change when Colonel Brandon cancels a picnic and hurries to London. Then Mrs Dashwood, Elinor and Margaret return home and find Willoughby in the cottage and Marianne crying. Willoughby tells them that he has to go to London on business and in the days following his departure, Marianne can neither eat nor speak.
A few weeks later, Elinor and Marianne go to stay at a friend's house in London. Marianne writes to Willoughby, but she hears nothing from him until she and Elinor attend a party.

5 **LI.05 Listen to the next part of the story. What is Willoughby's secret?**

6 **LI.05 Listen again. Choose the correct answers.**
1 At the party Elinor sees Willoughby
  a having dinner.
  b talking to an elegant young lady.
2 Elinor tells Marianne
  a to talk to Willoughby.
  b to try and control her feelings.
3 When they speak to Willoughby
  a he ignores Marianne and speaks to Elinor.
  b he holds his hands out to Marianne.
4 Willoughby looks
  a ashamed.
  b bored.
5 When Willoughby returns to the elegant young lady
  a Marianne feels unwell and sits down.
  b Marianne leaves the party immediately.
6 Elinor realizes
  a that Willoughby still loves Marianne.
  b that Willoughby doesn't love Marianne anymore.

7 **SPEAKING** **Work in pairs. Answer the questions.**
1 Why do you think Willoughby ends his friendship with Marianne?
2 Who do you think the elegant young lady is?
3 What would you do if a friend ignored you at a party?

Writing

8 **Write an email to a friend. Tell them about a friendship which is over. Say:**
- who you used to be friends with.
- how long you had been friends.
- why your friendship ended.
- how you feel about it.

Background to the story

After the death of Mr Dashwood, his second wife and their three daughters, Elinor, Marianne and Margaret, are poor. This is because property passes from father to son, and their half-brother John and his horrible wife Fanny now own Norland, their home. John and Fanny are wealthy, but they refuse to help John's half-sisters and their mother. Mrs Dashwood and the girls remain at Norlands for a few months because a friendship has developed between Fanny's brother Edward and Elinor. Sir John Middleton, a relative, offers them a small cottage in Devon.
Their life is very different now. Practical Elinor and romantic Marianne do not expect to meet anyone who will want to marry them, but they soon meet the wealthy and unmarried Colonel Brandon who falls in love with Marianne.

Sense and Sensibility

One morning, Marianne and Margaret, taking no notice of their mother's and Elinor's warnings of rain, decided to walk on one of these hills. They climbed to the top, delighted to see blue sky between the clouds, and laughing at the wind that caught at their hair and clothes.

'Nothing in the world could be better than this!' called Marianne. 'What a pity Mama and Elinor did not come with us!'

But in a few minutes, the blue sky disappeared, the dark clouds gathered, and driving rain began to beat down on their faces. Surprised and disappointed, they were forced to turn back. Fortunately, they were not far from home; it was just a matter of running with all possible speed down the steep side of the hill which led to their garden gate.

At first, Marianne was ahead, but a false step brought her suddenly to the ground, and Margaret, unable to stop herself, carried on down the hill and through the garden gate.

A gentleman, who was out shooting, was walking up the hill when Marianne's accident happened. He put down his gun and ran to help her. She had hurt her ankle, and could not stand. The gentleman offered his assistance, and in spite of Marianne's protests, took her up in his arms and carried her down the hill. He took her straight into the house and placed her carefully on a sofa in the sitting room.

Elinor and her mother rose in astonishment as the stranger entered, carrying Marianne. While they both looked at him, secretly admiring his unusually handsome appearance, he apologized most politely for his rude entrance. Even if he had been old, ugly and vulgar, Mrs Dashwood would have been extremely grateful to him for taking care of her child, but the influence of his looks and elegance touched her deepest feelings. She thanked him again and again, and asked the name of the person to whom she owed so much. He replied that his name was Willoughby, his present home was at Allenham, and he sincerely hoped that she would allow him to call tomorrow to enquire after Miss Dashwood. Permission was immediately given, and he then departed, to make himself still more interesting, in the middle of a heavy shower of rain.

From Oxford Bookworms Level 5: *Sense and Sensibility* by Jane Austen, retold by Clare West, 9780194614429

Exam Insight 1

Listing

Listening

Exam strategy

- Read the sentences carefully before you listen to the recording. They will prepare you for what you are about to hear.
- The information in the text is in the same order as the statements about it.

1 EXAM TASK 🔊EI.01 Listen to a conversation with Jenny, a teacher. Choose the correct answer.

1 Jenny met Halina
 a on this trip. **b** on a previous trip.
 ç on the beach.
2 Halina is
 a a local mother. **b** an English teacher.
 c a young girl.
3 Halina's family
 a is very poor. **b** was on holiday.
 c lives in Manila.
4 Aid Asia provides
 a 100 pounds a year to Halina's family.
 b books, paper and pens for Halina's school.
 c assistance to children in Halina's village.
5 Jenny visited the village for
 a half of her holiday. **b** a few days.
 c a year.

Reading

Exam strategy

- Read the text through quickly to get a general idea of what it is about.
- Next read the questions so you know what information you are looking for.
- Then read the text again slowly and carefully to find the information.

2 EXAM TASK Read the text and choose the correct answers.

1 At first Darren Brady was not allowed into court because he was wearing
 a shorts. **b** a T-shirt.
 c women's clothes. **d** a uniform.
2 James Wedderburn thinks that
 a his clients should just wear what they like.
 b his clients' appearance is important.
 c the decision of the jury only depends on the facts of the case.
 d judges and juries pay no attention to how people look.
3 James Harlow likes his clients to appear
 a casual. **b** elegant.
 c different. **d** responsible.
4 What is the main idea behind the article?
 a If you are a criminal, you should hide who you are by wearing a suit in court.
 b Wearing suitable clothing shows respect for the court and the people in it.
 c What you wear won't make any difference to the court's decision.
 d The court wants to see you as a real person, so you shouldn't change your appearance.

APPEARING IN COURT

Imagine you are appearing in court. What should you wear to help persuade the judge and jury that you are not guilty? Your usual clothes or something casual and comfortable? Something very smart or something sporty?

Last week, at Oxford Crown Court, Darren Brady surprised court officials by arriving in a skirt and blouse. Earlier in the day, wearing shorts and a short-sleeved shirt, he had been refused entry by uniformed security staff because he was 'not suitably dressed'. Brady walked round the corner to a local charity shop, bought a blue flowery skirt and a cotton blouse, and returned. 'It was 32 degrees,' he told reporters. 'I couldn't see what was wrong with shorts. I was hot.'

Even some of the lawyers that day found Brady's behaviour amusing. But would they recommend it to their clients? 'Absolutely not,' said James Wedderburn, of Buckley and Wedderburn. 'The judge and the jury will try to be fair, to listen to all the arguments, and to judge a case on the facts. But what they see will also influence their decision: your attitude towards the court, how you speak, your gestures and of course what you wear.'

In the US, a whole industry of court consultants has developed, especially around cases that get a lot of attention in the media. 'All sorts of things can make a difference to how people see you,' says James Harlow, a jury consultant. 'Jewellery, hairstyle, bright or dark colours, tie or no tie, all sorts of things.' Harlow recommends suits for both men and women. 'It's neutral,' he explains. 'An ordinary business suit suggests hard work and honesty. A person who wears a suit is not lazy and rich, nor are they living on the streets.'

'It's also a disguise,' he continues. 'It can hide things you don't want the court to know. A man or woman can step straight out of prison and put on a suit. Half an hour later in court nobody will have the slightest idea that this person already has a criminal record. I want the judge and jury to see my clients as "real people"; but I don't want them to see too much.'

What the suit also seems to say is: 'I understand the court and I believe in the law. I know what I'm supposed to wear and how I'm supposed to behave in here.' And that, in fact, may be the most important message that you can give to the judge and jury.

Use of English

Exam Strategy

- Skim the task to get the main ideas. Then, read each complete sentence to select the word to fill the gap.
- Re-read the entire task at the end to make sure it makes sense.

3 Complete the text with the correct options.

For the 1__________ of a lifetime, stay at the Eastern & Oriental hotel on Penang Island. Founded in 1885, the hotel has been the premier hotel in Penang for over 100 years.

We spent seven nights there in the most luxurious 2__________. All the rooms are suites with views either over the sea towards mainland Malaysia or looking across the rooftops of the old town. You can dine in the traditional 1885 restaurant or in the hotel coffee shop, one of the most famous in Penang.

There is everything here you would 3__________ from a top-class hotel: a swimming pool with a poolside restaurant, a gymnasium and full business 4__________ for those people unlucky enough not to be on holiday.

In addition to all this, the hotel is ideally 5__________ at the end of Penang Road. For tourists, the old castle and the state museum are a short distance away. Or you can walk down Penang Road, enjoying the sights and sounds of the shops, 6__________ delicious new tastes at the food stalls and restaurants, and finding oases of peace in churches, temples or mosques down quiet side streets.

1 a experiment b experience c situation d ultimatum
2 a path b design c style d way
3 a expect b look c take d invite
4 a activities b agencies c services d meetings
5 a populated b developed c settled d located
6 a meeting b discovering c producing d revealing

Speaking

Exam strategy

- Describe the photo with as much detail as possible. Use a wide range of vocabulary.
- Imagine you are talking to someone who cannot see the photo.

4 EXAM TASK Describe what you see in the photograph.

Exam strategy

- Answer each question with as much detail as possible.
- If the question asks for your opinion, choose one side and explain your reasons for your choice.

5 EXAM TASK EI.02 You will hear six questions. Listen to each question and then give your answer. Start speaking when you hear the tone.

6 What vocabulary might you need for talking about problems on a holiday?

airport security ▪ blanket ▪ check-in ▪ collection ▪ delay ▪ dissapointed ▪ lost ▪ relax ▪ seasick ▪ suitcase ▪ sunny ▪ ticket

7 EXAM TASK EI.03 You will hear four questions. Listen to each question and then give your answer. Start speaking when you hear the tone.

Writing

Exam strategy

- When writing an email, make sure you know who you are writing to and why. Answer each of the prompts.

8 EXAM TASK Read this email from a good friend. Write a reply email to Julie of about 100 words using your notes.

Answer this

Yes ... explain

Dear Alina,

I'm so excited for our upcoming beach holiday! I haven't had any time to prepare. What do I need to bring? Any formal clothes?

I know you have been making lots of plans for us. I really appreciate it. Will we be able to do any water activities? I really hope so – I don't want to just sit on the beach all day.

I'm really looking forward to this trip. My new job is just terrible and I need to get away.

See you soon!

Julie

Ask about this

Share your plans

Listening

Exam strategy

- Look at the three pictures before listening to the recording. What is different about them?
- Read the question carefully so you know what is being asked.

1 EXAM TASK 🔊 **EI.04 Listen to the recordings and choose the correct picture (A, B or C).**

1 A woman is calling a bike shop. How much will she pay for her bike rental?

A

B

C

2 Two friends are at the gym. Which class do they decide to take?

A

B

C

3 A friend is inviting Daniel to participate in a dance party fundraiser. What time will Daniel arrive at the event?

A

B

C

Reading

Exam strategy

- Read the descriptions first, noting the specific information about each one
- Next, read the profiles of the people and identify which is the best match.

2 EXAM TASK Five people are looking for a volunteer opportunity with a charity. Read the information about the people and the charities and choose the best charity for each person. Choose the correct answer (A, B or C) for questions 1–5.

CHARITIES

A Open Hearts Refugee Shelter. We receive over 100 refugees each month looking for shelter, food and legal assistance. Our guests come from all over the world, so being bilingual is an advantage. We are looking for volunteers to prepare meals and work in the laundry. We are open 24 hours a day, seven days a week. We ask that volunteers come the same day and time each week. We also need volunteers who can watch young children while their parents attend appointments Monday to Saturdays.

B Environmental Justice Now! We organize weekly protests around the city to demand change from businesses and governments on environmental issues. The days and times of these events vary; attend when you can. We always need help publicizing events, especially on social media. We are also looking for volunteers to participate in letter-writing and phone campaigns. You will contact government officials about pro-climate laws and regulations.

C Craft & Care. Our arts organization seeks creative types who enjoy working with special needs children. We run several after-school programmes around the city. Volunteers commit to one afternoon per week for the school year and must attend two training sessions before beginning work. You must be 21 years old and pass a background check. We also need a volunteer with reliable transport who can purchase and deliver the art supplies to the schools every Monday.

1 Mariana is a university student studying education. She wants to work with children. She attends classes on weekdays from 8 a.m. to 4 p.m. She has her own motor scooter.

2 Lionel, who works as a chef at a local Italian restaurant, is looking for a way to make a difference in the world. He works long hours in his job, and his schedule changes every week. He can borrow his flatmate's car when needed.

3 Jane is an elderly woman who enjoys meeting new people. She retired from her law career and has a lot of free time. Jane speaks Spanish and a little French, in addition to her native English. She relies on public transport.

4 Scott is an art lover who enjoys behind-the-scenes work rather than interacting with people. He owns his own IT business, where he works from Tuesday to Saturday. He has his own car.

5 Arwaa is a marketing specialist for a grocery store chain. She would like to use her skills to help a community organization. She works long hours during the week, but is available at weekends. She has her own car.

Exam Insight 2

Use of English

Exam strategy

- Skim read the text to find the topic and general meaning.
- Then, look at each gap and think of a single word that makes sense. Make sure your spelling and grammar are correct.
- Re-read the text to make sure it makes sense.

3 EXAM TASK Complete the text. Use one word for each gap.

WORLD HEART DAY

It is World Heart Day 1 ____________ 28th September and the theme this year is 'know your risk'. The main message is: It isn't difficult to reduce the possibility of getting heart disease. Some very simple changes to your lifestyle can actually 2 ____________ a considerable difference. The question is: what 3 ____________ these changes?

The Geneva-based World Heart Federation will use World Heart Day to stress the importance 4 ____________ a healthy lifestyle. Events will be held 5 ____________ over the world to promote the message that heart disease can be prevented. Free health tests will be provided in more than 100 countries. Major risk factors, such as high blood pressure, will be identified. There will also be walks, runs, concerts and sports competitions 6 ____________ raise money.

Speaking

Exam strategy

- Organize your ideas clearly. Explain your reasons with supporting details.

4 Read the exam task. Think about the vocabulary you need to describe each photo.

5 EXAM TASK 🔊EI.05 You have one minute to give a talk. First, read and listen to the task, and decide what you will say.

Your after-school club will participate in two community service projects this year. Pick two projects from the photos. Explain to your club members why they should choose these two projects.

Exam strategy

- Listen closely to the questions.
- As you answer, make sure you are using a range of vocabulary. Provide details and explanations.

6 EXAM TASK 🔊EI.06 You will hear six questions. Listen carefully and answer the questions after the tone.

Writing

Exam strategy

- Before you write an essay, make notes of your main points. Think of examples or explanations to support your points.
- Make sure you write about each point.

7 Look at the exam task. Think of at least two reasons to support your opinion.

8 EXAM TASK You have 25 minutes to write your essay. Write 100–160 words. You have been talking about protests in your English class. Your teacher has asked you to write an essay about this topic:

'Some people say teenagers are too young and inexperienced to fight for social change. Do you agree or disagree? Why / why not?'

Exam Insight 3

Listing

Exam strategy

- As you listen to and read the instructions, think about the context and what words you might expect to hear.
- During the first listening, listen for the main idea and choose the best option for each question. During the second listening, check your answers.

1 EXAM TASK 🔊EI.07 **For each question, choose the correct answer. You will hear an interview with psychologist Marilyn Hong.**

1 A common belief about shoplifters is that they
  a are teenagers impressing their friends.
  b have a mental illness.
  c are too poor to buy basic items.
2 When Dr Hong speaks about professionals, she means
  a experts helping people with shoplifting addictions.
  b shop owners concerned about shoplifting.
  c shoplifters who make a business from the items they steal.
3 Dr Hong works with patients who
  a don't tell anyone about their shoplifting experiences.
  b can't afford to pay for the items they shoplift.
  c think about stealing items before entering a shop.
4 When do Dr Hong's patients feel excited?
  a Before they shoplift.
  b While they are shoplifting.
  c After they shoplift.
5 What is usually most difficult for Dr Hong's patients?
  a Talking about their problem with shoplifting.
  b Recognizing their impulse to shoplift.
  c Replacing negative thoughts with positive ones.
6 Why did Karla start meeting with Dr Hong?
  a She wanted to control her impulses.
  b A judge required her to attend.
  c Her family asked her to get help.

Reading

Exam strategy

- Read the text and decide what situation it would appear in. Read the three options and look for the answer in the text.
- Compare your chosen option with the text again to make sure it is correct.

2 EXAM TASK For each question, choose the correct answer.

GIVEAWAY. Win these brand new headphones! Post your favourite song below to enter for a chance to win, then share this post with three friends who love music as much as you do.

1 **a** Three people who post will win headphones.
  b Three friends need to post their favourite songs.
  c The winner will post the name of a song.

Job Search

NEEDED: Experienced caregiver to help my elderly mother three days a week. Cooking, light cleaning and some driving to appointments. References required.

2 **a** Applicants must have worked previously with elderly people.
  b Applicants will take the woman to appointments three times a week.
  c Applicants have to clean the lamps in the home.

Leo: Join me at 5 a.m. at Fast Feet tomorrow? They have the new trainers and they open at 9! Matt

3 Matt wants Leo to
  a give him a lift to Fast Feet.
  b meet him early at Fast Feet.
  c buy trainers for him at Fast Feet.

Amazing coffee! Rich flavour, cool packaging design, and the sales go to the farmers, not to some giant corporation.
★★★★★ 5 STARS

4 The reviewer thinks the coffee
  a is delicious, but a little expensive.
  b benefits the people who make it.
  c comes in the perfect size.

DO NOT ENTER!

Shops on the second floor are accessible from the back car park only. Enter the first floor shops from the south entrance.

5 **a** Shops on the second floor are closed.
  b Shoppers need to park in the back car park.
  c Shoppers must go to a different entrance.

Use of English

3 Complete the phrasal verbs with the words below. Then match them to definitions a–d.

back ▪ in ▪ on ▪ out

1 print ______
2 get ______
3 put ______
4 sit ______

a enter a place or vehicle
b produce a paper document from a computer
c get comfortable and relax
d dress yourself in something

Exam strategy

- Read through the text quickly to get a general idea of what it is about. Then re-read each sentence.
- Concentrate on the words before and after each gap – they will help you complete the gaps.

4 EXAM TASK Read the text about a new gadget. Complete the text. Use one word in each gap.

THE MAGIC MIRROR

Do you ever have trouble buying jeans? You know, you try [1]______ one brand and they fit perfectly; then the same size in a different brand is a few centimetres too big, or too small.

Until now, the only solution to this problem has been to carry an armful of trousers in a variety of brands and sizes to the dressing room. Then you spend the next half an hour struggling in and out of them [2]______ find the ones you want. Sometimes, you just want to give [3]______ and go home!

Well, those days could soon be over. Scientists have developed a 'magic mirror', a 3D body scanner which will measure a man's or woman's body. All you have to do [4]______ get in the scanner. In just 12 seconds, the machine takes 300,000 measurements and creates a virtual image of you.

You can then sit back and watch while your on-screen image does the hard work of putting on the clothes. Once you have chosen the items you like, you pick them [5]______ and take them home, confident that you will look great.

This is the next big revolution in shopping – probably just until 3D printers are [6]______ advanced that you can download some new jeans and print them out.

Speaking

Exam strategy

- Talk about all of the visual prompts, including the advantages and disadvantages of each one. Don't reach your conclusion too quickly.

5 EXAM TASK EI.08 Your school received a £10,000 donation and is asking students how they should spend it. Here are some ways they could spend the money. Talk about the advantages and disadvantages of each, and then choose one as your final suggestion.

Exam strategy

- Give a full answer to the questions. Ask yourself the questions 'why?' and 'how?' to add more detail to your responses.

6 EXAM TASK EI.09 You will hear three follow-up questions. Listen carefully and answer the questions after the tone.

Exam strategy

- Answer each question with as much detail as possible. Explain your reasons for your choice.

7 EXAM TASK EI.10 You will hear six questions. Listen carefully and answer the questions after the tone.

Writing

Exam strategy

- Read the opening sentence carefully. Plan what you will write before you start.
- After writing, check your verb tenses, pronouns and vocabulary.

8 EXAM TASK Your teacher has asked you to write a story. Your story should be about 100 words and must begin with this sentence:

Sam picked up the wallet off the ground, opened it up and found €200 inside.

Exam Insight 4

Listening

Exam strategy

- You will hear each audio twice. Listen the first time for the gist, and choose an answer.
- On the second listen, confirm that your answer is correct.

1 EXAM TASK 🔊 **EI.11 Listen to recordings 1–5. Choose the correct answer.**

1 Why did the speaker change jobs?
  a to make more money
  b to have a permanent job
  c to learn new skills
2 The woman says that Tom
  a changed her life.
  b taught her fire eating.
  c told her to leave school.
3 The man's friend
  a studied literature with him at university.
  b has worked for three years in her job.
  c is climbing the management ladder.
4 The woman
  a writes funny articles for a national newspaper.
  b began in the advertising department of a newspaper.
  c has written for two different newspapers.
5 The man
  a didn't like his job at the law firm.
  b changed his mind about working with children.
  c was pressured by his family to go into law.

Reading

Exam strategy

- Read the text for the gist. Decide if any answer choices are obviously wrong.
- Then read the text more carefully to determine which of the remaining answer choices is correct.

2 EXAM TASK Read the texts and choose the correct answers.

1 According to the text, what is surprising about the *Paranormal Activity* film series?
  a The story is simple enough for all to understand.
  b The first movie was made at a very low cost.
  c It is based on a true story about a young couple.
  d Oren Peli did the editing and special effects.
2 Oren Peli
  a had another job while planning his film.
  b wanted to move to a different house.
  c asked others to help him with the editing.
  d planned to make seven films from the start.
3 What is the writer's intention?
  a To persuade readers to watch the films.
  b To inform readers how to make a horror film.
  c To evaluate the performance of the actors.
  d To explain the unusual origin of a film series.

SURPRISINGLY SUCCESSFUL

The movie *Paranormal Activity* is an amazing success story. The independent horror movie was filmed for $15,000, and has made over $193 million worldwide. And that's just the first movie in this series that now includes seven successful films.

The director, Oren Peli, didn't start out in the film industry. In fact, he was working full-time as a computer software engineer when he came up with the idea for the movie. He had moved to a new house, was living alone and was hearing strange noises during the night. Peli was a film-lover, but he had never worked a day on a film set, nor did he have any contacts in the movie industry. Nevertheless, he thought he could make a horror movie based on what happens in our houses while we sleep. He shot the film with actors in his own house over seven days. Peli says his background helped him with the editing and special effects. He was comfortable with computers and figured out the technical aspects easily.

The result was a simple yet frightening story. A young couple investigate some strange happenings by filming everything that happens in their house at night.

Peli never imagined that his idea for a movie would become the blockbuster series it now is. He was just using his creativity to tell a story that others found incredibly scary.

4 What was the problem in the writer's house?
  a There was water leaking out of the shower.
  b There was a hole in the ground outside the house.
  c There was a water leak outside the house.
  d The water company needed to move some pipes.
5 What does the writer think about dowsing?
  a It doesn't really work.
  b It isn't as good as radio waves.
  c It's an incredible skill.
  d It's too old to be of any use.

WHAT A MORNING!

I woke up this morning, wanting to have a shower, and there was no water in any of the taps in the house. I called the water company and they sent Brian. He told me there was probably a hole in one of the underground pipes leading into the house. 'They're old pipes,' he said. 'Sometimes there's movement in the ground and you get a hole and water starts leaking out.'

I wondered how he was going to find the leak. Hi-tech equipment? Radio waves? No, he went to the back of his van and came out with two short wooden sticks. He held one in each hand, with the sticks just touching at the end, and started walking backwards and forwards in front of the house five or six times. Then suddenly the sticks jumped in his hands and made a cross. 'That's where it is!' he said. And he dug a hole, found the leak and fixed it.

Honestly, what is going on? I mean, how can someone find water underground using a couple of old sticks? Of course, I looked it up on the internet. It's called 'dowsing', and it's an ancient skill. Good dowsers can find all sorts of things: water, oil, even gold. And they can make a lot of money. Scientists think they can prove scientifically that it doesn't work. But I saw it! And if it doesn't work, why would people pay dowsers lots of money to find things?

Use of English

Exam strategy

- Read the text for the main idea. Identify any choices that are clearly wrong.
- Check your answer fits logically as well as grammatically in the sentence.

3 EXAM TASK Complete the text with the correct options.

A spokesperson for Farnsworth Town Council publicly [1]____________ for destroying a valuable piece of art. Karen Wilde said: 'Our decision seemed [2]____________ at the time. If only we had known the artist was someone famous.' When the old department store in Camford Street was demolished last month, builders were amazed to find what looked like an enormous piece of graffiti covering up the entire wall of the residential building behind. The council was so eager to clean up any [3]____________ of vandalism that they did not consult any [4]____________ on who had created the painting and when. The wall was first sandblasted to remove the graffiti, then painted over in beige. The large-scale mural [5]____________ out to be the work of prominent expressionist painter Alastair Horgenson. He painted it in the early 1930s to [6]____________ the suffering of World War I. The department store was built in 1953, the year in which Horgenson himself passed away. Ms Wilde promised the town council she would set up a foundation in honour of Alastair Horgenson to support local street artists.

	a	b	c	d
1	explained	apologized	detailed	wondered
2	difficult	mistaken	logical	effective
3	factors	ways	parts	signs
4	experts	critics	defenders	accounts
5	resulted	found	turned	ended
6	recover	memorize	catch	remember

Speaking

Exam strategy

- Describe the photo in as much detail as possible. Imagine you are talking to someone who cannot see the photo.
- Use a wide range of vocabulary. If you don't know the exact word, it is okay to paraphrase (use other words to explain what you mean).

4 EXAM TASK Describe what you see in the photo.

Exam strategy

- Read and listen to the instructions carefully.
- Make sure you reply to all of the points in the exam task in your voicemail.

5 EXAM TASK EI.12 You have 40 seconds to leave a voicemail message. First read and listen to the task, and decide what you want to say. Start speaking when you hear the tone.

You want your friend to help you give a party. Leave a voicemail message for your friend. In your message you should:

- ask your friend to help you with the plans.
- describe the party, including the time and day.
- explain the specific tasks you need help with.

6 EXAM TASK EI.13 You have 40 seconds to reply to a voicemail message. First read and listen to the task, and decide what you want to say. Start speaking when you hear the tone.

Listen to the message from your friend about a decision she needs to make about university. Then, leave a voicemail message for your friend. In your message you should:

- congratulate your friend.
- ask some questions about her two choices.
- give her advice about what to do.

Writing

Exam strategy

- When writing an article, remember to give it a title.
- A good title attracts the attention of the reader, and clearly outlines what the text is about.

7 Read the exam task and choose the best title for your article. Why is it the best title?

- A summer to remember.
- The importance of a summer job.
- Make money this summer!

8 EXAM TASK You see this notice on an English language website. Write an article for the website.

ARTICLES

WANTED!

What tips do you have for helping other teenagers find paid work this summer?

Share your advice and experience.

Write a 100-word article about this topic and we will publish it on our website.

Listening

Exam strategy

- Remember, the statements won't always be the exact same words as the speakers' words in the recording. They may be paraphrased or implied.

1 EXAM TASK EI.14 You will hear two students talk about a documentary on graffiti. Match the opinion to the person who says it. Choose the correct answer (the woman, the man or both) for each statement (1–5). You have 30 seconds to look at the task.

1. Graffiti is done by angry young people. ________
2. Street art can be beautiful and creative. ________
3. City streets are the property of all citizens, not just property owners. ________
4. The city should not pay to remove graffiti from private property. ________
5. A street art tour is a great way to spend a weekend afternoon. ________

Reading

Exam strategy

- Read the whole text first to get the gist. Find key words in sentences A–G in the exam task.
- Look for related ideas before and after each gap to help you choose the right answer. Make sure the sentence fits grammatically and logically.

2 EXAM TASK Read the text. Some parts of the text have been removed. Match sentences A–G to gaps 1–6 in the text. There is one sentence that you do not need.

A Many people claim that Berners-Lee's greatest achievement is that the web carries no fees, no charges and no restrictions.

B His parents had met while working on the Ferranti Mark 1, the first commercially available computer.

C Its main purpose is to promote universal and fairly priced internet access

D In 2004 he was given a special honour for his pioneering work by Queen Elizabeth II and he became Sir Tim Berners-Lee.

E Visitors could also learn more about hypertext, find out how to create their own webpages, and how to search the web for information.

F Although the 'internet' already existed in some form, in those days it consisted of separate unconnected networks.

G He explains that he was just one of many people at the forefront of computer technology at the time.

TIM BERNERS-LEE

The GREATEST LIVING BRITON

Voted the Greatest Living Briton, Tim Berners-Lee was born in East Sheen, an unremarkable part of south-west London. He grew up in a family where computers and mathematics were seen as a fun, everyday part of life. [1]________ From an early age he picked up on their enthusiasm and recalls early conversations with his father about the potential of computers.

Berners-Lee left school to study at Queen's College, Oxford, where he built his first computer from an old television. Gaining a first-class degree in physics, he went into software development for a number of different companies, before finally ending up at CERN in Switzerland.

It was at CERN that the ideas which would make him famous began to take shape. [2]________ The different systems were unable to communicate with each other. He began to address this problem during his first period at CERN. But it wasn't until Berners-Lee returned there in 1984 that he was able to turn his ideas into reality.

By 1989, CERN had the biggest internet site in Europe. Berners-Lee's vision was that computers all over the world would be able to talk to each other using a language – hypertext – that he would create. In 1991, he put the first website online. This provided an explanation of the World Wide Web. [3]________ The rest, as they say, is history.

Berners-Lee is modest about his achievements. [4]________ He also feels that if he had not invented the web, someone else would have done. However, if that had been the case, the internet might have been something very different. It might, for example, not have been free. [5]________ John Poole of Image Computer Systems, who employed Berners-Lee in the 1970s, admires his position: 'What impresses me is that he was not in it for the money. His dream was a free interchange of information, and he stood by his principles.'

Berners-Lee left CERN in 1994 to set up the World Wide Web Consortium (W3C), an organization whose aim is to improve the quality of the web. It is also committed to maintaining the idea that the web should be free.

These days, Berners-Lee devotes much of his time to activities around the foundation he helped set up, the Alliance for Affordable Internet. [6]________ During the Covid-19 pandemic, the web allowed people to work, study and socialize from home. According to Berners-Lee, this has revealed the urgency for all people, regardless of their income or social status, to have access to fast, reliable internet. It's a cause he considers of utmost importance.

Exam Insight 5

Use of English

Exam strategy

- Skim-read the entire text first to get the general idea.
- Then, think of one word that can fill each gap.

3 EXAM TASK Read the text about a device and complete the text. Write one word for each gap.

You enter a concert hall. You're excited and already thinking of the photos you'll share with your not-so-lucky friends who didn't get tickets. You ¹__________ wait to post on Instagram to show the world that you were here.

Well, think again. As you enter, an assistant hands you a small bag, just a bit larger ²__________ your phone. You put your phone on silent and slip it into the bag, which locks with a magnet. You can keep the bag with you, but you can't open it. No videotaping, no photos, no social media. If you need to make a call or send a text, you exit to the lobby, tap the bag to an unlocking device, and take your phone ³__________.

Welcome to the world of Yondr, a product created to separate us from our smartphones and let us fully be in the moment. With Yondr, users are focused on the event. In addition, the performer's work is protected from being uploaded to YouTube for the world to see ⁴__________ free. Some schools have even got ⁵__________ board with Yondr and require students to lock their phones away during the school day.

Critics claim that Yondr separates users from a vital lifeline in case of an emergency. However, the schools and artists using Yondr think the benefits outweigh the negatives. Concert-goers are still undecided. If you can't post about a concert, ⁶__________ it really happen?

Speculating

4 Read the exam task. Think about the vocabulary you would need to talk about each picture.

Exam strategy

- Organize your ideas clearly. Explain your reasons.

5 EXAM TASK 🔊EI.15 You have one minute to give a talk. First read and listen to the task, and decide what you want to say.

You are going to give a talk to your English class about different kinds of dance classes.
Choose two photographs of classes you would like to take. Tell your class why you prefer taking these dance classes.
You have 30 seconds to think about what you want to say.

hip hop

ballet

Latin dancing

traditional folk dancing

Exam strategy

- Listen closely to the questions.
- As you answer, use a range of vocabulary. Provide details.

6 EXAM TASK 🔊EI.16 You will hear six questions. Listen carefully and answer the questions after the tone.

Writing

Exam strategy

- When writing an email, make sure you know who you are writing to and why.
- Answer each of the prompts.
- When you finish, re-read your email to check for clear organization, a variety of vocabulary and correct grammar.

7 EXAM TASK Read this email from an art project organizer and the notes you made. Write a reply of about 100 words.

because ...

answer this

From: Sophie Hebert, Project Organize

Re: Community Mural

Hello! We're so pleased that you've signed up to help paint our community mural on the wall of the old bank building. Before we can accept you as a volunteer artist, we need to know more about your experience with painting and also why you want to participate in this project.

You will need to bring your own supplies. We will provide lunch and drinks for all participants. Let us know if you have friends or family who would like to help out. We still need five more artists.

We look forward to seeing you next Saturday.

Best,

Sophie Hebert

Yes! My friend Jack

Don't have any! Ask about this

Setting goals is an important part of getting what we want out of life. The thing is, they need to be just the right level of challenge: achievable for us to be able to reach, but demanding enough to motivate us.

On the one hand, if the goal is too easy to achieve we are unable to get the sense of pride we're looking for when we finally reach our target. There's almost no point in being able to do what anyone else can do. We want to be unique and different and get the feel-good factor.

On the other hand, if we aim too high, there's a chance that we'll give up or lose interest. And that would leave us with a sense of failure. A task that is too big will leave us unmotivated and disappointed.

So choose your goals wisely and you'll get to where you want to be eventually!

1 Read the article. Are the sentences true (T) or false (F)? Correct the false ones.

1 Goals should be extremely challenging.
2 We feel pleased with ourselves even with small goals.
3 It's important to achieve something many others can't.
4 We become bored with things that are too tough.
5 Failure is the result of being overambitious.
6 If you choose carefully, goals can be met quickly.

2 Can you remember what the SMART acronym stands for? Complete the table.

1 Specific	What e__________ do you want to achieve and why?
2 M__________	How will you know when your goal has been reached?
3 Actionable	What is your p__________ of action?
4 R__________	Can you actually do this in the time you've given yourself?
5 Time-bound	When will you c__________ your goal?

3 Complete the sentences with the correct form of the verbs below.

achieve ▪ overcome ▪ set ▪ track ▪ use

1 I'm __________ my progress each week so that I can see how far I get.
2 Our boss has __________ us an unrealistic deadline.
3 The only way they __________ their goal was by having a plan and sticking to it.
4 The project has already had to __________ several problems the company didn't predict.
5 Clara __________ a tried and tested strategy for setting up a new business.

4 Look at the poster and choose the correct words.

GO FOR IT!

Motivation is the key to success, so why not join our weekly classes to discover the ingredients of success!

Don't be too [1]**ambitious / able / motivated** – think big, but start small.

[2]**Respect / Reward / Relax** yourself – do nice things for yourself when you achieve something.

Help each other – sharing plans with others can be [3]**amusing / foolish / motivating**.

[4]**Reflect / Visualize / Reach** your goal – imagine yourself after your success. What new [5]**risks / promotions / opportunities** will you have?

5 Think about a plan for your English language study over the next six months to a year. Use the SMART guide and the poster in exercise 4 to help you. Then design a poster with your partner about how to reach your goal(s). Think about:

- what your goal(s) is / are.
- what problems there might be.
- how you can measure your goal(s).

Assess your progress

	Mark (1–3)
1 What are three important things to consider? I can understand the elements of a realistic goal.	
2 Give three out of the five words from the SMART acronym and explain their meaning. I can understand the SMART acronym.	
3 Think of verbs which collocate with the following nouns. a deadline ▪ a goal ▪ a problem ▪ a strategy ▪ your progress I can use collocations related to setting goals.	

How can I improve?

PRESENTATIONS VIEW ALL >

You are going to make a presentation. You have spent time preparing what you have to say, making notes and practising in front of the mirror. You're almost there. Now for the slides. They're going to be a piece of cake in comparison, right? Well, not exactly. There's much more to consider than you might think. And it probably makes sense to create these as you write the presentation, rather than after it has been written. Slides go a long way towards supporting and adding value to what you're talking about. In this way, the message is clearer. Some of your audience will have a preference for visual information and others for spoken information. Therefore, you need to please both sets of people.

Think of slides not as an extra but as a central part of a presentation. They will not only help you organize a plan for your presentation, but also communicate your message in a better way.

1 Read the text and answer the questions.

1 What does the writer suggest people focus on when planning speeches in the first paragraph?
2 What do you think 'a piece of cake' means?
3 When is it a good idea to prepare slides?
4 In what ways do slides help a presentation?
5 What two types of audience member do you have to think about?
6 How important should slides be for someone preparing a presentation? Why?

2 What sort of thing do you need to look at when you are creating slides for a presentation? Tick (✓) the boxes.

1 audience ☐
2 colour ☐
3 paragraphs ☐
4 font ☐
5 background ☐
6 pictures and graphics ☐
7 volume ☐
8 bullet points ☐

3 Read the notes about visual aids and complete the table with the words below.

appearance ▪ appropriate ▪ clear font ▪ consistent ▪ effects ▪ graphics ▪ text and background ▪ uncluttered

Text
Choose a [1] ____________
Use bullet points

Colours
Use contrasting colours for the [2] ____________
Consider the meaning and emotional [3] ____________ of different colours

[4] ____________
Make sure they have a clear purpose
Don't include too many: keep slides simple and [5] ____________

Overall style and [6] ____________
This should be [7] ____________ for the topic, presentation and audience
Be [8] ____________: use the same font and colour on each slide

4 Choose the correct adjective to complete the sentences.

1 You don't need every slide to have a different style. Be **consistent** / **inconsistent**.
2 Your information has to be **legible** / **illegible** or the audience won't get the message.
3 If the slides look **neat** / **messy** they will be easy to read.
4 If anything is **clear** / **unclear** on the slides, the audience will ask questions.

5 Work in small groups. Choose a topic and create five slides for a mini-presentation.

1 Choose one of the following topics:
- Success at school
- Good use of free time
- Why sleep is important

2 Prepare your presentation together with your five slides.
3 Give your presentation.
4 Listen to the audience's feedback and advice.

Assess your progress

	Mark (1–3)
1 What are three ways slides can help a presentation?	
I can understand why slides are important.	
2 Think about things related to the following areas. ▪ colour ▪ overall style ▪ pictures ▪ text	
I can understand how to evaluate slides.	
3 What is the opposite of the following words? ▪ appropriate ▪ clear ▪ cluttered ▪ consistent ▪ legible	
I can use prefixes to make adjectives negative.	

How can I improve?

Global skills Understanding cultures

It was only when I studied abroad that I realized the importance of culture. Before that, growing up in the countryside, it wasn't something I had to think about very much. Most of us had the same kind of habits, language and customs. I only had to think about one way of life.

Then I got the chance to study in Italy for a few months. That really opened my eyes. Here was a place that wasn't that far from the UK as the crow flies but it did many things differently – from socializing to the way people spoke. I had a lot to learn and I'll admit that some things weren't easy. For a start, I got very hungry around six in the evening but had to wait until nine to eat!

What I didn't expect was that I would end up preferring some Italian habits when I went home. I have kept them in my life to this day. For example, English people tend to speak in an indirect way. Italians are much more direct. I prefer this as there is no miscommunication. You know exactly how someone feels. More importantly, it made me think about my culture as different, rather than better.

1 Read the article and answer the questions.

1 What first made the writer think about culture?
2 Why didn't the writer need to think about culture before this time?
3 What do you think 'as the crow flies' means?
4 What did the writer find difficult about Italian life?
5 What surprised the writer on his return?
6 How does he now view his own culture?

2 Complete the tips with the verbs below.

avoid ■ belong ■ learn ■ look ■ reflect ■ respect ■ treat ■ try

Message to all students

- Please remember to [1]________ other cultures.
- People [2]________ to different cultures and we can all [3]________ from each other.
- [4]________ at the similarities, not just differences.
- [5]________ on your own culture. How might it seem different to others?
- [6]________ to be flexible.
- [7]________ everyone as an individual and [8]________ stereotypes.

3 Read the sentences and choose the correct word.

1 People shouldn't **mind** / **generalize** about a culture.
2 Everyone has their own **values** / **stereotypes**.
3 The best thing to do is to **make** / **keep** an open mind.
4 **Individuals** / **Stereotypes** about a culture can be negative.
5 Many people are proud of their **cultural** / **open** identity.

4 Match words 1–6 to the correct definitions a–f.

1 halls of residence	a understand the good points about something
2 constantly	b without stopping
3 appreciate	c change
4 complex	d complicated
5 adapt	e accommodation for students
6 upset	f make someone unhappy

5 In groups, compare and contrast two cultures.

New Zealand	Switzerland
Languages: English, Maori	Languages: German, French, Italian and Romansh

1 Choose two of the topics or your own ideas. How are the ideas, attitudes and rules different or similar?
2 How do people from other cultures think differently about these two topics?
3 Present your ideas to the class.

Assess your progress

	Mark (1–3)
1 What can studying abroad teach you?	
I can understand the importance of learning about different cultures.	
2 Give two things to avoid doing with someone from another culture.	
I can understand what NOT to do when I meet new people.	
3 Explain the meaning of. ■ cultural identity ■ keep an open mind ■ values	
I can use words related to talking about culture.	

How can I improve?

Global skills Dealing with conflict

Are you the type of person who has an argument with someone and is still upset or angry about the situation days later? Or are you someone who is able to walk away from conflict or not let it spoil your whole week?

Researchers at Oregon State University, who interviewed over 2,000 people, found that when a person holds onto stress after an argument, it can have a big negative effect on their overall health. The results showed that it is much better for people to try to move on from a bad situation that has happened.

This also appeared to be age-related. People over the age of 68 were 40% less likely than people under 45 to continue to be stressed by a conflict. The reason is unclear, but it could be a result of life experience and having the ability to choose your battles.

Conflict is never going to disappear completely. However, being able to get on with people after an argument is clearly an important life skill for all involved.

1 Read the article and answer the questions.

1 What is the difference between the kinds of people in the first paragraph?
2 How does it affect a person if they remain stressed after a conflict?
3 What should people try to do instead?
4 According to the study, what age lets go of stress easier?
5 Does the writer suggest people should try not to argue?

2 Match tips 1–6 to the extra information a–f.

1 Keep calm.
2 Listen and ask questions.
3 Explain how you feel.
4 Focus on the 'common ground'.
5 Analyse the problem.
6 Look for a win-win solution.

a Try to communicate your emotions. Don't accuse or attack.
b Take some deep breaths, try to relax and think before you speak.
c Find a solution that you're both happy with.
d Think logically and break down what is making you disagree.
e When they speak show you are focussed on them. Don't assume you understand how they feel.
f Don't just look at how much you differ. You will usually have some shared ideas and goals.

3 Complete the conversation with the words below.

both ▪ explain ▪ feel ▪ how ▪ main ▪ shall

A I 1__________ frustrated when you don't clean the kitchen after meals.
B 2__________ we talk about it?
A Yes, that would be good.
B Can you 3__________ a bit more about it? I think we 4__________ want a clean house and I do other things around the house, like vacuuming.
A Yes, you do. The 5__________ issue is that I just don't want to do the same jobs all the time.
B So how should we share the jobs?
A 6__________ about we make a rota?

4 Work in pairs. Prepare a role-play which demonstrates how to handle the situation below.

Friend A: You want to go on a holiday with your friend as you've just finished school and will start work soon.
Friend B: You don't have any money and are upset that your friend keeps suggesting holidays you can't afford.

1 Analyse the situation.
2 Write your script.
3 Rehearse your role-play.
4 Now listen and comment on other groups' role-plays. How did they handle the conflict situation?

Assess your progress

	Mark (1–3)
1 What did the Oregon State University study teach us?	
I can understand why it's important to let go of conflict.	
2 Give three tips about how to handle a conflict with someone.	
I can understand how to deal with conflict.	
3 Think of a phrase to ▪ calm someone down ▪ explain how I feel ▪ find common ground ▪ suggest a solution	
I can express myself in a conflict.	

How can I improve?

In the job market these days there is a lot of competition. Why should someone pick you out of so many others? Here's how to stand out from the crowd.

1 Put in a good application. Take your time. If you rush it, you'll make mistakes and create a bad impression.
2 Dress well for the interview. First impressions count so dress for the job you want.
3 Plan your journey. You don't have to go into the interview ahead of time, but know where you're going and get there with time to spare.
4 Be friendly. The interviewer wants to know you are good with people. This isn't easy to do when you're nervous, but it's just as important as the questions.
5 Don't give up. Few get the first job they apply for. You might not be the best candidate for the job or you might need a bit more interview practice. It will all be worth it when you get that special phone call!

1 Read the text and answer the questions

1 What does 'stand out from the crowd' mean?
2 What happens if you're in a hurry?
3 What does the writer mean by 'look the part'?
4 What do you need to know about your journey?
5 Why do people find it hard to be friendly in interviews?

2 Look at some advice about how to answer interview questions. Choose the correct word to complete the sentences.

... STAR is a good way to remember how to give an interview question a clear, structured answer. *S* stands for [1]**solution / situation**: where did this event take place? *T* stands for [2]**trouble / task**: what was your [3]**result / goal** and how was it a challenge? *A* stands for [4]**action / answer**: what did you do to [5]**solve / make** the problem? Finally, *R* stands for [6]**result / research**: what happened in the end and what did you learn from this [7]**mistake / experience**? ...

3 Match words 1–5 to the correct definitions a–e.

1 role — a have the job of doing something
2 responsible — b knowledge of doing something
3 demonstrate — c makes you feel good
4 experience — d show
5 rewarding — e position

4 Choose the best word to complete the sentence.

1 Be ___________ interested in the job.
a genuinely b truly c quite
2 Use words like '___________ player' in your interview.
a group b team c only
3 It can be difficult to ___________ employers.
a greet b chat c impress
4 Ask friends or family to ___________ you feedback.
a make b give c help
5 Think about how you can ___________ your skills.
a support b demonstrate c find

5 Look at the job adverts. Work in pairs.

1 What skills are employers looking for?
2 Answer each question using the STAR structure.
3 Practise your answer in front of your partner.
4 Did you answer well? Why / why not?

Seeking summer camp activity leaders — Give an example when something went wrong at school or at home. How did you solve the problem?

Help wanted in busy café — Think of a time when someone complained to you. What did you do?

Assistant required for local vet — Give an example of how you work in a team. How did you help achieve your common goal?

Assess your progress

	Mark (1–3)
1 Give two points mentioned in the text about how to stand out.	
I can stand out from the crowd.	
2 What does STAR stand for?	
I can understand what STAR means.	
3 Explain the following words. ■ challenging ■ experience ■ responsible ■ rewarding	
I can use vocabulary related to applying for a job.	

How can I improve?

Unit 1

achieve (a goal) (v) /ə'tʃiːv/ to succeed in reaching a goal: *She has worked hard to achieve her goal.*

arrogant (adj) /'ærəgənt/ thinking that you are better and more important than other people: *I have little respect for people who are arrogant.*

assertive (adj) /ə'sɜːtɪv/ expressing your opinion clearly and firmly so that people listen to you or do what you want: *You should be more assertive.*

at the back (adv) /ət ðə 'bæk/ in the part or on the side of sth that is furthest from the front: *I sat at the back of the class.*

at the front (adv) /ət ðə 'frʌnt/ in the most forward part of sth; in the area that is just outside of or before sb / sth: *There is a small garden at the front of the house.*

attractive (adj) /ə'træktɪv/ (used about a person) beautiful or nice to look at: *He was attractive.*

beautiful (adj) /'bjuːtɪfl/ *The view from the top of the hill was really beautiful.*

behind (prep) /bɪ'haɪnd/ in, at or to the back of sb / sth: *There's a forest behind the house.*

Bermudas (n pl) /bə'mjuːdəz/ casual knee-length shorts: *I often wear Bermudas in the summer.*

blonde-haired (adj) /'blɒnd heəd/ with fair or yellow hair: *Both my sisters are blonde-haired.*

blue-eyed (adj) /'bluː aɪd/ with blue eyes: *What a beautiful blue-eyed baby!*

bob (n) /bɒb/ a style in which a woman's hair is cut short and to the same length all around the head so that it hangs above the shoulders: *Her hair was cut in a neat bob.*

broad-shouldered (adj) /brɔːd 'ʃəʊldəd/ having wide shoulders: *A lot of jackets don't fit me because I'm broad-shouldered.*

bun (n) /bʌn/ hair fastened tightly into a round shape at the back of the head: *She has a bun.*

camisole top (n) /'kæmɪsəʊl tɒp/ a women's loose top which is held up by shoulder straps: *She wears camisole tops and shorts in the summer.*

cardigan (n) /'kɑːdɪgən/ a warm piece of clothing, often made of wool, which you wear on the top half of your body; cardigans have long sleeves and fasten at the front, usually with buttons: *It was cold, so I put on my cardigan.*

cargo pants / trousers (n pl) /'kɑːgəʊ pænts, traʊzəz/ loose trousers that have pockets in various places, for example on the side of the leg above the knee: *Do you have these cargo trousers in a larger size?*

chic (adj) /ʃiːk/ fashionable and elegant: *I love your new coat – it's very chic!*

curly (hair) (adj) /'kɜːl/ full of curls; shaped like a curl (= a piece of hair that curves round): *He's got curly hair.*

deadline (n) /'dedlaɪn/ a point in time by which something must be done: *I prefer to work to a deadline.*

designer (adj) /dɪ'zaɪnə(r)/ having been made by a famous fashion designer: *I wear designer jeans.*

determined (adj) /dɪ'tɜːmɪnd/ having firmly decided to do sth or to succeed, even if it is difficult: *He is determined to leave school at 16.*

dyed hair n /daɪd heə(r) / to change the colour of something by using a special liquid or substance: *Dyed hair is common among punk musicians.*

easy-going (adj) /ˌiːzi 'gəʊɪŋ/ (used about a person) calm, relaxed and not easily worried or upset by what other people do: *Her parents are very easy-going. They let her do what she wants.*

elegant (adj) /'elɪgənt/ attractive and of good style or design: *She was elegant in her new dress.*

emotional (adj) /ɪ'məʊʃənl/ having strong emotions and showing them in front of people: *He always gets very emotional when I leave.*

face (a problem) (v) /feɪs/ if you face a particular situation, you have to deal with it: *We need to talk about the problems faced by homeless people.*

fair-haired (adv) /ˌfeə 'heəd/ with light or blonde hair: *He's fair-haired and he's quite tall.*

fleece (n) /fliːs/ a type of soft warm cloth that feels like sheep's wool; a warm piece of clothing made from this cloth, which you wear on the top half of your body: *Are you wearing a fleece today?*

goal (n) /gəʊl/ something that you hope to achieve: *You need to set yourself some long-term goals.*

handsome (adv) /'hænsəm/ (often used about a man) attractive: *He's a handsome man in his twenties.*

hoody (n) /'hʊdi/ a jacket or sweatshirt with a hood (= the part of a coat, etc. that you pull up to cover your head and neck in bad weather): *I took off my hoody because it was very warm.*

impression (n) /ɪm'preʃn/ an idea, a feeling or an opinion that you get about sb / sth: *What's your first impression of the new director?*

in front (of sth) (adv) /ɪn 'frʌnt/ further forward than sb / sth: *A car has stopped in front of the bus.*

in the (top / bottom / right-hand / left-hand) corner (adv) /ɪn ðə 'kɔːnə(r)/ in the part of a photograph near where two of the edges meet: *There's a dog in the top left-hand corner of the photo.*

in the background (adv) /ɪn ðə 'bækgraʊnd/ in the part of a view, scene, picture, etc., which is furthest away from the person looking at it: *You can see the hills in the background of the photo.*

in the foreground (adv) /ɪn ðə 'fɔːgraʊnd/ in the part of a view, scene, picture, etc. that appears closest to the person looking at it: *There are three children in the foreground of the photo.*

in the middle (adv) /ɪn ðə 'mɪdl/ in the part or position that is at about the same distance from the two ends or sides of sth: *There was a large table in the middle of the room.*

innovative (adj) /'ɪnəvətɪv/ created using new methods, ideas, etc.: *The car has an innovative design.*

joggers (n pl) /'dʒɒgə(r)z/ a warm pair of soft trousers that you wear for sports practice: *I wear joggers when I go running.*

lazy (adj) /'leɪzi/ (used about a person) not wanting to work: *Don't be lazy. Give me a hand!*

leggings (n) /'legɪŋz/ a piece of women's clothing that fits tightly over both legs from the waist to the feet, like a very thin pair of trousers: *She often wears leggings and a dress when it's cold.*

maxi dress (n) /'mæksi dres/ a piece of clothing worn by a girl or a woman; it covers the body from the shoulders to the ankles: *Maxi dresses were very trendy last summer.*

mini skirt (n) /'mɪnɪ skəːt/ a very short skirt: *Mini skirts first became popular in the 1960s.*

modest (adj) /'mɒdɪst/ not talking too much about your own abilities, good qualities, etc.: *He was very modest about his excellent exam results.*

on the right / left (adv) /ɒn ðə 'raɪt, ɒn ðə 'left/ at the side of sth that is mentioned: *There's a bank on the left and a church on the right.*

original (adj) /ə'rɪdʒənl/ new and different: *His work has a lot of original ideas.*

overcome (a problem) (v) /ˌəʊvə'kʌm/ to succeed in dealing with or controlling a problem that has prevented you from achieving something: *He finally managed to overcome his problem.*

overweight (adj) /ˌəʊvə'weɪt/ too heavy: *I'm a bit overweight – I might do more exercise.*

pale-skinned (adj) /peɪl skɪnd/ having skin that is light in colour: *She's tall and pale-skinned.*

plait (n) /plæt/ three or more long pieces of hair that have been crossed over and under each other to make one thick piece: *She often has a plait.*

polo shirt (n) /'pəʊləʊ ʃɜːt/ an informal shirt with short sleeves and a few buttons at the neck: *He wears polo shirts in the summer.*

ponytail (n) /'pəʊniteɪl/ long hair that is tied at the back of the head and that hangs down in one piece: *She wears a ponytail when she does sport.*

retro (adj) /'retrəʊ/ using styles or fashions from the recent past: *She dresses in a 1980s retro style.*

second-hand (adj) /ˌsekənd 'hænd/ already used or owned by sb else: *Second-hand cars are much cheaper than new ones.*

sensitive (adj) /'sensətɪv/ showing that you are conscious of and able to understand people's feelings, problems, etc.: *She always tries to be sensitive to other people's feelings.*

set (a deadline) (v) /set/ to choose a point in time by which something must be done: *We have set a deadline of 1st June to finish the work.*

shaved (head) (adj) /ʃeɪvd/ having had the hair removed: *The football player had a shaved head.*

short-sighted (adj) /ˌʃɔːt 'saɪtɪd/ able to see things clearly only when they are very close to you: *I wear glasses because I'm short-sighted.*

shy (adj) /ʃaɪ/ nervous and uncomfortable about meeting and speaking to people; showing that sb feels like this: *She's very shy with strangers.*

slim (adj) /slɪm/ thin: *She's a tall, slim woman.*

spiky (hair) (adj) /'spaɪki/ (about hair) sticking straight up from the head: *He has short, spiky hair.*

straight (hair) (adj) /streɪt/ not in a curve or at an angle: *She wore her long, straight hair loose.*

(use a) strategy (n) /'strætədʒi/ a plan for achieving a particular goal: *Which strategy are you going to use?*

stubborn (adj) /'stʌbən/ not wanting to do what other people want you to do; refusing to change your plans or decisions: *He's a very stubborn man.*

stunning (adj) /'stʌnɪŋ/ very attractive, impressive or surprising: *The hotel had a stunning view.*

stylish (adj) /'staɪlɪʃ/ fashionable and attractive: *She's a stylish dresser.*

sun-tanned (adj) /'sʌn tænd/ (used about sb's skin) brown as a result of spending time in the sun: *She's got beautiful sun-tanned skin.*

to the right / left (of sth) (prep) /tə ðə 'raɪt, tə ðə 'left/ on the side of sth that is mentioned: *There's a newsagent's to the right of the post office.*

track (your) progress (v) /træk ... 'prəʊgres/ to follow the progress or development of something: *Setting goals can help you track your progress.*

ugly (adj) /'ʌgli/ unpleasant to look at or listen to: *I thought her new jacket was ugly.*

unattractive (adj) /ˌʌnə'træktɪv/ not attractive: *Those new buildings are very unattractive.*

vest (n) /vest/ a sleeveless top: *He wore jeans and a vest.*

vintage (adj) /'vɪntɪdʒ/ in a style or fashion from the past: *We enjoy shopping for vintage clothes.*

wavy (hair) (adj) /'weɪvi/ having curves; not straight: *She had long, wavy hair.*

work towards (a goal) (phr v) /wɜːk tə'wɔːdz/ to try to reach or achieve a goal: *They are all working towards the same goal.*

Unit 2

adventure holiday (n) /əd'ventʃə(r) ˌhɒlədeɪ/ a holiday where you do outdoor sports such as rock climbing, canoeing, etc.: *We did lots of different sports on our adventure holiday in France.*

aisle (n) /aɪl/ a passage between the rows of seats on a plane, bus, etc.: *Do not leave suitcases or bags in the aisle.*

(go) ashore (adv) /ə'ʃɔː(r)/ onto the land from the sea, a river, etc.: *The passengers went ashore for an hour while the ship was in port.*

backpacking holiday (n) /'bækpækɪŋ ˌhɒlədeɪ/ a holiday where you go travelling with your clothes, etc. in a backpack: *We went on a backpacking holiday round Europe last summer.*

beach resort (n) /'biːtʃ rɪˌzɔːt/ a place near the sea where a lot of people go to on holiday: *We spent the summer at a beach resort in Spain.*

buffet car (n) /'bʊfeɪ kɑː(r), 'bʌfeɪ kɑː(r)/ part of a train where passengers can buy food and drinks: *The buffet car is situated at the rear of the train.*

cabin (n) /'kæbɪn/ a small room in a ship or boat, where a passenger sleeps; the part of a plane where the passengers sit: *You can only take small bags into the cabin of the plane.*

carriage (n) /'kærɪdʒ/ one of the separate parts of a train where people sit: *The train conductor asked people to move along to the next carriage.*

city break (n) /'sɪti breɪk/ a short holiday in a city: *We went on a city break to Rome last spring.*

coach tour (n) /'kəʊtʃ tɔː(r)/ a journey on a large bus that you make for pleasure, during which you visit many places: *They went on a ten-day coach tour around Scotland.*

connect (with) (v) /kə'nekt/ to form an association or relationship with sb else: *I use this forum to connect with people who share my hobbies.*

crossing (n) /'krɒsɪŋ/ a journey from one side of a sea or river to the other: *We had a rough crossing.*

Wordlist

cruise (n) /kruːz/ a holiday in which you travel on a ship and visit a number of different places: *They're planning to go on a cruise.*

cut through (sth) (v) /kʌt θruː/ to go across, etc. sth, in order to make your route shorter: *It's much quicker if we cut through the field.*

deck (n) /dek/ one of the floors of a ship or bus: *The restaurant is on the upper deck.*

DIY holiday (n) /ˌdiː aɪ ˈwaɪ hɒlədeɪ/ a holiday where you choose and book the accommodation, transport, activities, etc. yourself: *We decided to go on a DIY holiday so we could get the cheapest flights.*

drive (along) (v) /draɪv/ to go or take sb somewhere in a car: *I drove along the motorway.*

enthusiastic (adj) /ɪnˌθjuːziˈæstɪk/ full of excitement and interest in sth: *The kids are very enthusiastic about sport.*

escape the crowds (v) /ɪˌskeɪp ðə ˈkraʊdz/ to get away from a place where there are lots of people: *I found a quiet beach to escape the crowds.*

excursion (n) /ɪkˈskɜːʃn/ a short journey or trip that a group of people make for pleasure: *They're going on an excursion to the seaside.*

expedition (n) /ˌekspəˈdɪʃn/ a short journey that you make for pleasure: *My brothers went on a fishing expedition together.*

flight (n) /flaɪt/ a journey by air: *They met on a flight to Australia.*

gate (n) /ɡeɪt/ the place at an airport where you get on or off a plane: *Flight 139 to Bali is now boarding at gate 16.*

get off the beaten track (idiom) /ɡet ˈɒf ðə ˌbiːtn ˈtræk/ to go to a place where people do not often go: *We got off the beaten track and ate at a quiet local restaurant.*

get to know sb (v) /ˌɡet tə ˈnəʊ/ to meet sb and gradually find out more about them: *Alex's partner seems interesting. I'd like to get to know her better.*

head (for sb / sth) (v) /hed/ to move in the direction mentioned: *The ship was heading for the harbour.*

hold (n) /həʊld/ the part of a ship or an aircraft where goods are stored: *Five men were found hiding in the ship's hold.*

honeymoon (n) /ˈhʌnimuːn/ a holiday that is taken by two people who have just got married: *We went to Hawaii for our honeymoon.*

house swap (n) /ˈhaʊs swɒp/ an arrangement where two people or families move into each other's houses for a holiday: *We're doing a house swap with a family who live in Paris.*

land (v) /lænd/ to come down from the air or to bring sth down to the ground; to go onto land or put sth onto land from a ship: *The plane landed at Heathrow airport.*

lead (to) (v) /liːd/ (used about a road or path) to go to a place: *I don't think this path leads anywhere.*

luggage rack (n) /ˈlʌɡɪdʒ ræk/ a piece of equipment on a train, bus, plane, etc., that you can put bags, suitcases, etc. in or on: *I got on the train and put my bags in the luggage rack.*

motorway (n) /ˈməʊtəweɪ/ a wide road where traffic can travel fast for long distances between large towns: *I love driving on the motorway.*

national park (n) /ˌnæʃnəl ˈpɑːk/ a large area of beautiful land that is protected by the government so that the public can enjoy it: *We saw lots of wildlife in the national park.*

overhead locker (n) /ˌəʊvəhed ˈlɒkə(r)/ a small cupboard above the seats on a plane, used for storing bags, suitcases, etc.: *Please put your bags in the overhead locker.*

package holiday (n) /ˈpækɪdʒ hɒlədeɪ/ a holiday where the accommodation, travel, activities, etc. are arranged for you by a company: *We booked a package holiday in Spain.*

pier (n) /pɪə(r)/ a large wooden or metal structure that is built out into the sea from the land; boats can stop at piers so that people or goods can be taken on or off: *We boarded the boat from the pier.*

platform (n) /ˈplætfɔːm/ the place where you get on or off trains at a railway station: *Which platform does the train to York leave from?*

public transport (n) /ˌpʌblɪk ˈtrænspɔːt/ a system of buses, trains, etc. which can be used by the public: *Do you go to work by public transport?*

runway (n) /ˈrʌnweɪ/ a long piece of ground with a hard surface where aircraft take off and land at an airport: *The plane landed safely on the runway.*

seat belt (n) /ˈsiːt belt/ a long, narrow piece of cloth that is fixed to the seat in a car or plane and that you wear around your body, so that you are not thrown forward if there is an accident: *Fasten your seat belt!*

self-catering holiday (n) /ˌself ˈkeɪtərɪŋ ˌhɒlədeɪ/ a holiday where you stay in a house or flat and cook for yourself: *We're going on a self-catering holiday because hotels are too expensive.*

set sail (v) /set ˈseɪl/ to begin a journey by sea: *Columbus set sail for India.*

sightseeing holiday (n) /ˈsaɪtsiːɪŋ ˌhɒlədeɪ/ a holiday where you visit the sights of a of a city, etc. as a tourist: *I went on a sightseeing holiday to Rome.*

slow down (v) /sləʊ ˈdaʊn/ to start to move, do sth or happen at a slower speed; to cause sb / sth to do this: *Can't you slow down? You're driving too fast.*

soak up the sun (v) /ˌsəʊk ʌp ðə ˈsʌn/ to take off most of your clothes and sit or lie in the sun in order to enjoy its warmth, relax, get a tan (= darker skin), etc.: *I can't wait to soak up the sun in Goa.*

speed up (v) /spiːd ˈʌp/ to go or make sth go faster: *The traffic sped up on the motorway.*

stand (n) /stænd/ a place at a bus or coach station where a bus or coach stops so that people can get on and off: *The bus leaves from stand C.*

staycation (n) /ˌsteɪˈkeɪʃn/ a holiday where you stay at home, and relax or go on day trips: *We're just having a staycation this year.*

take off (v) /teɪk ˈɒf/ (used about an aircraft) to leave the ground and start flying: *The plane took off an hour late.*

take part (in sth) (v) /teɪk ˈpɑːt/ to join with other people in an activity: *We all took part in the discussion.*

take time out (to do sth) (v) /teɪk taɪm ˈaʊt/ to stop doing your usual activities for a short time, in order to relax, go on holiday, etc.: *I'm going to take time out to read a few good books.*

tour (n) /tʊə(r)/ a journey that you make for pleasure, during which you visit many places: *We went on a tour of Oxford.*

tour guide (n) /ˈtʊə(r) ɡaɪd/ a person who shows tourists or people who are travelling where to go: *She works as a tour guide in Venice.*

tourist trap (n) /ˈtɔːrɪst træp, ˈtʊərɪst træp/ a place that has been created to attract tourists and encourage them to spend money: *That gift shop is a tourist trap. Let's go to the museum instead.*

tracks (n pl) /træks/ the two metal rails on which a train runs: *The train stopped because there was a tree across the tracks.*

travel (down) (v) /ˈtrævl/ to go from one place to another, especially over a long distance: *The bus travelled down a long country road.*

travel destination (n) /ˈtrævl destɪˌneɪʃn/ a place that is popular with people who are going on holiday: *Travel destinations like Rome and Paris are often very busy.*

trek (n) /trek/ a long, hard walk, lasting several days or weeks, usually in the mountains: *We went on a trek for two weeks in the Himalayas.*

trip (n) /trɪp/ a journey to a place and back again, either for pleasure or for a particular purpose: *How was your trip to Turkey?*

voyage (n) /ˈvɔɪɪdʒ/ a long journey by sea: *The voyage took three days.*

wind (around) (v) /waɪnd/ (used about a road, path, etc.) to have a lot of bends or curves in it: *The path winds around the hills.*

working holiday (n) /ˈwɜːkɪŋ ˌhɒlədeɪ/ a journey where you help a charity or the local people in the place you are visiting: *She's going on a working holiday to help build a school in India.*

Unit 3

ability (n) /əˈbɪləti/ the mental or physical power or skill that makes it possible to do sth: *She has the ability to pass the exam, but she must work harder.*

amazed (adj) /əˈmeɪzd/ very surprised: *I was amazed by the change in his attitude.*

annoyed (adj) /əˈnɔɪd/ slightly angry: *He's annoyed with himself for failing the exam.*

appalled (adj) /əˈpɔːld/ feeling horror or disgust at sth unpleasant or wrong: *We were appalled by the poverty and starvation we saw everywhere.*

appropriate (adj) /əˈprəʊpriət/ suitable, acceptable or correct for the particular circumstances: *Now that the problem has been identified, appropriate action can be taken.*

astonished (adj) /əˈstɒnɪʃt/ very surprised: *I was astonished by the decision.*

backache (n) /ˈbækeɪk/ a pain in the part of the body between the neck and the bottom: *Dad had a backache after gardening all day.*

be down in the dumps (idiom) /bi ˌdaʊn ɪn ðə ˈdʌmps/ to be unhappy or sad: *She was down in the dumps because all her friends were on holiday.*

be on cloud nine (idiom) /bi ɒn ˌklaʊd ˈnaɪn/ to be very happy, pleased, etc.: *He was on cloud nine when he got his exam results.*

bruised (adj) /bruːzd/ having the blue, brown or purple marks that appear on the skin after you have fallen, been hit, etc.: *He had a bruised leg.*

bullet points (n pl) /ˈbʊlɪt pɔɪnts/ items in a list in a document, that are printed with a square, diamond or circle in front of them in order to show that they are important: *Please see the first and second bullet points on the first page.*

cheaply (adv) /ˈtʃiːpli/ for a low price: *You can travel quickly and cheaply all over the town by bus.*

chest pains (n pl) /ˈtʃest peɪnz/ unpleasant feelings in the top part of the front of your body: *I'm going to the doctor because I have chest pains.*

clearly (adv) /ˈklɪəli/ without doubt: *She clearly doesn't want to speak to you any more.*

commitment (n) /kəˈmɪtmənt/ being prepared to give a lot of your time and attention to sth because you believe it is right or important: *I admire her commitment to the basketball team.*

consistent (adj) /kənˈsɪstənt/ always behaving in the same way, or having the same opinions, standards, etc.: *We must be consistent in applying the rules.*

contrasting (adj) /kənˈtrɑːstɪŋ/ very different in style, colour or attitude: *The book explores contrasting views of the poet's early work.*

cough (n) /kɒf/ an illness or infection that makes you cough (= to send air out of your throat and mouth with a sudden loud noise) a lot: *Kevin's got a bad cough.*

cross (adj) /krɒs/ angry or annoyed: *I was really cross with her for leaving me with all the work.*

delighted (adj) /dɪˈlaɪtɪd/ extremely pleased: *She was delighted that she got the job.*

devastated (adj) /ˈdevəsteɪtɪd/ extremely shocked and upset: *They were devastated when their team lost the cup final.*

discipline (n) /ˈdɪsəplɪn/ the practice of training your mind and body so that you control your actions and obey rules; a way of doing this: *It takes a lot of discipline to study for three hours a day.*

disgusted (adj) /dɪsˈɡʌstɪd/ not liking or approving of sb / sth at all: *We were disgusted at the standard of service we received.*

dizzy (adj) /ˈdɪzi/ feeling as if everything is turning round and that you might fall: *I get dizzy in high places.*

excited (adj) /ɪkˈsaɪtɪd/ feeling or showing happiness and enthusiasm; not calm: *Are you getting excited about your holiday?*

extremely (adv) /ɪkˈstriːmli/ very: *Listen carefully because this is extremely important.*

feel blue (idiom) /fiːl ˈbluː/ to be sad or unhappy: *He'd been feeling blue all week.*

feel down in the mouth (idiom) /fiːl ˌdaʊn ɪn ðə ˈmaʊθ/ to be sad or unhappy: *I felt down in the mouth when you said you were leaving.*

feel on top of the world (idiom) /fiːl ɒn ˌtɒp əv ðə ˈwɜːld/ to be very happy: *Chris felt on top of the world when he got his new motorbike.*

frightened (adj) /ˈfraɪtnd/ afraid or scared: *Frightened children were calling for their mothers.*

furious (adj) /ˈfjʊəriəs/ very angry: *Kat was furious with Warren for losing the car keys.*

generosity (n) /ˌdʒenəˈrɒsəti/ the quality of being generous: *He thanked her for her kindness and generosity.*

happiness (n) /ˈhæpinəs/ a feeling of pleasure: *Money doesn't always bring happiness.*
headache (n) /ˈhedeɪk/ a pain in your head: *I've got a splitting (= very bad) headache.*
hurt (adj) /hɜːt/ upset and offended by sth that sb has said or done: *Madeleine was deeply hurt that she had not been invited to the party.*
incredibly (adv) /ɪnˈkredəbli/ extremely: *We have had some incredibly strong winds recently.*
itchy (adj) /ɪtʃi/ making you want to rub or scratch your skin: *My skin is all itchy.*
kindness (n) /ˈkaɪndnəs/ the quality of being kind; a kind act: *Thank you for your kindness.*
laziness (n) /ˈleɪzinəs/ the quality of not wanting to work: *I put his bad exam results down to laziness.*
legible (adj) /ˈledʒəbəl/ clear enough to read: *The signature was still legible.*
meaning (n) /ˈmiːnɪŋ/ the thing or idea that a sound, word, sign, etc. represents: *What's the meaning of this word?*
necessity (n) /nəˈsesəti/ something that you must have: *Clean water is an absolute necessity.*
numb (adj) /nʌm/ not able to feel anything; not able to move: *My fingers were numb with cold.*
painful (adj) /ˈpeɪnfl/ that causes pain: *My ankle is still too painful to walk on.*
petrified (adj) /ˈpetrɪfaɪd/ very frightened: *Phil is petrified of dogs.*
pleased (adj) /pliːzd/ happy or satisfied about sth: *Heather was very pleased with her new car.*
prosperity (n) /prɒˈsperəti/ the state of being successful, and having a lot of money: *Tourism has brought prosperity to many parts of Spain.*
purpose (n) /ˈpɜːpəs/ the intention, aim or function of something; the goal that something is supposed to achieve: *The purpose of the book is to provide a complete guide to the university.*
quickly (adv) /ˈkwɪkli/ fast; in a short time: *I'd like you to get here as quickly as possible.*
rapidly (adv) /ˈræpɪdli/ very quickly: *The quality of her work progressed rapidly.*
rash (n) /ræʃ/ an area of small red spots that appear on your skin when you are ill or have a reaction to sth: *He came out in a rash where the plant had touched him.*
really (adv) /ˈrɪəli/ very: *I'm really tired.*
runny nose (n) /ˌrʌni ˈnəʊz/ a nose that is producing too much liquid: *Their children always seem to have runny noses.*
scared (adj) /skeəd/ in a state of fear: *Are you scared of the dark?*
self-esteem (n) /ˌself ɪˈstiːm/ your opinion of yourself: *Richard has low self-esteem.*
self-reliance (n) /ˌself rɪˈlaɪəns/ the ability to manage without depending on help from anyone else: *Going to university teaches students self-reliance.*
self-sacrifice (n) /ˌself ˈsækrɪfaɪs/ giving up what you need or want in order to help others: *Rebuilding the country after war demanded hard work and self-sacrifice.*
shivery (adj) /ˈʃɪvəri/ shaking slightly, especially because you are ill: *I feel weak and shivery.*
shocked (adj) /ʃɒkt/ to feel upset, angry or surprised: *We were shocked by his death.*
sick (adj) /sɪk/ not well: *His baby is sick again.*
similarly (adv) /ˈsɪmələli/ in a way that is like sb / sth but not exactly the same: *The plural of 'shelf' is 'shelves'. Similarly, the plural of 'wolf' is 'wolves'.*
single-mindedness (n) /ˌsɪŋgl ˈmaɪndɪdnəs/ the quality of having one clear aim or goal which you are determined to achieve: *I admired her single-mindedness and her determination to win.*
sore (adj) /sɔː(r)/ painful: *My feet were sore from walking so far.*
sportsmanship (n) /ˈspɔːtsmənʃɪp/ the quality of being fair, generous and polite when you are playing a game or doing sport: *The players showed sportsmanship when they shook hands after the match.*
stamina (n) /ˈstæmɪnə/ the ability to do sth that involves a lot of physical or mental effort for a long time: *You need stamina to run a marathon.*
stomach ache (n) /ˈstʌmək eɪk/ a pain in the front part of your body below your chest and above your legs: *Prawns give me a stomach ache.*
surprised (adj) /səˈpraɪzd/ feeling or showing surprise: *I was very surprised to see Jim at the party.*
surprisingly (adv) /səˈpraɪzɪŋli/ *Surprisingly few people got the correct answer.*
swollen (adj) /ˈswəʊlən/ thicker or wider than usual: *Her ankle was swollen after she twisted it.*
team spirit (n) /ˌtiːm ˈspɪrɪt/ an attitude of loyalty (= continuous support) towards a group that you belong to, especially a group of people who you play sports with: *The group had plenty of team spirit.*
tiredness (n) /ˈtaɪədnəs/ the feeling that you need to rest or sleep: *Tiredness causes accidents.*
uncluttered (adj) /ˌʌnˈklʌtəd/ not containing too many objects, details or unnecessary items: *It's a tidy, uncluttered room.*
unhappy (adj) /ʌnˈhæpi/ not happy, sad: *She's terribly unhappy about losing her job.*
unwell (adj) /ʌnˈwel/ ill; sick: *You should go home if you are unwell.*
upset (adj) /ʌpˈset/ unhappy or worried: *She was looking really upset about something*
weak (adj) /wiːk/ (used about the body) having little strength or energy: *He was weak with hunger.*
worryingly (adv) /ˈwʌriɪŋli/ in a way that makes you think that sth bad might happen or has happened: *Worryingly, I can't find my house keys.*

Unit 4

address (issues / a problem) (v) /əˈdres/ to try to deal with a problem, etc.: *The government is finally addressing the issue of corruption.*
aid (poor people / developing countries) (v) /eɪd/ to help sb / sth: *The government paid for food and medicine to aid developing countries.*
believe in sth (v) /bɪˈliːv ɪn/ to think that sb / sth is good or right: *He doesn't believe in eating meat.*
belong to sth (v) /bɪˈlɒŋ tə/ to be a member of a group or an organization: *Do you belong to any political party?*
campaign (v) /kæmˈpeɪn/ to take part in a planned series of activities in order to make sth happen or to prevent sth: *Local people are campaigning for lower speed limits in the town.*
campaigner (n) /kæmˈpeɪnə(r)/ a person who takes part in a planned series of activities in order to make sth happen or to prevent sth: *He's an animal rights campaigner.*
care (about sb / sth) (v) /keə(r)/ to be worried about or interested in sth: *I only care about money.*
charity worker (n) /ˈtʃærəti ˌwɜːkə(r)/ a person who is employed by a charity (= an organization that collects money to help people who are poor, sick, etc. or to do work that is useful to society): *Shelters for stray dogs are run by charity workers.*
climate change (n) /ˈklaɪmət ˌtʃeɪndʒ/ changes in the Earth's weather, including changes in temperature, wind patterns and rainfall, especially the increase in the temperature of the earth's atmosphere that is caused by the increase of particular gases, especially carbon dioxide: *Some people blame climate change on pollution.*
co-exist (v) /ˌkəʊɪgˈzɪst/ to live or be together at the same time or in the same place as sb / sth: *Can different ethnic groups co-exist peacefully?*
compete (v) /kəmˈpiːt/ to try to win or achieve sth, or to try to be better than sb else: *The world's best athletes compete in the Olympic Games.*
competitor (n) /kəmˈpetɪtə(r)/ a person or an organization that is competing against others: *There are ten competitors in the first race.*
contaminate (v) /kənˈtæmɪneɪt/ to add a substance which will make sth dirty or harmful: *The town's drinking water was contaminated with poisonous chemicals.*
co-operate (v) /kəʊˈɒpəreɪt/ to work with sb else to achieve sth: *We are co-operating with a new firm on this project.*
deforestation (n) /ˌdiːfɒrɪˈsteɪʃn/ cutting down trees over a large area: *Deforestation is a major cause of global warming.*
devastate (v) /ˈdevəsteɪt/ to destroy sth or damage it badly: *The town was devastated by an earthquake.*
die out (v) /daɪ ˈaʊt/ to stop happening or disappear: *Dinosaurs died out millions of years ago.*
disease (n) /dɪˈziːz/ an illness of the body in humans, animals or plants: *Malaria is a disease.*
distribute (v) /dɪˈstrɪbjuːt/ to give things to a number of people: *They distributed emergency food supplies to the areas that were most in need.*
distributor (n) /dɪˈstrɪbjətə(r)/ a person or company that transports and supplies goods to a number of shops and companies: *The company is the main distributor of mobile phones in the area.*
donate (money / clothes) (v) /dəʊˈneɪt/ to give money or goods to an organization, especially one for people or animals who need help: *She donated a large sum of money to Cancer Research.*
donor (n) /ˈdəʊnə(r)/ a person who gives money or goods to an organization that helps people or animals: *The charity is supported by donors.*
drought (n) /draʊt/ a long period without rain: *The country had two years of severe drought.*
earthquakes (n pl) /ˈɜːθkweɪks/ sudden, violent movements of the earth's surface: *Thousands of people were left homeless by the earthquakes.*
evacuate (v) /ɪˈvækjueɪt/ to move people from a dangerous place to somewhere safer; to leave a place because it is dangerous: *Hundreds of people were evacuated from the war zone.*
famine (n) /ˈfæmɪn/ a lack of food over a long period of time in a large area that can cause the death of many people: *There is a severe famine in many parts of Africa.*
floods (n pl) /flʌds/ large amounts of water that have spread from a river, the sea, etc. and that cover an area which should be dry: *He was forced to leave his home because of the floods.*
fundraiser (n) /ˈfʌndreɪzə(r)/ a person whose job is to find ways of collecting money for a charity or an organization: *Would you like to work as a fundraiser for a charity?*
insist (on sth) (v) /ɪnˈsɪst/ to say strongly that you must have or do sth, or that sb else must do sth: *Dan insisted on coming too.*
interact (v) /ˌɪntərˈækt/ (used about people) to communicate or mix with sb, especially while you work, play or spend time together: *He is studying the way children interact with each other.*
international (adj) /ˌɪntəˈnæʃnəl/ involving two or more countries: *He came second in an international piano competition.*
manager (n) /ˈmænɪdʒə(r)/ a man or woman who controls an organization or part of an organization: *He is the manager of a shoe shop.*
organize (v) /ˈɔːgənaɪz/ to plan or arrange an event, activity, etc.: *The school organizes trips to various places of interest.*
organizer (n) /ˈɔːgənaɪzə(r)/ a person who plans or arranges an event, activity, etc.: *The organizers of the concert said that it had been a great success.*
overcrowded (adj) /ˌəʊvəˈkraʊdɪd/ (used about a place) with too many people inside: *The trains are overcrowded on Friday evenings.*
overflowing (adj) /ˌəʊvəˈfləʊɪŋ/ so full that the contents go over the sides: *The tap was left on and the bath was overflowing.*
participant (n) /pɑːˈtɪsɪpənt/ a person who takes part in sth: *Hundreds of participants joined the demonstration.*
participate (v) /pɑːˈtɪsɪpeɪt/ to take part or become involved in sth: *Students are encouraged to participate in the running of the college.*
pollution (n) /pəˈluːʃn/ the act of making the air, water, etc. dirty and dangerous; substances that pollute: *The rivers are full of pollution.*
poverty (n) /ˈpɒvəti/ the state of being poor: *Millions of people in this country live in poverty.*
preserve (v) /prɪˈzɜːv/ to keep sth safe or in good condition: *They've managed to preserve most of the wall paintings in the caves.*
promote (v) /prəˈməʊt/ to advertise sth in order to increase its sales or make it popular: *This cream is being promoted as a miracle cure for wrinkles.*

promoter (n) /prəˈməʊtə(r)/ a person who organizes or provides the money for an event: *The promoters believed that the party was a success.*

protest (against sth) (v) /prəˈtest/ to say or show that you do not approve of or agree with sth, especially publicly: *Students have been protesting against the government's decision.*

raise (money) (v) /reɪz/ to get money from people for a particular purpose: *We are doing a sponsored walk to raise money for charity.*

raise (awareness) (v) /reɪz/ to increase the level of sth or to make sth better or stronger: *The wristbands were sold to raise awareness of the campaign.*

reappear (v) /ˌriːəˈpɪə(r)/ to appear again or be seen again: *If any signs of the illness reappear, see your doctor immediately.*

rebuild (v) /ˌriːˈbɪld/ to build sth again: *Following the storm, many houses will have to be rebuilt.*

relocate (v) /ˌriːləʊˈkeɪt/ to move to a new place to live or to run a business: *My parents are relocating to the South of France.*

rely on sb / sth (v) /rɪˈlaɪ/ to need sb / sth and not be able to live or work properly without them or it: *The old lady had to rely on other people to do her shopping for her.*

semi-circle (n) /ˈsemisɜːkl/ one half of a circle; something that is arranged in this shape: *Please sit in a semi-circle.*

semi-permanent (adj) /ˈsemi ˈpɜːmənənt/ something which doesn't last forever, temporary: *We've decided to live in France on a semi-permanent basis.*

set up (sth) (v) /ˌset ˈʌp/ to start a business, an organization, a system, etc.: *The company has set up a new branch in Wales.*

sponsor (n) /ˈspɒnsə(r)/ a person who agrees to pay money to a charity if sb else completes a particular activity: *I need sponsors for a bike ride to Brighton in aid of Cancer Research.*

sponsor (v) /ˈspɒnsə(r)/ to agree to pay money to a charity if sb else completes a particular activity: *I'm running a marathon for charity – will you sponsor me?*

spread (v) /spred/ to affect a larger area or a bigger group of people; to make sth do this: *Rats and flies spread disease.*

support (a charity / a campaign) (v) /səˈpɔːt/ to help sb / sth by saying that you agree with them or it, and sometimes giving practical help such as money: *My company is supporting the project.*

supporter (n) /səˈpɔːtə(r)/ a person who supports a political party, sports team, etc.: *All the applause came from the politician's own supporters.*

survive (v) /səˈvaɪv/ to continue to live or exist in or after a difficult or dangerous situation: *Only three people survived the crash.*

transform (lives / a situation) (v) /trænsˈfɔːm/ to change sb / sth completely, especially in a way which improves sb / sth: *Having a baby has transformed my life.*

underdeveloped (adj) /ˌʌndədɪˈveləpt/ (used about a country, society, etc.) having few industries and a low standard of living: *She's helping to build schools in underdeveloped countries.*

unemployment (n) /ˌʌnɪmˈplɔɪmənt/ the number of people who are unemployed: *The economy is doing badly and unemployment is rising.*

urbanization (n) /ˌɜːbənaɪˈzeɪʃn/ the process in which areas of the countryside become part of towns and cities: *Animals' homes are being destroyed by urbanization.*

volcanic eruptions (n pl) /vɒlˌkænɪk ɪˈrʌpʃnz/ times when a mountain with a hole in the top throws out steam, lava (= hot melted rock), fire, smoke, etc.: *The volcanic eruptions covered the town in a layer of ash.*

volunteer (n) /ˌvɒlənˈtɪə(r)/ a person who offers or agrees to do sth without being forced or paid to do it: *Are there any volunteers to do the washing-up?*

volunteer (time / help) (v) /ˌvɒlənˈtɪə(r)/ to offer sth or to do sth which you do not have to do or for which you will not be paid: *He often volunteers for extra work because he really likes his job.*

wash sb / sth away (v) /ˌwɒʃ əˈweɪ/ (used about water) to carry sb / sth away: *The floods had washed away the path.*

work for charity (v) /ˌwɜːk fɔː(r) ˈtʃærəti/ to do work for an organization that collects money to help people who are poor, sick, etc. or to do work that is useful to society: *He's working for charity this summer.*

Unit 5

admit (to sth) (v) /ədˈmɪt/ to agree that sth unpleasant is true or that you have done sth wrong: *He refused to admit to the theft.*

approve (of sb / sth) (v) /əˈpruːv/ to be pleased about sth; to like sb / sth: *His father didn't approve of him becoming a dancer.*

armed robber (n) /ˌɑːmd ˈrɒbə(r)/ a person who steals from a place or a person using a weapon: *An armed robber held up the cashier at gunpoint.*

armed robbery (n) /ˌɑːmd ˈrɒbəri/ the crime of stealing from a place or a person using weapons: *Two men were found guilty of armed robbery.*

be responsible (for sth) (v) /rɪˈspɒnsəbl/ being the thing or person whose caused sth to happen: *Who was responsible for the accident?*

bias (n) /ˈbaɪəs/ a strong feeling in favour of or against one group of people, or one side in an argument, often not based on fair judgement: *There's a strong bias against drill music.*

blame sb (for sth) (v) /bleɪm/ to think or say that a certain person or thing is responsible for sth bad that has happened: *He blamed me for the accident.*

come up with sth (v) /kʌm ˈʌp wɪð/ to find an answer or a solution to sth: *Engineers have come up with new ways of saving energy.*

community service (n) /kəˌmjuːnəti ˈsɜːvɪs/ work helping people in the local community that sb does without being paid, either because they want to, or because they have been ordered to by a court as a punishment: *She was sentenced to three months of community service for vandalism.*

compulsory (adj) /kəmˈpʌlsəri/ that must be done, by law, rules, etc.: *Maths and English are compulsory subjects on this course.*

(take) control (n) /kənˈtrəʊl/ the power to make decisions about things: *He decided to take control over his own life.*

cultural identity (n) /ˈkʌltʃərəl aɪˈdentətiː/ the feeling of belonging to one or more cultural groups: *Living abroad has given me a clearer sense of my own cultural identity.*

deter sb (from doing sth) (v) /dɪˈtɜː(r)/ to make sb decide not to do sth, especially by telling them that it would have bad results: *The council is trying to deter visitors from driving in the city centre.*

disagreement (n) /ˌdɪsəˈgriːmənt/ a situation in which people have a different opinion about sth and often also argue: *It's normal for couples to have disagreements.*

disbelief (n) /ˌdɪsbɪˈliːf/ the feeling of not believing sb / sth: *'It can't be true!' he shouted in disbelief.*

dishonesty (n) /dɪsˈɒnɪsti/ the act of trying to make sb believe sth that is not true: *The footballer accused the referee of dishonesty.*

disrespect (n) /ˌdɪsrɪˈspekt/ a lack of respect for sb / sth that is shown in what you do or say: *Do not show disrespect towards your parents.*

fair (adj) /feə(r)/ treating each person or side equally, according to the law, the rules, etc.: *It wasn't fair on her to ask her to stay so late.*

fall out (with sb) (v) /fɔːl ˈaʊt/ to argue and stop being friendly (with sb): *Alan and Michael have fallen out. They aren't speaking to each other.*

forgive sb (for sth) (v) /fəˈgɪv/ to stop being angry towards sb for sth that they have done wrong: *I can't forgive him for his actions last night.*

gang violence (n) /ˌgæŋ ˈvaɪələns/ damage or harm caused to sb physically as a result of fights between groups of young people or criminals: *There is a lot of gang violence in that part of the city.*

generalize (v) /ˈdʒenrəlaɪz/ to assume that every person in a group is the same and not look at the details: *It would be foolish to generalize from a single example.*

get away with sth / doing sth (v) /get əˈweɪ wɪð/ to do sth bad and not be punished for it: *He lied, but he got away with it.*

get round to sth / doing sth (v) /get ˈraʊnd tə/ to find the time to do sth, after a delay: *I want to read that book but I haven't got round to it yet.*

have the right (to sth) (v) /ˌhæv ðə ˈraɪt/ to be allowed to do sth according to the law; to have a moral authority to do sth: *In Britain everybody has the right to vote at 18.*

illegal (adj) /ɪˈliːgl/ not allowed by the law: *It is illegal to drive a car without insurance.*

impact (n) /ˈɪmpækt/ the powerful effect that something has on somebody / something: *The book had a huge impact on me.*

inspiration (n) /ˌɪnspəˈreɪʃn/ a person or thing that makes you want to be better, more successful, etc.: *She became an inspiration and a role model for a new generation of women.*

internet fraud (n) /ˈɪntənet ˌfrɔːd/ (an act of) cheating sb in order to get money, etc. illegally, using the internet: *Have you ever been a victim of internet fraud?*

keep an open mind (v) /kiːp ən ˈəʊpən maɪnd/ to be prepared to accept new ideas: *Try to keep an open mind until you've heard all the facts.*

knife crime (n) /ˈnaɪf kraɪm/ illegal behaviour or activities in which knives are used as weapons: *There has been an increase in knife crime among young men since this time last year.*

legal (adj) /ˈliːgl/ allowed by law: *It is not legal to drive a car without insurance.*

life sentence (n) /ˈlaɪf sentəns/ the punishment by which sb spends the rest of their life in prison: *He was given a life sentence for murder.*

limiting (adj) /ˈlɪmɪtɪŋ/ putting limits on what is possible: *The rules about what shoes you can wear to school are very limiting.*

live up to sth (v) /lɪv ˈʌp tə/ to be as good as expected: *Children sometimes find it hard to live up to their parents' expectations.*

misbehaviour (n) /ˌmɪsbɪˈheɪvjə(r)/ to behave badly: *Paul was punished for his misbehaviour.*

misfortune (n) /ˌmɪsˈfɔːtʃuːn/ (an event, accident, etc. that brings) bad luck or disaster: *He has learned a lot from his misfortunes.*

mistreatment (n) /ˌmɪsˈtriːtmənt/ cruelty to a person or animal: *The owner of the zoo was accused of mistreatment of his animals.*

mugger (n) /ˈmʌgə(r)/ a person who attacks and steals from sb in the street: *The mugger was white, aged 18 to 20, and was wearing a dark jacket.*

mugging (n) /ˈmʌgɪŋ/ *The mugging took place around midnight.*

obligatory (adj) /əˈblɪgətri/ that you must do: *It is obligatory to get insurance before you drive a car.*

offence (n) /əˈfens/ a crime; an illegal action: *Deliberate damage to public property is a criminal offence.*

offender (n) /əˈfendə(r)/ a person who breaks the law or commits a crime: *Young offenders should not be sent to adult prisons.*

optional (adj) /ˈɒpʃənl/ that you can choose or not choose: *Optional extras with the car include electric windows and a CD player.*

own up (to sth) (v) /əʊn ˈʌp/ to tell sb that you have done sth wrong: *None of the children owned up to breaking the window.*

prison term (n) /ˈprɪzn tɜːm/ a period of time for which sb is in prison: *He faces a long prison term.*

prohibit sb / sth (from doing sth) (v) /prəˈhɪbɪt/ to say that sth is not allowed (by law): *English law prohibits anyone under 18 from buying cigarettes.*

prohibited (adj) /prəˈhɪbɪtɪd/ *Smoking is prohibited on this train.*

punish sb (for sth) (v) /ˈpʌnɪʃ/ to make sb suffer because they have done sth bad or wrong: *The children were punished for telling lies.*

put sth down to sth (v) /pʊt ˈdaʊn tə/ to believe that sth is caused by sth: *I put his bad exam results down to laziness rather than a lack of ability.*

put up with sb / sth (v) /pʊt ˈʌp wɪð/ to suffer sb / sth unpleasant and not complain about it: *I don't know how they put up with this noise.*

release sb (from sth) (v) /rɪ'li:s/ to allow sb to be free: *He's been released from prison.*
reputation (n) /ˌrepju'teɪʃn/ the opinion that people have about what somebody / something is like: *He has a bad reputation.*
restrictive (adj) /rɪ'strɪktɪv/ limiting; preventing people from doing what they want: *London has restrictive parking rules.*
rob sb / sth (of sth) (v) /rɒb/ to take money, property, etc. from a person or place illegally: *Several people on the train were robbed.*
rude (adj) /ru:d/ not polite: *She was very rude to me about my new jacket.*
sentence sb (to sth) (v) /'sentəns/ (used about a judge) to tell sb who has been found guilty of a crime what the punishment will be: *The judge sentenced her to three years in prison.*
shoplifter (n) /'ʃɒplɪftə(r)/ a person who steals sth from a shop while pretending to be a customer: *Shoplifters will be prosecuted.*
shoplifting (n) /'ʃɒplɪftɪŋ *He was arrested for shoplifting.*
speeding fine (n) /'spi:dɪŋ faɪn/ a sum of money that you have to pay for driving a car, etc. faster than the legal speed limit: *He received a speeding fine of £200.*
stereotype (n) /'steriətaɪp/ a fixed (and often false) idea that a lot of people have about a particular group: *He doesn't conform to the usual stereotype of the businessman with a dark suit and briefcase.*
stop sb / sth (from) doing sth (v) /stɒp/ to make sb / sth end or finish an activity; to prevent sb / sth from doing sth: *They've built a fence to stop the dog getting out.*
take account of sb / sth (v) /teɪk ə'kaʊnt ɒv/ to consider sth, especially when deciding or judging sth: *We'll take account of your comments.*
theft (n) /θeft/ the crime of stealing sth: *There have been a lot of thefts in this area recently.*
thief (n) /θi:f/ a person who steals things from another person: *A thief snatched her handbag containing her new mobile phone.*
treat (sb) as an individual (v) /tri:t 'sʌmbədi əz ən ˌɪndɪ'vɪdʒuəl/ to recognize that each person is unique: *Every child is treated here as an individual.*
value (n) /'vælju:/ a belief about what is right and wrong and what is important in life: *We need to be guided by our moral values.*
vandal (n) /'vændl/ a person who damages sb else's property on purpose and for no reason: *Vandals had wrecked the school hall.*
vandalism (n) /'vændəlɪzəm/ *There has been a marked increase in vandalism in recent years.*
voluntary (adj) /'vɒləntri/ done or given because you want to do it, not because you have to do it: *He took voluntary redundancy and left the company last year.*

Unit 6

advertising campaign (n) /'ædvətaɪzɪŋ kæmˌpeɪn/ all of the advertisements, posters, billboards, etc. that are created to promote a product or service at a particular time: *The advertising campaign for the new MP3 player was very popular with teenagers.*
banner (n) /'bænə(r)/ a long, narrow advertisement on a website: *There are too many banners on this web page.*
billboard (n) /'bɪlbɔ:d/ a large board near a road where advertisements are put: *There were several billboards on the main road into the city.*
brand image (n) /'brænd ˌɪmɪdʒ/ the general impression that a product, company, organization, etc. gives to the public: *Polluting the environment would damage the company's brand image.*
classified ad (n) /ˌklæsɪfaɪd 'æd/ a small advertisement that you put in a newspaper if you want to buy or sell sth, employ sb, find a flat, etc.: *If you need a babysitter, you could look at the classified ads.*
commercial (n) /kə'mɜ:ʃl/ an advertisement on TV or the radio: *This TV channel shows far too many commercials!*
considerable part of (n) /greɪt 'pɑ:t əv/ most of; the majority of: *She spent a considerable part of her life in Paris.*
consumer (n) /kən'sju:mə(r)/ a person who buys things or uses services: *Consumers should complain if they are not satisfied with the service they receive.*
design (n) /dɪ'zaɪn/ a decorative pattern: *These scarves come in a range of beautiful designs.*
design (v) /dɪ'zaɪn/ to plan and make a drawing of how sth will be made: *She designs the interiors of shops.*
display (n) /dɪ'spleɪ/ an arrangement of things in a public place for people to see: *The bakery had a beautiful display of cakes and biscuits.*
display (v) /dɪ'spleɪ/ to put sth in a place where people will see it or where it will attract attention: *Posters for the show were displayed at school.*
endorsement (n) /ɪn'dɔ:smənt/ a public statement that you give official support or agreement to a plan, statement, decision, etc.: *Celebrities are often paid to give endorsements of expensive products.*
experience (n) /ɪk'spɪəriəns/ something that has happened to you (often sth unusual or exciting): *She wrote a book about her experiences in Africa.*
experience (v) /ɪk'spɪəriəns/ to have sth happen to you; to feel: *It was the first time I'd ever experienced failure.*
flyer (n) /'flaɪə(r)/ a small sheet of paper that advertises a product or an event and is given to a large number of people: *He's handing out flyers for a new club.*
free samples (n pl) /ˌfri: 'sɑ:mplz/ small amounts of products that you don't have to pay for, which are given to you to test, try out, taste, etc.: *They're giving out lots of free samples to promote the new perfume.*
glossy magazine (n) /ˌglɒsi mægə'zi:n/ a type of large, thin book with a shiny paper cover that you can buy every week or month containing articles, photographs, etc. often on a particular topic: *There were adverts for the shampoo in all the glossy magazines.*
industry (n) /'ɪndəstri/ the people and activities involved in producing sth, providing a service, etc.: *The new high-tech industries are replacing manufacturing industries in many areas.*
influence (n) /'ɪnfluəns/ the power to affect, change or control sb / sth: *TV can have a strong influence on children.*
influence (v) /'ɪnfluəns/ to have an effect on or power over sb / sth so that he/she/it changes: *You must decide for yourself. Don't let anyone else influence you.*
insider knowledge (n) /ɪnˌsaɪdə(r) 'nɒlɪdʒ/ information that a person has who knows a lot about a group or an organization because they are a part of it: *His insider knowledge was very useful when he moved to a rival company.*
jingle (n) /'dʒɪŋgl/ a short tune that is easy to remember, often used in advertising: *That bank's jingle is very easy to remember.*
launch (v) /lɔ:ntʃ/ to start sth new or to show sth for the first time: *They've just launched a new car.*
logo (n) /'ləʊgəʊ/ a printed symbol or design that a company or an organization uses as its special sign: *The company logo was very modern.*
luxury goods (n) /'lʌkʃəri ˌgʊdz/ products that are beautiful and very expensive: *Luxury goods, such as perfume, are popular with rich tourists.*
(vast) majority (n) /mə'dʒɒrəti/ the largest number or part of a group of people or things: *This product is available in the vast majority of stores.*
manufacture (v) /ˌmænju'fæktʃə(r)/ to make sth in large quantities using machines: *The local factory manufactures furniture.*
market (n) /'mɑ:kɪt/ a country, an area or a group of people that buys sth; the number of people who buy sth: *The company is hoping to expand into the European Market.*
market (v) /'mɑ:kɪt/ to sell sth with the help of advertising: *It is marketed as a healthy snack.*
marketing agency (n) /'mɑ:kɪtɪŋ ˌeɪdʒənsi/ a company that creates advertising for other companies' products: *They hired a marketing agency to design the posters.*
massive (adj) /'mæsɪv/ very big: *He suffered a massive heart attack.*
(tiny) minority (n) /maɪ'nɒrəti/ the smaller number or part of a group; less than half: *Only a minority of students become involved in politics.*
modest (adj) /'mɒdɪst/ not very large: *She received a modest pay increase.*
overwhelming (adj) /ˌəʊvə'welmɪŋ/ extremely great or strong: *I had an overwhelming desire to go.*
persuade (v) /pə'sweɪd/ to make sb do sth by giving them good reasons: *It was difficult to persuade Tom to change his mind.*
pop-up ad (n) /ˌpɒp ʌp 'æd/ an advertisement that appears on your computer screen suddenly while you are browsing the internet: *This website has so many pop-up ads – they're really annoying!*
present (n) /'preznt/ something that you give to sb or receive from sb: *The toy was a lovely present.*
present (v) /prɪ'zent/ to show sth that you have prepared to people: *Good teachers try to present their material in an interesting way.*
profit (n) /'prɒfɪt/ the money that you make when you sell sth for more than it cost you: *We made a profit on our house when we sold it.*
promise (n) /'prɒmɪs/ a written or spoken statement or agreement that you will or will not do sth: *You should never break a promise.*
promise (v) /'prɒmɪs/ to say definitely that you will do or not do sth or that sth will happen: *She promised to phone every week.*
promote (v) /prə'məʊt/ to advertise sth in order to increase its sales or make it popular: *The new face cream is being promoted as a miracle cure for wrinkles.*
(large) proportion (adj) /prə'pɔ:ʃn/ a part or share of a whole: *A large proportion of the earth's surface is covered by sea.*
purchase (n) /'pɜ:tʃəs/ something that you buy: *These shoes were a poor purchase – they're falling apart already.*
purchase (v) /'pɜ:tʃəs/ to buy sth: *Many employees have the opportunity to purchase shares in their company.*
refund (n) /'ri:fʌnd/ a sum of money that is paid back to you, especially because you have paid too much or you are not happy with sth you have bought: *There's a hole here. Can I have a refund?*
refund (v) /rɪ'fʌnd/ to pay sb back a sum of money, especially because they have paid too much or they are not happy with sth they have bought: *Your travelling expenses will be refunded.*
research (n) /rɪ'sɜ:tʃ, 'ri:sɜ:tʃ/ detailed and careful study of sth to find out more information about it: *We are carrying out market research to find out who our typical customer is.*
research (v) /rɪ'sɜ:tʃ, 'ri:sɜ:tʃ/ to do detailed and careful study of sth to find out more information about it: *They're researching ways of reducing traffic in the city centre.*
retailer (n) /'ri:teɪlə(r)/ a person or company that sells goods to the public: *The supermarket has caused problems for local retailers.*
risk (n) /rɪsk/ a possibility of sth dangerous or unpleasant happening; a situation that could be dangerous or have a bad result: *The risks involved in the enterprise were considerable.*
risk (v) /rɪsk/ to do sth that may mean that you get into a situation which is unpleasant for you: *If you don't work hard now, you risk failing your exams.*
sample (n) /'sɑ:mpl/ a small number or amount of sb / sth that is looked at, tested, examined, etc. to find out what the rest is like: *The interviews were given to a random sample of shoppers.*
significant amount (n) /sɪgˌnɪfɪkənt ə'maʊnt/ a quantity or number of sth that is important or large enough to be noticed or to have an effect: *He donated a significant amount of money to the charity.*
slogan (n) /'sləʊgən/ a short phrase that is easy to remember and that is used in politics or advertising: *Anti-government slogans had been painted all over the walls.*
spam (n) /spæm/ advertising material sent by email to people who have not asked for it: *This email program can recognize spam and delete it for you.*

special offer (n) /ˌspeʃl ˈɒfə(r)/ a low price for sth in a shop, usually for a short time: *See below for details of our special offer.*

stealth marketing (n) /ˌstelθ ˈmɑːkɪtɪŋ/ the practice of promoting products in a way that does not appear to be advertising, such as by product placement (= showing products in films or television programmes): *Do you think stealth marketing is ethical?*

target (v) /ˈtɑːɡɪt/ to try to have an effect on a particular group of people: *The advertising campaign is targeted at teenagers.*

trend (n) /trend/ a general change or development: *He always followed the latest trends in fashion.*

trick (v) /trɪk/ to persuade sb to do sth by making them believe sth that is not true: *He tricked me into lending him money.*

whopping (adj) /ˈwɒpɪŋ/ (informal) very big: *He earns a whopping £200,000 a year.*

Unit 7

analyse a problem (v) /ˈænəlaɪz ə ˈprɒbləm/ to think about a problem logically and decide on the best solution: *We need to analyse the problem before trying to come up with a solution.*

argue (v) /ˈɑːɡjuː/ to say things, often angrily, that show that you do not agree with sb about sth: *I never argue with my parents about money.*

blink (v) /blɪŋk/ to shut your eyes and open them again very quickly: *Oh dear! You blinked just as I took the photograph!*

cheer (v) /tʃɪə(r)/ to shout to show that you like sth or to encourage sb who is taking part in competition, sport, etc.: *The audience clapped and cheered when the band came on stage.*

chewy (adj) /ˈtʃuːi/ (used about food) difficult to break up with your teeth before it can be swallowed: *This toffee is very chewy and sticky.*

conclude (v) /kənˈkluːd/ to form an opinion as the result of thought or study: *From the man's strange behaviour I concluded that he was unhappy.*

conclusion (n) /kənˈkluːʒn/ an opinion that you reach after thinking about sth carefully: *Have you reached any conclusions from your studies?*

consider (v) /kənˈsɪdə(r)/ to think about sb / sth in a particular way: *He considered the risk (to be) too great.*

creamy (adj) /ˈkriːmi/ containing cream; thick and smooth like cream: *He cooked some chicken in a creamy sauce.*

crumbly (adj) /ˈkrʌmbli/ easy to break into very small pieces: *This cheese has a crumbly texture.*

crunchy (adj) /krʌntʃ/ making a loud noise when crushed: *She ate a crunchy apple.*

decide (v) /dɪˈsaɪd/ to think about two or more possibilities and choose one of them: *There are so many to choose from – I can't decide!*

decision (n) /dɪˈsɪʒn/ a choice or judgement that you make after thinking about various possibilities: *Have you made a decision yet?*

detect (v) /dɪˈtekt/ to notice or discover sth that is difficult to see, feel, etc.: *I detected a slight change in his attitude.*

differentiate (v) /ˌdɪfəˈrenʃieɪt/ to see or show how things are different: *It is hard to differentiate between these two types of seed.*

distinguish (v) /dɪˈstɪŋɡwɪʃ/ to see, hear or recognize with effort: *I listened but they were too far away for me to distinguish what they were saying.*

entirely (convinced) (adv) /ɪnˈtaɪə(r)/ wholly or completely: *I'm not entirely convinced by your argument.*

exclaim (v) /ɪkˈskleɪm/ to say sth suddenly and loudly because you are surprised, angry, etc.: *'I just don't believe it!' he exclaimed.*

express (v) /ɪkˈspres/ to show sth such as a feeling or an opinion by words or actions: *I found it very hard to express what I felt about her.*

expression (n) /ɪkˈspreʃn/ the look on sb's face that shows what they are thinking or feeling: *He had a puzzled expression on his face.*

fairly (tasteless) (adv) /ˈfeəli/ quite, not very: *He is fairly tall.*

focus on the 'common ground' (v) /ˈfəʊkəs ɒn ðə ˈkɒmən ɡraʊnd/ to focus on the opinions, ideas and goals that are shared between different people: *It's important to try to focus on the 'common ground' when you don't agree on something.*

highly (beneficial) (adv) /ˈhaɪli/ to a high degree; very: *Their children are highly intelligent.*

impress (v) /ɪmˈpres/ to make sb feel admiration and respect: *She's always trying to impress people with her new clothes.*

juicy (adj) /ˈdʒuːsi/ containing a lot of juice: *She bought a bag of sweet, juicy oranges.*

keep calm (v) /kiːp kɑːm/ to not get excited, nervous or upset: *He always stays calm under pressure.*

look for a win-win solution (v) /lʊk fə(r) ə wɪn wɪn səˈluːʃən/ to try to find a solution that is good for everyone involved: *Let's look for a win-win solution that everyone will be happy with.*

lumpy (adj) /ˈlʌmpi/ full of or covered with lumps (= a piece of sth solid): *The sauce tastes nice but it's a bit lumpy.*

moist (adj) /mɔɪst/ slightly wet: *The chocolate cake was lovely and moist.*

notice (v) /ˈnəʊtɪs/ to see and become conscious of sth: *I noticed that he was driving a new car.*

oily (adj) /ˈɔɪli/ covered with oil or like oil: *This pasta is much too oily and slippery.*

peer (v) /pɪə(r)/ to look closely or carefully at sb / sth, for example because you cannot see very well: *He peered at the photo, but it was blurred.*

protect (v) /prəˈtekt/ to keep sb / sth safe; to defend sb / sth: *Parents try to protect their children.*

protection (n) /prəˈtekʃn/ the act of keeping sb / sth safe so that he/she/it is not harmed or damaged: *After the attack the man was put under police protection.*

react (v) /riˈækt/ to do or say sth because of sth that has happened or been said: *If she's rude I won't react. I don't want an argument.*

reaction (n) /riˈækʃn/ something that you do or say because of sth that has happened: *Could we get your reaction to the latest news, Prime Minister?*

realize (v) /ˈriːəlaɪz/ to know and understand that sth is true or that sth has happened: *I'm sorry I mentioned it; I didn't realize how much it upset you.*

runny (adj) /ˈrʌni/ containing more liquid than is usual or than you expected: *I think the sauce needs more flour. It's a bit too runny.*

shout (v) /ʃaʊt/ to say sth in a loud voice: *The captain shouted instructions to his team.*

sigh (v) /saɪ/ to say sth with a sigh (= a long, deep breath that shows you are tired, sad, disappointed, etc.): *'I'm so tired,' he sighed.*

situate (v) /ˈsɪtʃueɪt/ to put sth in a particular place or position: *The hotel is conveniently situated close to the beach.*

situation (n) /ˌsɪtʃuˈeɪʃn/ the things that are happening in a particular place or at a particular time: *The situation in the north of the country is extremely serious.*

smooth (adj) /smuːð/ (used about a liquid mixture) without lumps: *Stir the sauce until it is smooth.*

snore (v) /snɔː(r)/ to breathe noisily through your nose and mouth while you are asleep: *She heard her father snoring in the next room.*

snuffle (v) /ˈsnʌfl/ (used about people and animals) to make a noise through your nose: *The dog snuffled around the lamp post.*

soft (adj) /sɒft/ not hard or firm: *Warm butter is soft.*

somewhat (difficult) (adv) /ˈsʌmwɒt/ rather; to some degree: *We missed the train, which was somewhat unfortunate.*

stammer (v) /ˈstæmə(r)/ to speak with difficulty, repeating sounds and pausing before saying things correctly: *He stammered an apology and left.*

stare (v) /steə(r)/ to look at sb / sth for a long time because you are surprised, shocked, etc.: *Everybody stared at his hat.*

thick (adj) /θɪk/ (used about a liquid) that does not flow easily: *This paint is too thick.*

universally (accepted) (adv) /ˌjuːnɪˈvɜːsəli/ by everyone in the world or everyone in a particular group: *No political viewpoint is universally accepted.*

utterly (repulsive) (adv) /ˈʌtəli/ completely; totally: *I find raw fish utterly repulsive.*

vibrate (v) /vaɪˈbreɪt/ to make continuous very small and fast movements from side to side: *When a guitar string vibrates it makes a sound.*

vibration (n) /vaɪˈbreɪʃn/ continuous very small and fast movements from side to side: *Even at full speed the engine causes very little vibration.*

view (v) /vjuː/ to think about sb / sth in a particular way: *He views holidays as a waste of time.*

whine (v) /waɪn/ to complain about sth in an annoying, crying voice: *The children were whining all afternoon.*

whisper (v) /ˈwɪspə(r)/ to speak very quietly into sb's ear, so that other people cannot hear what you are saying: *She whispered something in his ear.*

widely (spread) (adv) /ˈwaɪdli/ existing or happening over a large area or among many people: *Internet fraud is more widely spread than I thought.*

Unit 8

actor (n) /ˈæktə(r)/ a person whose job is to act in a play, film or on TV: *She's one of the country's leading actors.*

athlete (n) /ˈæθliːt/ a person who is good at sports like running or jumping: *Many great athletes have competed in the Olympic Games.*

back down (v) /bæk ˈdaʊn/ to stop saying that you are right: *I think you are right to demand an apology. Don't back down now.*

be thrown in at the deep end (idiom) /bi ˌθrəʊn ɪn ət ðə ˈdiːp end/ to start or be made to start a new and difficult activity that you are not prepared for: *New doctors always feel like they have been thrown in at the deep end.*

boycott (n) /ˈbɔɪkɒt/ refusal to buy things from a particular company, take part in an event, etc. because you do not approve of it: *We ask people to take part in a boycott of companies that use child labour.*

challenging (adj) /ˈtʃælɪndʒɪŋ/ forcing you to make a lot of effort: *Chess is an intellectually challenging game.*

change your mind (v) /ˌtʃeɪndʒ jɔː(r) ˈmaɪnd/ to change your decision or opinion: *I'll have the green one. No, I've changed my mind – I want the red one.*

come up with (a scheme) (v) /kʌm ˈʌp wɪð/ to find an answer or a solution to sth: *Engineers have come up with new ways of saving energy.*

conceive (an idea) (v) /kənˈsiːv/ to think of a new idea or plan: *He conceived the idea for the novel during his journey through India.*

dead-end (job) (adj) /ˈded end/ that is a point, situation, etc. from which you can make no further progress: *He thought working in the supermarket was a dead-end job.*

demonstration (n) /ˌdemənˈstreɪʃn/ a public protest for or against sb / sth: *The police used force to break up the demonstration.*

discrimination (n) /dɪˌskrɪmɪˈneɪʃn/ treating one person or group worse than others: *Discrimination against disabled people is illegal.*

dream up (an idea) (v) /driːm ˈʌp/ to have an idea, especially a very unusual or silly one: *Trust you to dream up a crazy idea like this!*

ease off (v) /ˌiːz ˈɒf/ to become less strong or unpleasant: *Let's wait until the rain eases off.*

efficient (adj) /ɪˈfɪʃnt/ able to work well without making mistakes or wasting time and energy: *I must find an efficient way of organizing my time.*

engage in sth (v) /ɪnˈɡeɪdʒ ɪn/ to take part in sth: *I don't engage in that kind of gossip!*

face up to sth (v) /feɪs ˈʌp tə/ to accept a difficult or unpleasant situation and do sth about it: *She had to face up to the fact that she was wrong.*

fight back (v) /faɪt ˈbæk/ to attack sb who has attacked you: *If he hits you again, fight back!*

firefighter (n) /ˈfaɪəfaɪtə(r)/ a person whose job is to stop fires: *Firefighters raced to the factory.*

flight attendant (n) /ˈflaɪt əˌtendənt/ a person whose job is to serve and look after the passengers on a plane: *The flight attendant brought us some drinks.*

give in (to sb / sth) (v) /ɡɪv ˈɪn/ to stop fighting against sb / sth; to accept that you have been defeated: *We argued for ages but he finally gave in and said I could borrow his car.*

glamorous (adj) /ˈɡlæmərəs/ especially attractive and exciting, and different from ordinary things or people: *Actresses always look glamorous.*

go ahead (with a plan) (v) /ɡəʊ əˈhed/ to do sth after not being sure that it was possible: *They decided to go ahead with the plan without me.*

have a lot on your plate (idiom) /hæv ə lɒt ɒn jə(r) ˈpleɪt/ to have a lot of work, problems, etc. to deal with: *With a full-time job and two children, she has a lot on her plate.*

head teacher (n) /ˌhedˈtiːtʃə(r)/ the teacher in charge of a school: *Who is the new head teacher?*

high-flying (adj) /ˌhaɪ ˈflaɪɪŋ/ very successful: *He's a high-flying businessman.*

highly skilled (adj) /ˈhaɪli ˌskɪld/ having an ability to a very great degree, especially because of training, practice, etc.: *She's a highly skilled vet.*

injustice (n) /ɪnˈdʒʌstɪs/ the fact of a situation being unfair; an unfair act: *People are protesting about the injustice of the new tax.*

make a decision (v) /ˌmeɪk ə dɪˈsɪʒn/ to make a choice or judgement after thinking about various possibilities: *Have you made a decision yet?*

make up your mind (v) /ˌmeɪk ʌp jə(r) ˈmaɪnd/ to decide: *I can't make up my mind which top to buy.*

march (n) /mɑːtʃ/ an organized walk by a large group of people who are protesting about sth: *The peace march went through the centre of town.*

opposition (n) /ˌɒpəˈzɪʃn/ the feeling of disagreeing with sth and the act of trying to change it: *He expressed strong opposition to the plan.*

police officer (n) /pəˈliːs ɒfɪsə(r)/ a person whose job is to make sure that people obey the law, and to prevent and solve crime: *Two police officers ran after the thief.*

postal worker (n) /ˈpəʊstl ˈwɜːkə(r)/ a person who works in the industry connected with sending and receiving and delivering letters, etc.: *My grandfather was a postal worker and delivered letters in our town.*

put your feet up (v) /ˌpʊt jə(r) ˈfiːt ʌp/ to sit down and relax, especially with your feet off the floor and supported: *I'm so tired that I just want to go home and put my feet up.*

reconsider (a decision) (v) /ˌriːkənˈsɪdə(r)/ to think again about sth, especially because you may want to change your mind: *Public protests have forced the government to reconsider their policy.*

repetitive (adj) /rɪˈpetətɪv/ not interesting because the same thing is repeated many times: *Factory work can be very repetitive.*

rise to the challenge (v) /ˌraɪz tə ðə ˈtʃælɪndʒ/ to show that you are able to deal with a problem, etc. successfully: *Do you think she will rise to the challenge of the job?*

(have) second thoughts (n pl) /ˌsekənd ˈθɔːts/ a change of mind or opinion about sth; doubts that you have when you are not sure if you have made the right decision: *I'm starting to have second thoughts about accepting their offer.*

show sb the ropes (idiom) /ʃəʊ ðə ˈrəʊps/ to show sb how a job should be done: *My new manager showed me the ropes.*

spokesperson (n) /ˈspəʊkspɜːsn/ a person who is chosen to speak for a group or an organization: *A party spokesperson condemned the bombing.*

stand up for sb / sth (v) /stænd ˈʌp fɔː(r)/ to say or do sth which shows that you support sb / sth: *I admire him. He really stands up for his rights.*

start / get the ball rolling (idiom) /ˌstɑːt, ɡet ðə bɔːl ˈrəʊlɪŋ/ to start sth (an activity, a conversation, etc.) that involves or is done by a group: *I told a joke first, to start the ball rolling.*

step up (v) /step ˈʌp/ to increase the amount, speed, etc. of sth: *The Army has decided to step up its security arrangements.*

stressful (adj) /ˈstresfl/ causing worry and pressure: *Being a police officer is a stressful job.*

struggle (n) /ˈstrʌɡl/ a fight in which sb tries to do or get sth when this is difficult: *All countries should unite in the struggle against terrorism.*

take on sb / sth (v) /teɪk ɒn/ to fight against sb / sth: *The people were taking on the country's ruler because they wanted political reforms.*

the bottom line (n) /ðə ˈbɒtəm ˌlaɪn/ the most important thing to consider when you are discussing or deciding sth: *For Jeremy, the bottom line was doing something meaningful.*

threat (n) /θret/ a warning that sb may hurt, kill or punish you if you do not do what they want: *He says he'll resign, but he won't carry out his threat.*

throw sb out (v) /θrəʊ aʊt/ to force sb to leave a place: *He was thrown out of the flat because he hadn't paid the rent.*

varied (adj) /ˈveərid/ having many different kinds of things or activities: *I try to make my classes as varied as possible.*

worthwhile (adj) /ˌwɜːθˈwaɪl/ important, enjoyable or interesting enough to be worth the cost or effort: *Working for so little money just isn't worthwhile.*

Unit 9

actually (adv) /ˈæktʃuəli/ really; in fact: *I don't agree. I thought the film was very good, actually.*

appear[1] (v) /əˈpɪə(r)/ to become visible or noticeable: *Scientists are unsure when the virus first appeared.*

appear[2] (v) /əˈpɪə(r)/ seem to be something: *She didn't appear at all surprised at the news.*

attach (v) /əˈtætʃ/ to add a picture, document, etc. to an email message: *I attached the photos and clicked 'Send'.*

break down (v) /ˌbreɪk ˈdaʊn/ to lose control of your feelings and start crying: *He broke down in tears when he heard the news.*

catch up (with sb) (v) /kætʃ ˈʌp/ to find out about things that have happened to sb: *I caught up with Victor last night. He's got a new job.*

challenging (adj) /ˈtʃælɪndʒɪŋ/ difficult in an interesting way that tests your ability: *I have had a challenging and rewarding career as a teacher.*

click (v) /klɪk/ to press one of the buttons on a computer mouse: *To open a file, click on the menu.*

consequently (adv) /ˈkɒnsɪkwəntli/ as the result of sth else: *She didn't work hard enough, and consequently failed the exam.*

consistently (adv) /kənˈsɪstəntli/ in the same way; in a way that does not change: *We must try to maintain a consistently high standard.*

convenient (adj) /kənˈviːniənt/ suitable or practical for a particular purpose; not causing difficulty: *I'm willing to meet you on any day that's convenient for you.*

currently (adv) /ˈkʌrəntli/ at present; at the moment: *He is currently working in Spain.*

delete (v) /dɪˈliːt/ to remove sth that is written or printed, or that has been stored on a computer: *Your name has been deleted from the list.*

demonstrate (v) /ˈdemənstreɪt/ to show something clearly by giving proof or evidence: *These paintings demonstrate his extraordinary ability as a portrait painter.*

download (v) /ˌdaʊnˈləʊd/ to copy a computer file, etc. from a large computer system to a smaller one: *You can download unlimited e-books for free.*

eventually (adv) /ɪˈventʃuəli/ in the end; finally: *He eventually persuaded his parents to let him buy a motorbike.*

expensive (adj) /ɪkˈspensɪv/ costing a lot of money: *Houses are very expensive in this area.*

experience (n) /ɪkˈspɪəriəns/ the knowledge and skill that you have gained through doing something for a period of time: *Do you have any previous experience of this type of work?*

fragile (adj) /ˈfrædʒaɪl/ easily damaged or broken: *This bowl is very fragile. Please handle it carefully.*

friendly (adj) /ˈfrendli/ behaving in a kind and open way: *I found the people there very warm and friendly.*

get over sb / sth (v) /ɡet ˈəʊvə(r)/ to feel normal again after being ill or having an unpleasant experience: *It took her a long time to get over her operation.*

hit it off (with sb) (v) /ˌhɪt ɪt ˈɒf/ to like sb when you first meet them: *When I first met Tony's parents, we didn't really hit it off.*

imagery (n) /ˈɪmɪdʒəri/ language that produces pictures in the minds of the people reading or listening: *His poems are characterized by their strange imagery.*

inexpensive (adj) /ˌɪnɪkˈspensɪv/ low in price: *The town is full of inexpensive eating places.*

install (v) /ɪnˈstɔːl/ to put a piece of equipment, etc. in place so that it is ready to be used: *We are installing a computer system in the library.*

latest (adj) /ˈleɪtɪst/ no later than a time or date; up-to-date: *Women in Paris always wear the latest fashions.*

log in (v) /lɒɡ ˈɪn/ to perform the actions that allow you to start using a computer system: *You need to key in your password to log in.*

log out (v) /lɒɡ ˈaʊt/ to perform the actions that allow you to finish using a computer system: *Remember to log out when you have finished reading your emails.*

make up (with sb) (v) /meɪk ˈʌp/ to become friends again after an argument: *Has she made up with him yet?*

metaphor (n) /ˈmetəfə(r), -fɔː(r)/ a word or phrase that is used to show that one thing has the same qualities as another; a way of making a comparison: *'Her words were a knife in his heart' is a metaphor.*

open up (to sb) (v) /ˌəʊpən ˈʌp/ to talk about what you feel and think: *She was shy at first, but she finally opened up to me and told me how she felt.*

ordinary (adj) /ˈɔːdnri/ normal; not unusual or different from others: *It's interesting to see how ordinary people live in other countries.*

out-of-date (adj) /ˌaʊt əv ˈdeɪt/ not fashionable; no longer useful; no longer able to be used: *We have to stop using these out-of-date methods.*

personification (n) /pəˌsɒnɪfɪˈkeɪʃn/ a description of an object or a feeling as if it were a person: *In this poem, he uses personification to describe the wind as a mysterious woman.*

pick on sb (v) /ˈpɪk ɒn/ to behave unfairly or in a cruel way towards sb: *Lee gets picked on at school.*

poem (n) /ˈpəʊɪm/ a piece of writing arranged in short lines. Poems try to express thoughts and feelings with the help of sound and rhythm.: *He wrote poems about the beauty of the countryside.*

portable (adj) /ˈpɔːtəbl/ easy to carry or move: *The device is lightweight, portable and easy to store.*

possibly (adv) /ˈpɒsəbli/ perhaps: *Tony phoned to say he would possibly be late home.*

post (v) /pəʊst/ to put information or pictures on a website: *The photos have been provided by fans who post on the message board.*

prose (n) /prəʊz/ written language that is not poetry: *I admire the author's clear, elegant prose.*

reliable (adj) /rɪˈlaɪəbl/ that you can trust: *Japanese cars are usually very reliable.*

responsible (for doing sth) (adj) /rɪˈspɒnsəbəl/ having the job or duty of doing something, so that you may be blamed if something goes wrong: *Mike is responsible for designing the entire project.*

rewarding (adj) /rɪˈwɔːdɪŋ/ if an activity is rewarding, it makes you feel happy because you think you have done something useful or important: *Teaching is a very rewarding job.*

rhyme (n) /raɪm/ a word that has the same sound as another: *Can you think of a rhyme for 'peace'?*

rhythm (n) /ˈrɪðəm/ a regular repeated pattern of sound or movement: *I'm not keen on the tune but I love the rhythm.*

role (n) /rəʊl/ the function or position that somebody has or is expected to have in an organization, in society or in a relationship: *It is important that everyone has clearly defined roles and responsibilities.*

run into sb (v) /rʌn ˈɪntə/ (informal) to meet sb by chance: *I ran into Nikki outside the library.*

share[1] (v) /ʃeə(r)/ to divide sth between two or more people: *The four of us shared the pizza.*

share[2] (v) /ʃeə(r)/ have sth in common with other people: *They shared a common interest in sports.*

Wordlist

share³ (v) /ʃeə(r)/ post sth on social media: *Please share this on Twitter so we can get the word out.*

simile (n) /ˈsɪməli/ a word or phrase that compares sth to sth else, using the words 'like' or 'as'; the use of such words and phrases.: *'A face like a mask' and 'as white as snow' are similes.*

stanza (n) /ˈstænzə/ a group of lines that form a unit in some types of poem: *The poem has three stanzas.*

status (n) /ˈsteɪtəs/ the position you have in society: *She achieved celebrity status overnight.*

status (n) /ˈsteɪtəs/ where you are and / or what you are doing: *What is the current status of our application for funds?*

stick up for sb / sth (v) /stɪk ˈʌp fə(r)/ to support or defend yourself / sb / sth: *Don't worry. I'll stick up for you if there's any trouble.*

symbol (n) /ˈsɪmbl/ a person, sign, object, etc. which represents sth: *Some people think a fast car is a symbol of power.*

sympathetic (adj) /ˌsɪmpəˈθetɪk/ showing that you understand other people's feelings, especially their problems: *When Suki was ill, everyone was very sympathetic.*

theme (n) /θiːm/ the subject of a talk, a piece of writing or a work of art: *The theme of today's discussion will be 'Our changing cities'.*

undo (v) /ʌnˈduː/ to destroy the effect of sth that has already happened: *If you make a mistake when you are typing, you can undo it by clicking here.*

update (v) /ˌʌpˈdeɪt/ to put the most recent information into sth; to give sb the most recent information: *She updated the website with the new concert dates.*

upload (v) /ˌʌpˈləʊd/ to move data to a larger computer system from a smaller one: *Upload your videos and share them with friends and family online.*

verse (n) /vɜːs/ a group of lines which form one part of a song or poem: *This song has five verses.*

waterproof (adj) /ˈwɔːtəpruːf/ that doesn't let water through or that cannot be damaged by water: *My waterproof coat kept my clothes dry despite the heavy rain.*

Unit 10

acclaimed (adj) /əˈkleɪmd/ publicly praised or welcomed: *The author will be signing copies of her highly acclaimed new novel.*

actor (n) /ˈæktə(r)/ a person whose job is to act in a play, film or on TV: *This year the award for best actor went to an American.*

amazing (adj) /əˈmeɪzɪŋ/ very surprising and difficult to believe: *She shows amazing potential.*

amusing (adj) /əˈmjuːzɪŋ/ causing you to laugh or smile: *He's very amusing and he makes me laugh.*

appeal (to an audience) (v) /əˈpiːl/ to be attractive or interesting to sb: *The idea of living in the country doesn't appeal to me at all.*

artist (n) /ˈɑːtɪst/ a person who paints or draws pictures: *Many artists are known for their unusual clothes.*

attend (a performance) (v) /əˈtend/ to go to or be present at a place: *We'd like as many people as possible to attend the performance.*

beauty (n) /ˈbjuːti/ the quality which gives pleasure to the senses; the state of being beautiful: *I was amazed by the beauty of the mountains.*

biographer (n) /baɪˈɒɡrəfə(r)/ a person who writes the story of sb else's life: *The politician's biographer interviewed her about her childhood.*

captivating (adj) /ˈkæptɪveɪtɪŋ/ very attractive and interesting: *It was a captivating performance from my favourite actor.*

(provide a) catering service (n) /ˈkeɪtərɪŋ/ the work of providing food and drink at events or in places that a lot of people go to: *Who's going to provide the catering service at the wedding?*

comical (adj) /ˈkɒmɪkl/ that makes you laugh; funny: *That film was extremely comical.*

composer (n) /kəmˈpəʊzə(r)/ a person who writes music: *Vivaldi was a famous composer.*

cutting-edge (adj) /ˌkʌtɪŋ ˈedʒ/ of the newest, most highly developed stage of sth: *He works on cutting-edge computer technology.*

dedication (n) /ˌdedɪˈkeɪʃn/ wanting to give your time and energy to sth because you feel it is important: *I admire her dedication to her career.*

designer (n) /dɪˈzaɪnə(r)/ a person whose job is to make drawings or plans showing how sth will be made: *She's a fantastic designer – she's so creative.*

dramatic (adj) /drəˈmætɪk/ noticeable or sudden and often surprising: *The novel reaches a dramatic conclusion in the final chapter.*

eagerly-awaited (adj) /ˌiːɡəli əˈweɪtɪd/ waited for with a lot of desire or interest: *The singer has finally released his eagerly-awaited new album.*

elaborate (adj) /ɪˈlæbərət/ very complicated; done or made very carefully: *The vase was covered in elaborate patterns.*

family-oriented (adj) /ˈɔːrientɪd/ aimed at and suitable for children and their parents: *'Finding Nemo' is a family-oriented film.*

far and wide (adv) /ˈfɑː(r) ænd ˌwaɪd/ over a large area: *We searched far and wide for our lost cat.*

fascinating (adj) /ˈfæsɪneɪtɪŋ/ attracting or interesting sb very much: *It was such a fascinating book that I couldn't put it down.*

feature-length (adj) /ˈfiːtʃə(r) ˌleŋθ/ of the same length as a typical film/movie: *There's a feature-length documentary on the television tonight.*

first-time (adj) /ˈfɜːst taɪm/ doing sth having never done it before: *Most of the entries at the film festival were by first-time directors.*

flowing (adj) /fləʊɪŋ/ smooth and continuous: *He paints with beautiful flowing lines.*

genius (n) /ˈdʒiːniəs/ very great and unusual intelligence or ability: *Shakespeare's tragedies show true genius.*

headline a festival (v) /ˈhedlaɪn/ to be one of the main advertised bands, singers, musicians, etc. at a music festival (= a series of musical performances held regularly in one place): *Coldplay are headlining Glastonbury Festival this year.*

hilarious (adj) /hɪˈleəriəs/ extremely funny: *That joke was absolutely hilarious!*

hold (an event) (v) /həʊld/ to organize an event; to have a meeting, an election, a concert, etc.: *They're holding a party for his fortieth birthday.*

lifelike (adj) /ˈlaɪflaɪk/ looking like a real person or thing: *The silk flowers are very lifelike.*

little-known (adj) /ˈlɪtl ˌnəʊn/ unknown to most people: *We had a quiet meal at a little-known cafe.*

maturity (n) /məˈtʃʊərəti, məˈtjʊərəti/ the quality of behaving in a sensible, adult way: *University can help students to develop maturity.*

moving (adj) /ˈmuːvɪŋ/ causing strong feelings, especially of sadness: *The end of the film was so moving that I started to cry.*

musician (n) /mjuˈzɪʃn/ a person who plays a musical instrument or writes music, especially as a job: *He was a fine musician in his youth.*

novelist (n) /ˈnɒvəlɪst/ a person who writes novels: *Jane Austen is a famous novelist.*

open-air (adj) /ˌəʊpən ˈeə(r)/ not inside a building: *We were lucky that it didn't rain when we went to the open-air concert.*

original (adj) /əˈrɪdʒənl/ new and interesting; different from others of its type: *There are no original ideas in his work.*

originality (n) /əˌrɪdʒəˈnæləti/ the quality of being new and interesting: *His teacher was impressed by the originality of his essay.*

painter (n) /ˈpeɪntə(r)/ a person who paints pictures: *Picasso was a famous painter.*

pick and choose (v) /ˈpɪk ænd ˌtʃuːz/ to choose only the things that you like or want very much: *You can pick and choose which subjects to take at university.*

playwright (n) /ˈpleɪraɪt/ a person who writes plays for the theatre, TV or radio: *It must give a playwright great satisfaction to see his or her work performed.*

poet (n) /ˈpəʊɪt/ a person who writes poems: *The poet won a prize for her poem about the spring.*

recruit (volunteers) (v) /rɪˈkruːt/ to find new people to join a company, an organization, the armed forces, etc.: *We need to recruit more young people to the teaching profession.*

remarkable (adj) /rɪˈmɑːkəbl/ unusual and surprising in a way that people notice: *She certainly is a remarkable woman.*

renowned (adj) /rɪˈnaʊnd/ famous and respected for doing sth especially well: *The region is renowned for its food.*

romantic (adj) /rəʊˈmæntɪk/ having a quality that strongly affects your emotions or makes you think about love: *The low lighting gave a romantic atmosphere to the room.*

scriptwriter (n) /ˈskrɪptraɪtə(r)/ someone who writes instructions about what happens and what the actors say in a play, film, TV programme, etc.: *The scriptwriter gave advice to the director on the film set.*

sculptor (n) /ˈskʌlptə(r)/ a person who makes sculptures (= works of art that are figures or objects made from stone, wood, metal, etc.): *The sculptor made a beautiful sculpture of a tree.*

(manage) security (n) /sɪˈkjʊərəti/ things that you do to protect sb / sth from attack, danger, thieves, etc.: *A big company is going to manage security at the festival.*

singer (n) /ˈsɪŋə(r)/ a person who sings, or whose job is singing, especially in public: *The audience clapped as soon as the singer walked onto the stage.*

(appear on) stage (n) /steɪdʒ/ a platform in a theatre, concert hall, etc. on which actors, musicians, etc. perform: *More than 50 bands will be appearing on stage at the festival.*

(run a) stall (n) /stɔːl/ a small shop with an open front or a table with things for sale: *I'm running a book stall at the summer fair.*

style (n) /staɪl/ the way that sth is done, built, etc.: *The writer's style is very clear and simple.*

success (n) /səkˈses/ the fact that you have achieved what you want; doing well and becoming famous, rich, etc.: *Hard work is the key to success.*

take place (v) /teɪk ˈpleɪs/ (used about a meeting, an event, etc.) to happen: *The ceremony took place in glorious sunshine.*

talked-about (adj) /ˈtɔːkt əˌbaʊt/ widely discussed: *It's the most talked-about film of the year!*

thought-provoking (adj) /ˈθɔːt prəvəʊkɪŋ/ making sb think about or become interested in sth: *I've just read a very thought-provoking book.*

trial and error (n) /ˌtraɪəl ænd ˈerə(r)/ trying different ways of doing sth until you find the best one: *No one taught me to cook, so I've learned by trial and error.*

ups and downs (n) /ˈʌps ænd ˌdaʊnz/ both good times and bad times: *We're happy together but we've had our ups and downs.*

(get a good) vantage point (n pl) /ˈvɑːntɪdʒ pɔɪnt/ a place from which you have a good view of sth: *The bridge seemed a good vantage point to watch the race from.*

(find a) venue (n) /ˈvenjuː/ the place where people meet for an organized event, for example a concert or a sports event: *I hope we find a venue for the party in time.*

vision (n) /ˈvɪʒn/ a picture in your imagination: *They have a vision of a world without weapons.*

world-famous (adj) /ˌwɜːld ˈfeɪməs/ known about by people everywhere in the world: *James Cameron is a world-famous film director.*